# Abou

CW01465307

Clive Hart lives in the             .ds
as much time as he cai             He
is a small part of an i             to
recreating medieval mounted combat as close as it originally was.

The horses on the cover are Charlie and Icaro of Historic Equitation.

For information on other books, please
visit www.clivehart.net

## By Clive Hart:

The Rise and Fall of the Mounted Knight

The Legend of Richard Keynes series (six books):
Book One: Golden Spurs
Book Two: Brothers in Arms
Book Three: Dogs of War
Book Four: Knight Errant
Book Five: King Breaker
Book Six: Crusader

### Copyright © 2024 Clive Hart

All rights reserved. All characters in this publication are fictitious and any resemblance to real persons, living or dead, is purely coincidental.

# Contents

# Historical Foreword: Kingdom of Heaven

There is a particular Hollywood movie that introduced many people, the author included, to the Holy Land in the twelfth century. As it will form the backdrop for many who read this book, the film therefore deserves some consideration. As a visual spectacle, Kingdom of Heaven gives a fantastic feel to the time and place: the clothing, armour, and setting are all good and give the audience an exotic flavour of the time. Kingdom of Heaven was filmed in North Africa, and as such depicts the Holy Land to be a more barren place than it actually was. The land to the west of Jerusalem was fertile and productive, although further to the east and south of the Dead Sea, the land does become very dry and inhospitable to outsiders.

Beyond the general feel of the film however, it seems that facts started to get in the way of a good story. King Baldwin, the famous leper king, is seen on screen behind a silver mask to hide his disfigurement, but in reality Baldwin never shied away from his appearance, instead seeing it as a proof of his piety and strength. Likewise, Reynald of Chatillon, a most memorable character in the film, is portrayed as a member of the Knights Templar, which he never was. His adoption into the order for Kingdom of Heaven was probably done to make it clear he was on the 'bad' side, but in reality he was a secular lord. He actively fought against Saladin on the frontiers of the kingdom, but under his own banner, not the Templar's black and white piebald flag.

One thing the film gets right is the influence of the Knights Templar. They resembled a multinational corporation by this time, spread across the christian world to funnel money and fighting men into the Holy Land. Their forces and castles allowed the kingdom to survive, and their political manoeuvring made them and their ideals important. The order was rich as an entity, but the individual members lived lives of poverty without personal possessions or land. As a military force, they were so disciplined and experienced in the harsh conditions of the east that they formed a cavalry army that was truly feared by the enemy. Their Rule, the instruction manual for being a Templar, explains tactics and standard operating procedures that were harsh but effective. For example, a Templar couldn't leave formation or even replace a broken sword without permission. This book attempts to make the most accurate depiction of the Templar's military abilities and organisation yet seen in fiction.

Kingdom of Heaven's main character is where the film strays furthest from reality. Balian of Ibelin was in his forties when the events in the movie occurred. He had not come from England, nor been a blacksmith, and had an older brother (another Baldwin) who was senior to Balian. Balian held the castle at Ramla from his brother from 1169 and therefore was very much at home in the Holy Land. So if you have seen the film, imagine the following story to take place within its colourful world, but don't be surprised if the characters differ from the silver screen.

# UNHOLY LAND

Richard's eyes stung from the light and he had to fight to keep them open.

'I can't believe it's this hot in October,' Bowman shielded his eyes with a hand.

'It's November,' Sarjeant gripped the wooden sides of the Pisan ship which had carried them from Italy to the port of Jaffa in the Holy Land. His blue eyes reflected the bright sun above, but had little sparkle of their own.

Richard's eyes darted around at the harbour once they had become accustomed to the dazzling daylight, and he found a scene of colour and noise. They were the only arrivals, but a dozen other ships were being loaded and people were streaming onboard to depart the Holy Land.

Sarjeant made the sign of the cross and mumbled a prayer for their safe docking, for apparently the harbour was not the easiest to navigate. The large-framed man took a deep breath. 'Our trials only begin now, my boy.'

Richard wasn't listening because he was transfixed by the rows of bobbing ships, the hordes of dock workers, donkeys, mules, porters, officials, guards, sellers of everything and anything, and camels. He squinted at the camels, he'd never seen a camel. 'They look uncomfortable to ride,' he mumbled.

'Are you even listening to me?' Sarjeant asked.

'He's not,' Bowman rubbed his eyes, for he'd also been asleep when they'd docked. He sniffed the air. 'I can smell something other than just salt for the first time in a while.'

The Marshal pushed past Richard and onto the deck of their cog. His red surcoat had faded from hours of sitting in the ship's prow during their voyage, the red cloak of his deceased master always in his hands. The cloak itself had been sun-bleached too, streaks of faded pink alongside the still bright red areas which made the once regal garment look old. 'We need to get to Jerusalem,' the Marshal looked for a plank or ladder to take him to shore.

'I don't know what he's rushing for,' Bowman said, 'it'll be an age before the horses and carts are unloaded.'

'I'm not looking forward to that,' Richard glanced at the hold as a crane lifted something out of it. 'Solis is going to be furious.'

And it was the palomino horse who was lifted out of the hold by the crane first, swinging back and forth in a canvas sling with his ears pinned back.

'He's not forgiven you, then,' Bowman grinned.

Richard shook his head. 'No, and the wine has made him worse. He's refusing to drink water now unless there's wine in it. It's like having you around in horse form.'

'I told you bribing him to get back onto ships wasn't a good idea,' Bowman said.

'It got him here, didn't it?' Richard replied, although he wondered if Solis wouldn't have been better off staying in the west. The cross shaped scar on his flank was still an indent in his muscle, and he was still lame on the leg, although it didn't seem to bother the horse.

'We should get out of the sun,' Sarjeant said, 'there'll be shade on the shore, and food in the Pisan quarter. These sailors from Pisa know us now, so their quarter is the safest place to eat as they won't try to trick or rob us.'

Four dock workers rotated the crane round so Solis swung above the green water, which shimmered in the midday sun. His hooves lashed out at nothing.

'I'll go and look after Solie,' Richard said to Bowman, 'can you get the others disembarked?'

Richard didn't wait for an answer and followed the Marshal onto dry land. He was hit by a swirl of cooking smells which mixed with sea salt and the occasional waft of urine. Seagulls wheeled overhead and chatter bombarded Richard from all sides, a babbling of words he didn't understand. His leather shoes hit the stone of the harbourside and for a while he felt unsteady.

The Marshal paused for only a moment before, cloak over his shoulder, he marched up the paved street into Jaffa. A dark-skinned man held up a round, orange fruit to sell him, but the knight batted both man and fruit away.

Richard watched the orange fruit bounce, then roll off into the sea where it disappeared with a splash.

'It's called an orange,' Sarjeant clapped a hand on his shoulder.

'The Young King had them,' Richard said, 'but I didn't want to ask the name of the fruit and look like a country knight.'

'You are a country knight,' Sarjeant took a deep breath, 'a country knight with a king's ransom in silver in his possession.'

Richard squinted at the light which reflected off the seafront's white buildings, and for a brief moment he wished he was back in the quiet hold of the cog.

'I don't feel safe having it here,' he said, 'even with Guy and his company.'

Sarjeant looked back at the cog. 'As Christ is my witness, I'd feel safer without them.'

'We're stuck with them until Jerusalem,' Richard said, 'and I know you said you know the way, but we're better off together.'

Sarjeant looked up to where Solis's flailing hooves swung overhead. He was lowered down next to Richard.

The stallion snorted, and his thrashing hooves struck the stones and sent sparks flying through the air.

'Calm down,' Richard went to grab the loose rope attached to the horse's halter, but Solis snapped at him and Richard had to move to avoid being bitten.

Solis snorted and the dock workers made no effort to help Richard untie the sling. He held out a handful of horsebread to his horse, who put his ears forward and sniffed it. Solis turned his head away and stared at a group of camels instead.

Richard grabbed the rope, and with the horse in hand, he freed him from the canvas sling. He'd make Maynard lead the horse everywhere, Richard thought with some satisfaction. The squire had been violently seasick during the journey, to the point where he'd seemed unlikely to survive, but Richard had thrown a bucket of cold water over him and he'd just about made it to Jaffa alive.

Brian had been seasick, too, but he had recovered before they rounded the southern tip of Spain, and spent the rest of the voyage trying to teach the twins Latin. This had met with mixed success, but the boredom of the sailing had worked in the monk's favour.

Guy of Lusignan disembarked with Alice behind him, his sister dressed in a bright blue silk dress with white fur linings, and her silver circlet catching the sun and making her head glow.

'I'd wager she won't be wearing that fur in a week,' Sarjeant grinned, 'all the new folk wear their wools and their furs at the beginning, but by the time their six months is up, they're all in linens.'

'Or silk,' Richard hadn't seen her wear the silk before.

'They're trying to make an entrance,' Sarjeant said as Guy's company, blue and white banner above them, left the ship.

Guy's thin face had aged since Richard had first met him, but his eyes were strong and he strode down the boarding plank as quickly as he could.

'It's a shame there's no one here to welcome him,' Richard grinned.

Solis forgot about both the camels and his mood, and nuzzled at Richard to offer him the horsebread again. 'Fine,' Richard held his hand out and the stallion ate from it.

The dock workers toiled for the whole afternoon, taking off dozens of horses as well as the three covered carts laden with silver. Their crane strained at their weight, and Richard was thankful that they'd spread one full cartload of silver across the three of them. The last thing they needed was a fortune in silver spilling out across the quayside. As if thinking the same thing, Guy ordered his men to stay in the area until everything was ashore.

Once the carts were safely on dry land and the company gathered around them, the customs officials pounced.

A man with dark skin but clothed as a rich merchant spoke to them in a language Richard didn't understand. Richard frowned.

'Ah,' the man changed his language, 'you are new here. Is this the right tongue? Or are you German? You look pale enough to be from the Empire.'

'I can understand you,' Richard said, 'how much do you want?'

The customs official chuckled and nodded over to the carts. 'That depends on what is in there. All moveable goods are taxed.'

'I know,' Richard said, 'but how much for you not to have to look? I'd like to save you some time, your day must be busy.'

The official stroked his bearded chin. 'Twenty silver coins.'

Richard reached inside his tunic and under his arm, where he kept a pouch of silver. He retrieved it and counted out twenty coins.

'Now forty coins,' the official folded his arms.

'You just said twenty,' Richard looked up.

'But you did not argue with me,' the official said, 'so my lack of investigation is worth more than twenty coins.'

'Argue with him now,' Sarjeant said.

Richard sighed. 'I don't want him to raise it any more,' he held out the forty coins, which almost emptied the entire pouch.

The official took the money and slid it into a bag. 'Welcome to Jaffa,' he walked away, but turned around. 'But if you want my advice, find someone who knows how things work here. This isn't Normandy.'

'Normandy,' Richard mumbled, 'he's the first person who has ever thought I was from Normandy.'

Sarjeant laughed. 'From him, that was probably an insult. We should reclaim our letters of credit with the Templars, stock up on supplies, and be on our way.'

Richard twirled Solis's rope around in his hands. 'I don't think we should. It's just too much silver to be carting around. We can reclaim it in Jerusalem if we need to.'

Sarjeant scrunched his face up and turned away.

'We will have to deal with the Templars at some point.' Richard said. 'If we want to fulfil our crusading vows, it probably means working alongside them.'

'They were not my vows,' Sarjeant said as he climbed up to drive one of the carts.

Gerold manned the second and one of Guy's squires the third. Richard had worried that Gerold would suffer on the voyage, but the old knight, although gaunt after his illness, had never once seemed to suffer from the effects of the rolling waves.

Richard handed Solis to Maynard, the squire pale and thinner than previously, and went to find the blue roan in the herd of their horses that seemed to fill the whole port side.

The warhorse had travelled better than Solis, although Richard still wasn't going to ride him until at least the following day, when they would set out from Jaffa and towards Jerusalem. Jerusalem, the city at the heart of the world, and the place where Richard needed to go to ask after his father's fate.

They rode towards the rising sun of the morning, out of Jaffa's stone walls and through its pomegranate orchards. The red fruits were late to harvest and dotted the trees in vast quantities.

'The Franks planted those,' Sarjeant said from the cart Richard rode his horse next to.

Richard nodded.

'We're the Franks,' Sarjeant said, 'but those of us living here already are called poulains. It was they who planted all these pomegranate orchards. Dates too, figs, and bananas, but it is the sugar cane which is the most profitable and widespread.'

'None of those ever reached me in Normandy,' Richard said. He sniffed the air and it smelled of a certain dryness.

'And you're lucky that we reached here,' Sarjeant replied, 'especially as the sailing season is now over. The rains will begin here soon. This month it will rain as much as in Normandy, but next month it will rain far more here.'

'Really?' Richard asked, but he didn't really believe it. The early morning sun dazzled his eyes when he looked at it, and it warmed his skin to a pleasant level as the carts and Guy's company left the orchard and followed the road east. The road beyond the plantations of Jaffa tracked through flat ground that stretched off towards the horizon without so much as a small hill to break up the horizon. To Richard's surprise, the land was green. The ground itself was almost white, as if it was all made from crushed and crumbled stones, but out of it grew long grasses and trees which almost looked like those at home.

Richard wondered where home was as their company slowly moved through a cluster of palm trees. He looked up at their scaled trunks and spiked leaves and marvelled at the strangeness of this new land.

His children ran alongside the carts, excited to be free from the confinement of the ship, Judas the black dog panted heavily, but kept up with them. Richard hadn't managed to get much out of Alexander on the voyage, his son muttering only curt replies to any question Richard asked of him. Lora was happier, a beacon of life in the dark ship, but Richard ached for his son to at least acknowledge him.

'You shouldn't worry about them,' Sarjeant saw where Richard looked. 'They have been through much, time will heal them.'

'They've been through too much,' Richard felt a tear in his eye at the thought of Sophie, 'and this pilgrimage isn't helping.'

'It was your decision to bring them,' Sarjeant said, 'so cease complaining and concentrate on ensuring they stay alive.'

Richard cast his eyes ahead to the sun, which lifted itself above the horizon, a ball of white light and heat. 'I'm just as worried about the rest of us.'

'Do not fear the road to Jerusalem,' Sarjeant said, 'the stories of this land tell us that once it was a dangerous route, beset by brigands and mountain lions, but now the holy orders garrison castles and escort pilgrims from Jaffa. The armies of the Muslims no longer trouble the pilgrim trails.'

'Mountain lions?' Bowman asked from his black palfrey. 'What's a mountain lion?'

'They are large cats,' Sarjeant replied, 'thin and coloured yellow, and they used to attack stragglers and the sick. I only ever saw one in my whole time here, and it ran away when it saw us.'

Richard felt a surge of gladness to be accompanied by Guy's two dozen knights and squires as he found himself checking the undergrowth for hostile animals.

11

The company stopped to drink twice before they came across the first village on the road. A caravan of camels and thin Arabian horses came the other way, the camels braying with a sound halfway between a growl and a cough. Their handlers wore flowing white clothing which looked to Richard like tunics, and some wore wide-brimmed hats. They were not Christian and some of Guy's men cursed at them.

Richard choked on the dust they stirred up and took another drink before realising he'd already emptied the waterskin.

'That is what I meant about the drink,' Sarjeant said, 'there is never enough.'

Bowman threw his empty skin onto the back of Sarjeant's cart. 'This is as bad as the hottest day back home, and it's only November. I don't want to be here in the summer.'

Richard wiped grit from his eyes as the white dust from the caravan settled around them. The sun on his face and hands almost seemed to be pressuring him, pushing into his skin. Richard turned his head away from its rays and towards the village.

Fashioned out of white stone, it stood between the road and a river and had a church at its centre. Trees grew tall around the houses and down towards the river where two mill wheels turned in unison. The splashing of the water just made Richard more thirsty.

'They're milling a lot of bread,' Bowman said.

Sarjeant groaned. 'It isn't flour, it's sugar. The poulains crush the sugar cane and this village is solely here to do that.'

'Everyone here is a Christian?' Richard asked.

Sarjeant nodded. 'But remember, there were many Christians here before the Muslims conquered the Holy Land.'

Richard didn't understand, but he didn't really care, either. Buckets were laid out for the horses, who all sweated under the sun, but Solis kicked his over and spilled the precious water all over the white sand.

'Did anyone put wine in it?' Richard asked.

Maynard picked the bucket up and shrugged.

'You need to put wine in it,' Richard said, 'every time Solie doesn't drink, you don't drink.'

The squire grumbled but stomped off to the cart to find some wine to add to some more water.

Bowman watched him go. 'This is doing him good.'

'I hope so,' Richard said, 'but we need to be moving, we should be able to reach Jerusalem today.'

The blonde man glanced up at the sun. 'I hope it has shade.'

Sarjeant nodded. 'The street of bad cooking has a covering. A queen erected it to shade pilgrims.'

'The street of bad cooking?' Bowman groaned. 'I hope that's a joke.'

'The shade isn't,' Sarjeant replied.

The road to the holy city, however, had none. Halfway to Jerusalem, hills appeared, and the mules and horses had to strain in the heat to haul themselves up higher and higher. They passed the odd corpse by the side of the road, some already picked clean by wild animals, then more villages. Some of these villages were inhabited by Muslims, the strange sound of their prayers at first caused Guy's men to jump to arms, but Sarjeant was able to explain the alien sound was no threat.

'They don't have a church,' Bowman said, 'why are Muslims allowed to live in the Kingdom of Jerusalem?'

'They pay a tax in the same way Christians pay a tax in the Muslim lands,' Sarjeant shrugged.

'Aren't we here to rid the Holy Land of Muslims?' Bowman asked. 'Isn't that the point?'

Richard watched the Marshal cradling his cloak and wondered what the point really was. If he couldn't find the truth of his father's fate, he'd have to seek something else to occupy himself. The children for now probably, but what then?

Only once the sun dropped from its peak did Sarjeant admit that their progress had been too slow to reach their destination in a single day. 'We shall have to camp,' he said, 'but do not be fooled, without the sun this land is cold at night.'

The track followed a valley floor with white and grey rocks on one side. On that slope grew thin cyprus and cedar trees, small green bushes all around them, with long grass sprouting in tufts everywhere. The grasses may have been all bleached yellow, but this was not the barren desert Richard had expected.

Sarjeant nodded to a clearing. 'This would do,' he said.

Bowman laughed. 'Richard, remember the baptistry?'

'I do,' he replied, 'and I agree, we shouldn't camp in sight of the road. Ever.'

'Suit yourself, my boy,' Sarjeant paused. 'Although you are no longer a boy, I shall have to call you something else.'

'I have some ideas,' Bowman said as he led the company into the cedars on the flat side of the road. He went until they found a wall of rocks to camp against, a wall which the sun set behind and cast a cooling shadow over the tired company.

Richard felt a chill sweep over him as the sun left his skin.

Alexander and Lora leapt from the cart they'd taken to riding and ran over to a gnarled and hollow olive tree which they could both squeeze into the trunk of. It sat under the cooling rocks which were lined with bushes.

Judas ran with them, but skidded to a halt and snarled.

Bowman noticed, stopped what he was doing, and unslung his bow from his shoulder. He strung it.

'Children, come here,' Richard shouted.

Judas lowered his head and his black hackles raised.

'Bandits?' Richard asked.

'Or just a hare,' Sarjeant replied.

Bowman reached for an arrow as Sarjeant left his horse and walked over to the olive tree. 'Come here, Lora,' he stretched a hand out.

Judas barked, and everyone who'd been busy preparing the camp stopped to see what had triggered him.

A sand-coloured shape burst out of the bushes on top of the rock and towards the olive tree with a huge leap.

Bowman raised his bow as Richard kicked his horse on.

Lora looked out through the lumpy olive trunk and her young eyes bulged as the mountain lion landed on the earth without a sound. It peered at her with big yellow eyes.

Richard's horse was too far away and he fumbled for his sword, but Bowman's arrow flew.

Except it only glanced the skin on the cat's flank and it whirled round. The big cat saw Sarjeant approaching, hand held out towards Lora, and lunged at the hand.

In the tree Alexander screamed while the cat, both languid and elegant at the same time, knocked Sarjeant to the ground and went for his neck.

Richard's horse veered away from the animal and some of the horses nearby spooked and jumped at the commotion. At least one ran loose, but Richard pushed himself out of his saddle, which was no mean feat, and rolled when he hit the dusty ground.

Sarjeant screamed back at the lion as his hands fought to keep its jaws apart, but blood stained his tunic.

Alice ran over to the children, her dress swirling as she went, and picked Lora up and away from the tree.

Bowman's next arrow missed the lion again, and Richard had just enough time to wonder what was wrong with him. He drew Roland's sword from his waist and slashed at the mountain lion.

The blade cut deep enough for the cat to spin around, hiss, and jump back up from rock to rock until it disappeared back into the bushes. Two small birds flew out of the undergrowth, but the horses all watched the foliage with their ears pricked.

Richard fell to his knees and pushed Sarjeant's cloak out of the way.

'Can you breathe?' Richard asked.

'I don't know,' the older man cried, his fingers on his throat coming up bright red.

Bowman arrived and knelt down. 'I don't know what happened.'

'You missed,' Richard said. 'You never miss.'

The blonde man's mouth gaped and he stared at the blood oozing from the mountain lion's victim.

Richard pushed Sarjeant's tunic aside and felt for wounds.

Alexander sobbed in Alice's arms, but Richard concentrated on his task. His fingers felt some holes but no large gash. 'I don't think it's too bad,' he said.

Sarjeant's breathing was rapid. 'Not too bad? It nearly killed me.'

'I'm so sorry,' Bowman's face was white.

The Marshal walked over. 'It looked like a large hunting dog,' he said, 'but as nimble as a cat.'

'It was a cat,' Richard said.

'A cat?' the Marshal frowned. 'This land is bewildering. But you've upset the horses with it, they are sweating enough as it is with their winter coats. Until they shed them, we should avoid exciting them.'

'Avoid exciting them?' Richard looked up. 'We didn't ask the mountain lion to attack.'

The Marshal sniffed and walked away. Richard asked for some wine and washed Sarjeant's wound out. The former Templar sarjeant caught his breath and relaxed his body, his eyes looking up at the clear blue sky. 'I hate this place. Have I ever told you how much I hate this place?'

Richard nodded and had to shoo Solis away, who was attracted by the cleansing wine when Brian brought it. Brian tended to the wounded man while Richard tried to comfort his children, who now hid behind Alice and wouldn't leave a fire once one was lit.

Bowman sat by it and stared into the flames as the sun set and dusk brought a deepening chill to the air.

Brian tended to Sarjeant, and the former steward of Yvetot shivered and kept swallowing and touching his neck. He stammered his words and more than once glanced back to the bushes from where the mountain lion had sprung.

Richard sat down next to Bowman and they ate some bread and dates they'd bought in Jaffa. He'd never tasted dates, and marvelled at their sweet and strange taste, and ate more than he probably should have. The children tried some olives Brian offered, but didn't like them.

Bowman ate nothing, and when he refused a drink, Richard couldn't leave him alone any longer. 'It wasn't your fault, anyone can miss a shot.'

The blonde man's nostrils flared. 'I don't.'

'Forget about it,' Richard said, 'Sarjeant will be fine.'

Bowman looked him in the eyes. 'Even if he is, that's not the point.'

'You won't miss the next mountain lion,' Richard said. 'Have a drink. None of us can drink enough as it is.'

'He could have died,' Bowman pulled his cloak around himself and flickering orange flames reflected on his face.

The company spread out around several fires, and squires took axes to the local trees to ensure they had ready fuel for the impending night.

A few of Guy's men had set up to watch the road with Gerold, but just before the darkness became all-consuming, he returned to the camp.

Richard turned to welcome him and saw dark shapes behind him. Horses and men.

Some of Guy's men half drew swords, and Guy himself stood up. 'Who is with you?' he asked.

Gerold's face was barely visible in the gloom, but Richard saw him smile.

From behind his father's knight, a man walked into the firelight leading his horse. Behind him were pilgrims. The man wore a black surcoat with a white cross of St John blazoned across it. Slipped into his sword belt were two maces.

Richard squinted.

'Richard,' a familiar voice escaped from the black-clad Hospitaller.

'Otto?' Richard got up quicker than manners would dictate and rushed over to his old friend. Otto's weathered face had gained a scar since they'd parted after the Corbie tournament, but his happiness was clear to see.

'I told you to come and find me,' Otto stretched out his arms.

Richard embraced him. 'I forgot which city in Italy you said to find you in.'

'It matters not,' the German grinned and had at least one less tooth than before.

'You saw our fire from the road?'

Otto shook his head. 'No, but I could smell your scouts hiding in the trees.'

Richard offered Otto's party to join their camp, and they did, although they kept their distance from the Lusignan company.

Otto sat down next to Bowman and held his hands up to the fire. Bowman ignored him.

'What's wrong with him?' Otto asked.

'Nothing,' Richard said, 'but what are you doing here?'

'My job. Escorting pilgrims around the holy sites.'

'Oh,' Richard said. He could only picture Otto as a tournament knight and regarded his black and white surcoat with confusion. 'You don't look right in that.'

Otto hunched his neck. 'We should be vague about how you know me. I am only a knight of the Hospital here, nothing more.'

'Whatever you want,' Richard replied. 'Who are your pilgrims?'

Otto shrugged. 'Bohemians. They almost drink as much as you English do.'

Richard glanced at Bowman, but the blonde man neither returned the gaze nor spoke.

The German stretched out his legs. 'You are late to arrive here, why do you come now, and with such strange company? I am sure I heard Guy of Lusignan shout at me.'

'You did,' Richard said, 'and it's been complicated.' He told him about the Young King, although he left out more than he left in.

Otto rubbed his stubbled chin. 'The Marshal and Guy of Lusignan in the same company? Life always surprises us, does it not?'

'It does,' Richard replied. 'And this land surprises me. We never had a cat the size of a wolfhound jump out at us in Normandy, or even Ireland.'

Otto laughed. 'You are but newborn babies here. Innocent of the place and the people. You have a lot to learn before things will stop surprising you.'

'Like what?'

'This kingdom has a king younger than you.'

'That's not so surprising,' Richard said.

'No,' Otto's shining eyes smiled for him, 'but he is a leper.'

'A leper?' Richard cried. 'They are not favoured by God, how could he be allowed to rule a whole kingdom, let alone the most holy kingdom on earth?'

'Your surprise is making my point,' the German said. 'King Baldwin's face has dried up so much his eyes cannot blink and he grows blind. The skin on his face is so withered and stretched he looks like a corpse, but yet he is a good king.'

'A good king? How can a leper be a good king?'

'You will understand,' Otto said, 'if you live long enough, that is.'

'That's not funny.'

'Neither is this land. The villages and cities are prosperous and the land is green and bountiful, but a darkness hangs over it all.'

Richard went to point at the gloomy sky.

'And I don't mean the night,' Otto said. 'Yesterday I heard a rumour that the true cross is gone. It has been kept under safe keeping and out of public for years, but some say it has vanished. If that wasn't bad enough, the Saracens have a new king. They call him Saladin, and he has turned his attention towards us. He has defeated his infidel opponents and now rules from Egypt to Syria, he surrounds us. And what is worse, we Franks are not united. The Templars insist on pursuing a vendetta against my order, I can only think through a need to be the largest holy order in the kingdom.'

'I'd ask Sarjeant about it, but I think we should let him sleep,' Richard said.

'The sarjeants and common members of both orders have no quarrel with each other, it is only the leaders, the Grand Masters.'

The Marshal, his red cloak over his knees, looked up. 'I will be seeking the Grand Master of the Templars in Jerusalem, I will lay down my lord's cloak with him at my side.'

Otto scratched his nose. 'You can do whatever you want, no one here will care about your dead king. They care about their own king, who will soon join yours in the afterlife.'

'From the leprosy?'

'Of course,' Otto replied. 'And he has only a six year old son. He has a sister, Sibylla, but she is unmarried and different important men are fighting to foist their preferred husband on her.'

'Because he'll become the King of Jerusalem,' Guy walked to their fire and stood behind Otto.

The German nodded but looked uncomfortably at Guy's proximity.

'This Sibylla sounds like the rich heiress you've always wanted,' Richard said to the Marshal.

The knight ran his hand along the cloak. 'That dream seems so pointless now. So empty.'

Guy rolled his eyes. 'It sounds like an opportunity to me.'

19

Otto sighed. 'I pray that the Holy Land will bring you some humility, who do you think you are to become the King of Jerusalem? I hear you are nothing but the fourth son of an unimportant baron.'

Guy's sword was at the Hospitaller's neck before Richard had blinked, but Otto didn't flinch.

'You think that is how a king behaves?' the German asked. 'I think it is how a bandit behaves. However short of nobles we are here, you will not be welcomed.'

'Short of nobles?' Guy lowered his blade. His eyes twinkled.

'We aren't even in Jerusalem yet,' Richard said, 'keep your dreams of power to yourself until we can part ways. And please don't threaten murder in front of my children.'

Guy scoffed. 'At least one of your children is well accustomed to murder, from what I hear. But if the kingdom is short of nobles, they will welcome me with my knights and silver.'

'Survive the rainy season before your mind turns to glory,' Otto said. 'Many who come here succumb to disease before long, and many others ride out to battle and fall to the Saracens, whom they assume to be weak and effeminate.'

'Well, they are, aren't they?' Guy sheathed his sword. 'Devil-worshipping women. We'll push them back into the desert.'

Otto rubbed his forehead and looked at Richard. 'Do you at least understand? If it were that simple, we would no longer have a need for crusaders.'

Richard did, but it made him feel uneasy.

Guy put his hands on his hips. 'We'll find this Sibylla and I'll marry her. That will show King Henry who I am.'

Otto shook his head. 'You cannot simply marry her, Count Raymond of Tripoli is matching her with an ally already. He wishes that the next king will deal with Saladin diplomatically. Count Raymond realises the Saracens are too numerous to defeat purely by sword point, unlike the Templars who preach war.'

'That's blasphemous,' Guy said.

'I'm sure it is,' Otto groaned, 'and you will get on with the Templars, because they share your sentiments.'

The Marshal folded his cloak up. 'A well-organised charge will see to the Saracens, whoever they are. No knightly army should fear anyone.'

Otto locked eyes with Richard again. Richard shrugged back.

'Perhaps,' Otto said, 'it is true that Saladin besieged the castle at Kerak last year and was chased away, maybe he fears us. But you should all tread carefully until you have gained the measure of this land. In Jerusalem you will walk shoulder to shoulder with Muslims, Jews, and Christians whose beliefs would earn them a heretic's death in the west. You must temper yourselves, but be on your guard, there is change in the air. Saladin is making everyone nervous, and worrying omens have been sighted in the skies.'

'Which omens?' Brian perked up.

'At the start of the year, thunder was heard in the east,' Otto said.

Brian frowned. 'Which signals a year filled with blood.'

'Indeed,' the German nodded, 'and fire has travelled across the sky at night, lighting up the land beneath with flames.'

'Oh,' Brian said, 'that is always bad.'

'You see,' Otto said, 'you have arrived in a bad year. Nothing calamitous has yet befallen the kingdom, and there are only two months left in the year for it to occur.'

'Which means we are due blood and fire soon,' Richard said. 'That's just great, I'm guessing the mountain lion's attack doesn't count.'

'Sadly not,' Otto replied. 'Had you found me in Italy I would have warned you not to travel this year.'

'It is just a few omens,' Richard said.

'And Saladin,' Brian added, 'don't forget him.'

'The Saracens are not the only threat,' the German said, 'dangers greater than mountain lions stalk the night within the frontiers of our kingdom.'

'If you're trying to scare the children,' Richard said, 'it's working.'

'A Muslim sect uses murder as a weapon to shape the world to their desire,' the Hospitaller said, 'their fanatical members murder their enemies in violent and public attacks from which they never plan to survive.'

'That sounds horrible,' Brian said.

Otto nodded. 'If Guy here wishes to be king, he will need to avoid angering them.'

'What are they called?' Guy asked.

Otto took a deep breath. 'Their sect is named after the hashish they smoke before their crazed attacks. They are called the Assassins.'

# KNIGHT OF THE TEMPLE

Arnold of Torroja was the Grand Master of the Knights Templar, and he was feeling very old. That didn't surprise him, because at more than sixty of age he found himself feeling old more often than not. What's more, he also found himself doing what he considered to be the most demanding job in all of Christendom. He had triumphed in his home country of Spain, working hard on a treaty which bound the kingdoms of Aragon and Castile together. That treaty, fifteen years old, still held and had allowed the kingdoms to focus on their true enemy, the Muslims.

The task which awaited him in the Holy Land after his appointment as Grand Master had proved far harder to tame. Even as Arnold tried to funnel all of Christendom's wealth into the Templar coffers to fund military campaigns, others thwarted him. Apathy in the west for one, but also the Hospitallers, who insisted on dividing the holy orders with their greed, and of course the Saracens themselves. If that wasn't bad enough, he also had to deal with things which were not real. Rumours. Rumours spread like rats, Arnold thought, and the latest was a worry. A fragment of the true cross on which Christ had been crucified was apparently missing from the Templar vaults. Except that to Arnold's knowledge, the Templars had never had a piece of the true cross in the first place, indeed he would now have to send men to search for it just because he was being blamed for its loss. These were but some of the challenges Arnold had yet to conquer, and they weighed on his mind.

Which was why, as yet another party of pilgrim knights appeared before him, he did not appear to be hugely interested. What use would knights be who arrived so late in the year? The rains would soon be upon the kingdom and campaigning would in all likelihood cease. And who would be left to feed and house these knights until they could be of use? Arnold knew it would be him.

Richard was too awestruck to notice the Grand Master's lack of enthusiasm. Jerusalem had hit him with a wall of loud voices, smashing pottery, barking dogs, the smell of balsam and different spices, and vibrant colour. The Temple Mount seemed to Richard to take up a quarter of the whole city, a thick fortified wall of whites and yellows, which stood in a vast square to the east of the city. In the centre of the walled area stood the Dome of the Rock, an enamelled and bright structure with open space around it, contrasting with the tightly packed city outside. The main Templar area was along the southern wall, with a hall in one corner next to the Temple of Solomon, the temple from which the order took their name. Underneath all this were the storerooms, dormitories, and stables of the Templars. The clerk who had let them in told them proudly that two thousand horses were kept on site. Richard had scoffed and pretended to believe him.

The hall in which they were led to the Grand Master was nothing like the rest of Jerusalem, indeed it was as austere as the barren and bare monastery at Grandmont, the place where they had buried the eyes, bowels, and brain of the Young King. The walls were bare stone and only light from scattered candles served to illuminate anything at all.

But at least it was cool.

Arnold's expression was just as cool as he asked who was the senior member of the company.

Guy and the Marshal stepped forwards together, then exchanged angry glances.

The Marshal knelt down and held up his red cloak as if

23

offering up a sacred sword.

The Grand Master sat at a table with some of his officers around him, and he squinted at the cloak. He looked at his officers and raised his eyebrows.

'It's a cloak,' one said.

'I can see that,' Arnold snapped. 'Why is he holding it up?'

'Ask him.'

The Marshal frowned. 'This is the crusading cloak of Henry the Young King.'

'The king of where?' Arnold asked.

The Marshal's frown deepened.

Richard walked up and nudged him. 'They don't know who you are, and probably know of more than one king called Henry.'

'How can they not know who I am? I'm the Marshal.'

'Whose marshal?' Arnold asked. 'And what is your name?'

'That is my name,' the Marshal said, 'and I just happen to have served in the office of the same name for Henry the Young King of England.'

'Oh, how confusing.' Arnold coughed. 'That king. Has he come to fulfil his crusading vow? I remember he took the cross.'

The Marshal choked down his feelings and shook his head slowly. 'My lord is dead. I come with his cloak to present it at the Holy Sepulchre. It was his dying wish.'

Arnold sniffed. 'And how many knights did he send with you to us?'

The Marshal glanced sideways at Guy. 'I think it is only a few of us.'

'Quarter yourselves wherever you wish and do whatever you want,' Arnold said, 'there will probably be no fighting for months. We can find a castle that is lacking a garrison and you can overwinter there.'

'Overwinter?' the Marshal asked. 'I'm here to lay my lord's cloak down. Will you help me with that? He wanted to join your order, and I had hoped you would share with me the honour of laying it to rest.'

The Grand Master thought about it and sighed. 'Of course, it is only proper. We shall line the Sepulchre with every one of our knights in Jerusalem. It will show the Hospitallers how strong we are.'

The Marshal bowed and stepped back.

Guy remained where he was, dressed in a bright blue tunic with a white cloak. Richard hadn't seen that cloak before, it looked very new and shimmered in the faint candlelight.

'And who are you?' Arnold asked.

'I am Guy of Lusignan, and I have always admired the knights of the Temple of Solomon. Your piety and poverty set an example to the world.'

'That's quite a statement from a man wearing a silk cloak,' Arnold replied.

Guy blinked. 'I assure you that my admiration is genuine,' he said. 'I believe we share a common view of the world and that we have much to offer each other. I am also a man of the Lord.'

Richard waited for Bowman to make a comment, then remembered that the blonde man had refused to enter the complex at all. Alice and the children had not been allowed in because of their age and gender, so Otto had taken them off somewhere else.

'What can you offer the order?' Arnold asked Guy.

'Victory,' the Lusignan stepped up to their table and put his hands on it. He leant over towards the Grand Master and his companions. 'I can offer you a Holy Land free from the infidel.'

Arnold laughed despite the rudeness of the Lusignan. 'You would need to be king to make such an offer,' he said, 'and when the King of France crusaded here not that long ago, it ended in ruin and disaster.'

Guy stood up. 'That was then. This is now. I have a token of my good will to give to you,' he waved at some of his knights and squires, who carried in four chests.

'He cannot mean to,' Sarjeant started to say, but he was stopped by the crash of the chests on the wooden table.

Guy lifted the lid of one, and Arnold strained his eyes in the gloom to study the contents. 'Is it all silver?' he asked.

Guy grinned. 'My gift to you. I ask nothing in return.'

Richard stifled a laugh that turned into a snort.

Guy shot him an angry glance, but he was in full flow. 'I simply wish for you to remember me in the future. Nothing more.'

Arnold's fingers dug into the chest and pulled out a pouch. He unwound the lacing that sealed it and poured the contents onto the table. Silver scattered everywhere and plenty rolled off and onto the stone floor. One rolled up to Maynard's foot where it collided with his shoe. The squire shifted his foot over the top of it without looking down.

Richard sighed. He would have to do something about Maynard.

'Guy isn't doing anything more clever than bribery,' Richard whispered to Sarjeant.

'I think that's all politics is,' the tall man replied.

Arnold spoke to one of the men beside him and nodded towards Guy. 'The order thanks you for your most generous gift. Our treasury was emptied during that failed crusade and we have not yet quite recovered.'

'You shall recover more than gold or silver soon,' Guy locked his fingers together in front of him.

'So you say,' the Grand Master studied the Lusignan's face. 'Are you from good stock?'

A flicker of anger sparked in Guy's face, but the candlelight was too poor for it to be seen by Arnold.

'My father was a great baron in the south of France. He was a great crusader, too, in fact he gave his life for his faith. You may have heard of him, he was Hugh of Lusignan.'

Arnold raised his eyebrows. 'You may have to remind me.'

Guy sighed. 'He was captured at Harim twenty years ago. I recently learned he died in Muslim hands. But I come from the same part of the west that many of the great lords here do. I am one of them. One of you.'

'I come from Spain,' Arnold said, a hint of a smile twitching from the corners of his lips. 'However, we have been searching for a candidate for the regency if King Baldwin succumbs to his unfortunate condition.'

'That is why the Lord brought me to the east,' Guy said.

Richard turned to Sarjeant. 'This can't work, can it? Just walking in and telling everyone how important he is.'

Sarjeant shrugged, but his mountain lion wounds made him wince. 'Great men die here as quickly as the rest, so perhaps the requirements for power are lower.'

Guy nodded to the Templars. 'Once installed, I will support you from a position of secular power.'

'Does he even know what he's talking about?' Richard whispered.

Arnold thought so. 'Very good,' he said, 'we shall take you into consideration.'

'Consideration?'

'We must verify your identity,' Arnold replied, 'we are not some village fools to be dazzled by silver. If you are who you say you are, we may support your bid.'

Guy thanked them and withdrew.

Maynard made a point of tying the laces on his leather shoes, but Richard saw him scoop up the errant silver coin and slide it into the sleeve of his tunic.

The Grand Master surveyed the few knights left before him. 'You are still here. Does anyone else want anything?'

Richard felt a burning sensation within himself. This was his chance to find out something about his father, something real. He walked forward and bowed. 'Grand Master,' he said.

'What is your name? Do you wish to be a king, too?'

'No,' Richard said, 'I simply wish to ask you a question about my father.'

'Go on.'

'His name was William Keynes. He came to the east years ago with his brother, but never returned home. My uncle said he died here but would not speak of it. Another knight told me to ask the Templars of Jerusalem about him.'

Arnold picked up one of the silver coins and turned it over in his wrinkled fingers. 'Curious,' he said, 'you have come a very long way just to ask a question. What other business do you have in the Holy Land?'

'None,' Richard replied, 'other than to cleanse my soul and perform the usual pilgrimages.'

The Grand Master nodded. 'I am afraid I do not know of a William Keynes, for I served the order in Spain until relatively recently.' He turned to his officers and asked them if they knew the name.

A chorus of heads shook and faces frowned.

Richard's heart sank. 'William Keynes,' he said. 'He looked

like me, just without half an ear missing and no scar across his face.'

'And probably more fingers,' Sarjeant added.

Arnold shook his head again. 'It seems the name is not familiar to our high-ranking officers here, so I am very sorry that you have not found what you desired.'

Richard didn't have any words to reply with. Who was he supposed to turn to now? He had no other clues to follow, no names to track down, nothing to go on at all.

Sarjeant put a gentle hand on his shoulder. 'My lord, perhaps we should leave the Grand Master alone. We can think about what to do next.'

Richard looked pleadingly at Arnold, but the Grand Master still had no answers for him.

'You are free to ask any members of the order you wish,' Arnold waved a hand in the general direction of the rest of the Templar complex, 'but many hundreds or even thousands of knights have passed through the Holy Land, and a great many of them have died while doing so. Your father's story is not unique, or even remotely unusual. Unless he made an impression on someone who still lives, there may be no trace of him left.'

That wasn't what Richard wanted to hear.

'If you wish to serve the Lord to the fullest extent,' Arnold said, 'you are all welcome to join the order. Exchange your golden spurs for iron, your bright tunics for the white mantle and red cross. Save your souls and your religion.'

Richard rubbed his nose. He didn't want any of that; he wanted to know what had killed his father, but for now it looked like he wasn't going to find out, and before he plotted his next move, they had a red cloak to lay to rest.

The Holy Sepulchre's circular chamber was lined with stone columns which reached upwards, supporting further rings of arches until they reached the domed ceiling. At the very centre of that ceiling, a shaft of light burst through a round hole and shone down on the Tomb of Christ itself. The tomb was the focal point of the round sepulchre, and it was before the tomb that Arnold stood.

A hundred Templar knights in their mail armour and white surcoats lined the circular walls, standing between each arch in solemn silence. Bright red crosses on their chests almost look like a decoration of the building, so many were they. The Templar banner, half black and half white, was held next to the tomb and hung limply above the Grand Master. The hundred Templar knights were reckoned to be a full quarter of the fighting force of the order, and standing as still as the stone that surrounded them, Richard felt a little nervous in their presence.

The Marshal nodded to a few of them as he entered with his red cloak. Richard assumed he knew them from his time in the Young King or Queen Eleanor's courts, and it was relatively fashionable for knights to retire to the Holy Land and join the order.

Richard stayed at the entrance to the sepulchre with Guy and Sarjeant, Gerold somewhere to the rear of a small crowd.

A new sound of hurried footsteps echoed from behind that crowd, and a man swept through it followed by a handful of knights before taking a place next to Arnold.

The man was King Baldwin of Jerusalem, and Richard couldn't take his eyes off him.

Baldwin was in his early twenties at most, clad in an orange tunic and with a golden cloak on his shoulders. The beam of sunlight from the ceiling landed partly on him and the cloak shone as if the sun resided within it. But that did not detract from the leper king's face. His skin undulated like old leather, and his eyes were shrivelled and too white. Yet he held himself more regally than King Henry or even the Young King had.

'Arnold,' Baldwin said in a husky but firm voice, 'you should have told me what you were doing. I am most displeased. And you did not inform the Hospitallers either, one might think you wished to exclude and humiliate them.'

The Marshal fell to his knees before the King and Grand Master, Richard heard a sniff and a sob.

A trio of bishops began to speak grandly in Latin, and didn't stop until Richard had almost fallen asleep twice where he stood. They droned on in the way all churchmen seemed to, and managed to drain any hint of excitement or interest out of the chamber.

Incense was carried around the sepulchre and its heady scent caught in Richard's nose and stung it.

Guy grew bored and left for a while, but returned in time for Baldwin to raise his voice and address those present.

'King Henry of England vowed to take the cross,' he said with less anger than when he'd arrived, 'as did his son, and it is our loss that neither will now venture across the sea to aid us. I know our archbishop declared the family to be the spawn of Satan for their failure to crusade, but one cannot always be so quick to judge. Had he lived longer, the Young King I am sure would have led an army to drive away the dangers which threaten us. But we should not hide from the truth, anymore than I should not hide from my affliction. I display my disfigurement with pride so that all shall know how I endure what God has sent to test me. This is my truth. My scars are my badge. The Young King's badge is the tragedy of his premature death, although I fear I will not even reach the age he did. Our world is harsh, and we should be compassionate to all. As such, it is a fitting honour for the Young King's cloak to rest here in the most sacred space in the world. The Young King's offering shall honour the Tomb of Christ, and we should all reflect on the temporary nature of this material existence.'

Arnold took the red cloak from the Marshal and bowed to the knight.

The Marshal wiped tears from his face, and instead of getting to his feet, he fell to the floor and wept even more.

The Grand Master took the cloak inside the tomb itself, a structure within the chamber, and the red cloak was never to be seen again.

Arnold came back and knelt down by the Marshal, something which took him a moment to accomplish, and started to pray.

The Marshal struggled to his knees and put his hands together with his eyes closed.

Richard closed his own eyes and said a prayer for Sophie. She should have been alive, another who had died too young, another life left unfinished.

Arnold's Latin echoed around the sepulchre as if music, the hair on Richard's neck stood up, and he shivered. At that moment, he decided the children must come first. He must look after them because their mother could not. He would search a while longer for his father's truth, but he had a duty to the twins. Richard opened his eyes to find King Baldwin was looking right at him. But the white eyeballs meant Richard wasn't sure if the king would really see him or not. He fought an urge to look away from the disfigured face with its retreating and incomplete nose.

The Marshal got to his feet when Arnold declared the ceremony to be over.

'Finally,' Guy whispered under his breath and only then did Richard realise the Lusignan had been right behind him.

Guy pushed him aside and approached Baldwin.

Arnold whispered into the king's ear.

'You wish to replace me?' Balwin asked, his tone flat.

'Only once you're dead,' Guy said before realising how that sounded and grimaced at himself.

'I know your family,' Baldwin said, 'you have brothers here already. All of you have fled the west because you disturbed the peace there. Why will you be any less disruptive here?'

'I have never been disruptive,' the Lusignan replied, 'and I only wish to serve the Kingdom of Jerusalem.'

Baldwin walked towards him. 'Not while I still draw breath,' he strode at Guy, who at the last moment ducked to the side to avoid colliding with the king.

Richard stood aside too, and Baldwin swept out of the sepulchre more quickly than Richard expected him capable of.

Guy brushed himself down and frowned.

The Marshal turned his empty hands over and stared at them.

Arnold watched him. 'Your task is complete. Your duty is discharged.'

'I feel empty,' the Marshal said, 'empty of purpose. I should return home and join King Henry.'

The Grand Master smiled. 'You journey so far for such a short time?'

'I swore to serve my lord's family after his death, and they are in the west. I am now ready to fulfil my promise and become the man I declared I would, a man of loyalty and honour.'

'Grandiose words,' Arnold said.

Brian shuffled forwards and raised a hand. 'If I may,' he said to the Marshal, 'but what would the Young King have done in the Holy Land had he lived long enough to reach it?'

The Marshal rubbed his chest where he'd sewn a cross onto his tunic. 'He would have fought the Saracens.'

Brian smiled. 'So what would he want you to do here?'

The Marshal sighed. 'I am but one man.'

'I thought you were the world's greatest knight?' Richard asked.

Brian nodded. 'What better chance to redeem the soul of your lord than to fight for him here? Monks pray to lift great men out of purgatory, but surely fighting a holy fight in their name would lift them quicker.'

Arnold coughed. 'That is well said, monk. If you wish to do one last service for your dead king, Marshal, fight for him and therefore raise him all the more swiftly into heaven. You do not need to cast your life aside and wear the white cloak. Join us for two years, sign the contract and save your own soul at the same time.'

The Marshal thought about it, but only for a moment. 'I cannot argue with that,' he said, 'today I am reborn. I will join the order for two years, and before I die, I will join as a full brother.'

Richard exchanged a questioning glance with Sarjeant. 'Did I hear that right?'

Sarjeant groaned. 'He's drunk with this place, he'll return to his old self later, once it's too late.'

The Marshal looked up at Arnold. 'I have a great quantity of silver to my name. I give it freely to the order.'

Richard coughed. 'He's mad,' he whispered.

Guy laughed. 'The German was right, this land is constantly surprising. I think the fool even means it.'

'I mean it,' the Marshal whirled round. 'And you should join, too. You above all others have a need to repent.'

'Me? What have I done?'

The Marshal looked aghast. 'You? You murdered my uncle in front of me, tried to kidnap our queen, locked me up and refused to feed me, and then tried to murder my lord at a tournament.'

Guy licked his lips. 'I'd rather you didn't talk about any of that.'

'That's not the worst of it,' the Marshal continued, 'you are the reason the Young King died. You shut the gates of Rocamadour in his face and left him to camp in that godforsaken swamp.'

'It was hardly a swamp,' Guy said.

'Join the order,' the Marshal said, 'make amends for your wrongdoings. Then you might be respected enough in this kingdom for them to tolerate your advances.'

Richard could see Arnold's face reddening, so he stepped forward and stood between the arguing knights. 'That's enough,' he said, 'this is the most holy place in the world, we can't argue literally in front of Christ.'

The Marshal retreated.

Richard turned to him. 'Let Guy lose his soul if he wants, it is better if he is far away from us. The two of you need to be apart. I saw what he did to your uncle, and Earl Patrick was a good man. I liked him. But he's gone now, and you need to let it go.'

'Like you're letting your father go?' the Marshal asked.

Richard's eyes flashed red but he was very aware of the hundreds of knights that watched him. 'That is very different,' he said, 'let your uncle go and forget your vendetta with Guy.'

'I will for two years,' the Marshal replied, 'but once my contract is over, I will kill him.'

Guy looked to Arnold. 'You can't allow that, can you?'

The Grand Master sighed. 'I have had enough squabbling knights to last me a lifetime, I do not need the two of you despoiling the Temple of Christ. Leave the sepulchre.'

The Marshal turned to leave but stared at Richard. 'You promised to kill Guy, too. Bowman told me how you promised Long Tom before he died.'

'Long Tom is gone,' Richard said, 'the world moves on. So should you.'

The Marshal snarled one last time at Guy and stalked out of

the sepulchre.

Guy waited for his footsteps to cease their echo, then stormed out himself, followed by his knights.

Arnold watched Richard. 'You are not like either of those two. If you joined the order, I would believe your vows to be sincere.'

'Join the Templars?'

'Don't you dare,' Sarjeant whispered behind him.

'How long will you join us? For life?' Arnold asked.

Richard's pulse quickened. 'I have children with no mother, I cannot cast them aside for anything, even the Templars.'

Brian tapped him on the arm. 'You did swear to join the Templars, Bowman told me all about it. Back in Castle Tancarville when you and the Marshal were about to be sent back to England. You swore to join the Templars if God saw fit to save the two of you from England. And then, thanks to the Lord, war was declared.'

Richard's heart sank. 'That was just an idle promise made by a desperate boy,' he said. 'Why did Bowman have to tell you about that? He doesn't tell anyone anything.'

'It was when he was delirious in Ireland,' the monk said, 'but I think it would be fitting if you joined the Marshal to serve the Lord. Christ saved both of you from returning to England, so it seems only fair.'

'Only fair? To abandon my children? Whose side are you on?'

'Christ's side,' Brian said, 'you owe him. I've heard you pray on ships too, when the storms come. We all pray, but you swear to join the Templars.'

Richard swore.

'You will have to stop doing that,' Arnold said, 'blasphemy is very severely punished in the order.'

Richard scratched his tunic where the cross had once been. He knew Brian was right, and as much as he was angry at Bowman, he knew a promise to the divine wasn't to be taken lightly. The Young King had done just that, and he had paid a heavy price. He shook his head. 'I can't join you for even two years. I will not send my children off to a monastery to never see them. My son already hates me, he'll never speak to me again if I do it.'

'We must all pay a price for our faith,' the Grand Master said.

'My children come first,' Richard folded his arms, 'apparently before my own soul.'

Arnold chuckled. 'Children are not welcome in the order, that is true, but there is no need for you to become a brother in white. Like your friend with the cloak, you may join the order and wear the black mantle with the red cross. You may not touch your wife, but you may spend time with your relatives outside the order's buildings.'

Richard felt Brian's eyes burning into the back of his head, and didn't want to speak about Sophie in order to correct the comment about wives.

'You can't be considering it?' Sarjeant asked. 'Two years is a very long time.'

'But I can still see my children,' Richard said, 'and I have some things I need to do penance for. Quite a few things, actually. I don't want to end up like either Rob the Scot or the Young King.'

'The price for temporary membership is small,' Arnold said, 'merely half of your estate on your death.'

Half of nothing is still nothing, Richard thought. 'That sounds fine.'

'Your followers can join as knights in the black, or sarjeants in the brown if they please.'

'No, not again,' Sarjeant mumbled.

'I'm sorry,' Richard said to him, 'but my children need to spend some time in one place, they need to settle down. If we can build a life in the Holy Land, then their souls can be saved. This is the best thing I can do for them.'

'What about me?' Sarjeant said. 'And what will Bowman think about it?'

Richard swore quietly. 'I'll worry about him later.'

Arnold ordered the Templars who surrounded them to leave and return to their duties. The knights left in silence, uttering not a word to each other.

'You do not want to become like them,' Sarjeant said.

'Your man seems to be hostile to our order,' Arnold said.

'That's not what he intends,' Richard said, 'he's just had some bad times in the past in the Holy Land. He finds the warm weather disagreeable.'

'I shall just fail again,' Sarjeant moaned.

35

'Again?' the Grand Master asked.

'It's not important,' Richard said, 'joining the order as a sarjeant will be the best thing for him. It will give him a chance to right the wrongs of his past.'

Sarjeant backed away and bumped in Brian. The monk grabbed his hands and spoke softly to him.

Richard looked for Gerold behind him, the gaunt knight nodded back. 'I shall follow you into the order,' he said.

'Good,' Richard said, 'take Sarjeant away, take him to wherever Otto took the children and Bowman. I'll find you.'

Gerold nodded and Maynard helped him push the numb-looking Sarjeant out of the sepulchre.

'You are making the right decision,' Arnold said, 'it shall be a quiet and wet winter, but in the new year you will earn your salvation.'

Richard hoped so. It was no small matter to commit two years to the Templars, especially when half of his friends would disagree with the idea. But he had to do right by his children, and he couldn't make a home for them in the west, so he would do so in the east. He would serve his two years, make friends, earn some land, and build them a safe place to call home.

Arnold let out a deep breath. 'There is a long process to follow to initiate you, but you can take the black mantle and wear it from today as a sign of your commitment.'

'Thank you,' Richard said, 'I think we all need a cause larger than ourselves, and what can be larger than the cause of Christendom?'

'Wonderful words,' Arnold said, 'and I welcome you into the Knighthood of Christ.'


Gethsemane was on the other side of a valley to the Temple Mount, beyond the city of Jerusalem, and Richard admired the sturdy walls of the complex now from the outside. Gethsemane was at the foot of the Mount of Olives, a hill that rose up and soared away from Jerusalem. It was covered with olive trees that snaked up from the ground and provided much needed shade, although some clouds now tainted the blue sky.

The smell of balsam was strong and groups of pilgrims made their way back and forth all over the hill.

Richard's fur-lined and black linen mantle was warm to the touch when he saw Bowman throwing a stick for the black dog. It ran into a huddle of pilgrims who had stopped for a drink and sent two old women tumbling to the ground.

'Judas, no,' Bowman shouted and ran over to apologise.

The pilgrims were horrified. 'Do not invoke the name of the betrayer,' one shouted.

'How dare you,' cried their guide, a local man with a respectable beard.

The black dog retrieved his stick and swaggered off back down the hill to where the children sat on some rocks with Alice.

Bowman retreated from the angry pilgrims and spotted Richard. 'I don't think they are fond of dogs around here,' he said.

Brian groaned. 'Do you know where we are?'

'Jerusalem?' the blonde man answered.

The monk groaned. 'Gethsemane. The place where Judas betrayed Christ.'

'Oh,' Bowman glanced back up the hill to where the pilgrims made the sign of the cross and threw some curses at him.

'Maybe don't shout the dog's name out,' Richard said. 'Probably anywhere in the Holy Land, actually.'

'Probably a good idea,' Bowman said. The blonde man regarded Richard's new mantle, then glanced behind him at Sarjeant, whose face was red and puffy. 'Have I missed something? Richard, who trimmed your hair?'

Brian puffed his chest out. 'Richard has been saved.'

'Saved?' the blonde man thought for a moment. 'Oh, no, young lord, what have you done?'

'I didn't have much choice,' Richard said, 'the Marshal joined first.'

'Joined? Joined what?' Bowman's voice hardened.

Richard bit his lip.

'The holy order,' Brian beamed, 'he's a Templar for two years.'

'A what?' Bowman shouted so loudly that Judas dropped his stick and Alice stood up.

'We're all joining,' Brian said.

'Speak for yourself,' Sarjeant muttered.

Bowman went to speak, but his words failed him. But only for a moment. 'What is wrong with you? The Templars will get you killed. Two years? Two years? We won't live two months in this place. What about your children? What about me? I'm not joining them, they're insane.'

'Calm down,' Richard said, 'I'm still allowed to see the children. Arnold said we'd be garrisoned in a castle over winter together.'

'Garrisoned?' Bowman shouted. 'You know how much you hate being stuck in one place. You'll be bored within two weeks. A frontier castle is no place for children, what happens if they get stuck in one when the Saracens come and attack?'

Richard scratched his cheek. 'I hadn't thought of that.'

'No, you haven't,' the blonde man said, 'and you didn't think about anyone other than yourself. How much of your silver have they demanded? All of it?'

'The Marshal gave all of his to them,' Richard said.

Bowman frowned. 'Surely not. His eyes shone with greed as much as ours did. There is no way that man would do something as selfless as that.'

Richard shrugged. 'He did, he's given it all away and will serve for two years. He's wearing a black mantle now, he's already wearing it over his mail.'

'The world's gone mad,' the blonde man said. 'Why didn't you ask me about this first?'

'Because you refused to come inside, why don't you ever want to come inside churches, anyway?'

'That's hardly the point,' Bowman said, 'you've signed our lives away for some dust and sand. See all these pilgrims swarming over this hill? They are being milked dry by the guides, who charge them to enter every shrine, and then charge them to leave again. To light a candle, you have to buy it, and food and shelter for the night costs double for a pilgrim what it costs the locals. The whole thing is a scam.'

'Keep your voice down,' Richard said.

'And stop saying such terrible things,' Brian said, 'this is the most holy city in the world.'

'Is it?' Bowman asked.

Alice arrived and looked Richard up and down. 'What have you done?'

Bowman snorted. 'This might be the first thing we've ever agreed on. The young lord is an idiot.'

'Please tell me my brother hasn't been as foolish,' she asked, recognising the black mantle for what it meant.

Richard shook his head. 'Guy told the king he wanted to replace him, I think he's even more delusional than the Marshal these days.'

Alice smiled. A sweet smile. 'You know nothing of this land, Richard. Men can rise quickly. You could rise quickly.'

'Leave him alone,' Bowman said, 'you can't have him.'

'Why not?' Alice asked. 'Is he yours?'

Bowman flushed crimson on his cheeks. 'You are the devil here. Slither back to your brother and leave us alone.'

'The children like me.'

Richard nodded. 'They do, and I'm not going to be the one to order her away, they would hate me for it.'

Bowman spat onto the ground.

'You can't do that when you join the order,' Brian pointed out. The blonde man scowled at him. 'I'm not joining it.'

'We'll just have to see where I get posted,' Richard said.

'Hopefully to Normandy,' Bowman turned away and looked for Judas, who was fertilising an olive tree.

Sarjeant scanned the top of the hill. 'I hardly remember where the shrine is. I will pray there if it isn't too busy. We are lucky we're this late in the year, most of the pilgrims have left.'

'This is the quiet time?' Bowman asked.

Sarjeant nodded, then climbed up the hill one weary step at a time. He disappeared into the olive trees.

'I'm going to go with him,' Richard said and followed up the hill where his feet slipped on the loose white stones.

'Fine,' Bowman shouted up behind, 'just leave us again, then.'

Richard wanted the blonde man to have some time to cool off, and he also wanted to find the shrine himself. He came across Sarjeant as the older man looked around the olive grove and sighed. 'This is the wrong way,' he said.

'Don't worry,' Richard said, 'there's plenty of time to find it, it's only a short walk from the Temple Mount so we can return any time we wish.'

'Don't remind me,' Sarjeant caught his breath from the incline. 'I warned you against coming here.'

'You did,' Richard said, 'but we're here now. I've got two years to speak to every Templar I can find and ask them about my father. If none of them know of him, then I will accept failure and we can leave.'

'Two years is a long time, my lord. When the sun comes out in the spring and burns me, I know I'll falter. I'll find a drink and then I'll be lost. I'm too old to recover from the drink again.'

'This time I'm with you,' Richard said. 'We're all with you. The biggest failing of your life was to fail as a Templar sarjeant, this is your chance to succeed at it. I will still need you to protect my children after the two years are over, but our souls will then be saved and we can look to the future. When I have land I will need my steward.'

Sarjeant's eyes watered. 'You would still have me as steward?'

Richard nodded. 'You saved my children when Yvetot was destroyed, I don't trust anyone with them as much as I trust you. I'm joining the Templars for myself, and you can do the same. Prove to yourself you are stronger than before. Fulfil the duty of a sarjeant and redeem yourself in your own eyes.'

Sarjeant sniffed but held himself taller. 'Perhaps you are right. Where better to start than here?'

Richard breathed a sigh of relief, but knew Bowman would be harder to win over. He left Sarjeant to find his lost shrine and descended the hill to try.

'Have her, take her away,' Bowman shouted. Richard shouldn't see him as he was still obscured by olive trees, but his voice certainly carried. Richard rushed down the hill, dust flying up from his feet and yellowing his new surcoat.

Two well-dressed men stood next to Alice, who backed away from them.

The Red Child, no longer sitting on a rock, stood up and reached for his full-sized sword.

One of the men, dressed in fine light blue linen, laughed. 'The boy is more of a man than your guardian.'

'I'm not her guardian,' Bowman replied, 'I'm the very

opposite, just take her.'

'What's going on?' Richard shouted before he reached them.

The Red Child stayed his hand, but the light blue man's companion pulled out a dagger. He noticed Richard's new mantle and put it away. 'I am sorry, I did not realise a man of the Temple was here.'

Richard caught his breath. 'What is happening?'

'These vultures are circling already,' Alice said, 'it seems word travels fast here.'

'What do you want?' Richard asked the knights.

'We merely wish to arrange a marriage between Alice of Lusignan and either of ourselves,' the light blue knight answered.

'Marriage?' Richard asked. 'Do you even know who she is?'

'Of course,' the second man said, 'she is sister to the man the Templars wish to put on the throne once the king has died.'

'The throne?' Richard couldn't believe his ears. 'Guy is only looking to be regent.'

'That is not what I have heard,' the light blue knight said, 'and either way, we wish to be close to him. We are friends of the Templars, too.'

'Take her,' Bowman said, 'take her far away from here.'

'Don't take her,' Alexander said from the rock he and Lora still sat on, 'she's looking after us.'

'I'm looking after you,' Richard said, but even as the words came out, he didn't really think anyone else would believe them.

'I am not available,' Alice said to the knights, 'and you should leave. When this Templar has completed his term, I shall marry him.'

Richard was stunned into silence, but Lora clapped her hands together with joy.

'She twists words like a priest,' Bowman sneered and looked at Richard to deny her claim.

Richard said nothing as the two knights shrugged at each other. The light blue knight then drew his sword, and the second man's dagger flashed in the sunlight. 'Two years is a long time,' he said to Alice, 'you will be long married by then.'

'Enough, Gilbert,' a fresh voice rang from lower down the

hill.

The two knights glanced down at it and spoke hurriedly to each other. Then they fled into the olive trees.

A man laboured up the hill. He was a short man with dark eyebrows and tanned face. His beard had flecks of grey and wrinkles grew out of the side of his eyes to betray his middling age.

'I don't know what just happened,' Richard said, 'but thank you, I think.'

The man bowed. He wore a blue surcoat over a mail shirt. Richard half thought he'd seen him before. 'Think nothing of it,' the newcomer said.

'You knew them by name,' Richard said, 'why are you here?'

The man smiled, and his wrinkles accentuated. 'Straight to the point,' he said, 'not vague and slow like other knights.'

'You sound vague and slow to me,' Bowman crossed his arms.

'Then I will get to my point. I am known as Miles, they call me the Syrian.'

'Did you come to find us or those knights?' Richard asked.

'You.'

'If you are another suitor,' Alice said, 'you should leave before we drive you away.'

'Fear not,' Miles said, 'I was present in the sepulchre with the king when your friend laid down his cloak. I am very curious about Guy of Lusignan, it is seldom that a knight from the west arrives as such an unknown man and with such an assurance of his destiny.'

'Why do you care?' Alice narrowed her eyes.

'The sister,' Miles tilted his head as he looked at her. 'As fiery as Guy is, it seems. Guy has jumped into a fire, whether or not he knows it yet, and he has dragged you in with him. Men will seek to marry you to bind themselves to Guy's banner.'

'I'm not marrying anyone I don't choose to,' Alice said.

'How quaint,' Miles said, 'admirable, really, but if you are kidnapped and married, then married you shall be.'

'This land is barbaric,' Alice said.

'This land is harsh,' Miles said, 'and it makes the inhabitants harsh. But I wish for peace. I work alongside many men in the interest of it.'

'You serve the king?' Richard asked.

'I do,' Miles said, 'and I serve the Templars when they wish to know the king's designs. When the king wishes to know of Arnold's plans, I tell him.'

'You're not a very good spy if you work for everyone and are so happy to tell strangers about it,' Bowman said.

'The truth is,' Miles said, 'my allegiance is to neither party, and I fear Guy will upset the delicate balance we currently maintain. King Baldwin's sister is the key to the future and I believe the Templars will send Guy after her.'

'To kidnap her?' Alice asked.

'That idea won't bother him,' Bowman said.

'No,' Miles replied, 'to recuse her. Sibylla is being kept safely away from Jerusalem until the king dies. Then she shall marry a man of Count Raymond's choosing.'

'I don't understand,' Richard said, 'and why tell us about it?'

'Because you may have some sway over Guy.'

'I am very sorry to disappoint you,' Bowman said, 'but that lunatic is nothing to do with us. He certainly doesn't take advice from us.'

'His sister is here with you, is she not?' Miles asked. 'You are either his men or his friends.'

'My brother has no friends,' Alice said.

'And we certainly do not serve him,' Richard pointed at his new mantle, 'we serve the Templars.'

Miles sighed. 'Somehow I am already too late, then. I can only suggest that you try to talk Guy out of his foolish plans. A man of such low standing should not aim at kingship.'

'Low standing?' Alice said. 'Be careful what you say next.'

'If Guy's temper matches yours, then pray he never becomes regent.'

'I couldn't care less,' Alice said, 'I just want to settle down somewhere. I've had enough of men's games.'

'Haven't we all,' Miles said. He adjusted his surcoat. 'If Guy is sent into the desert after Sibylla, tell him not to bother. Raymond's men guard the castle she is in and there are no water sources nearby. It is impossible to capture her.'

'Raymond's men?' Richard asked. 'Although, truthfully I don't care, I want nothing to do with Guy or any princesses. We don't mix well with princesses.'

Bowman snorted. 'Speak for yourself.'

Miles turned away. 'If you wish to work for peace, for a bloodless agreement with Saladin, then find me.'

'I wouldn't count on it,' the blonde knight said.

'The Templars are agents of unrest,' Miles said, 'you may well become disillusioned with them. They seek a war that cannot be won.'

'I think that's blasphemy around here,' Richard said.

'Even if it's the truth? Richard, I know your name. Keynes, that is. I would work with you.'

'Wait,' Richard said as Miles started to leave. 'Do you know anything about William Keynes?'

'Perhaps,' Miles said, 'if my memory could be properly nudged. Keep me informed of the Templar's plans with Guy, and I may be able to remember if I know a William Keynes.'

Richard couldn't read the man's face. 'I will not spy for you,' he said, 'not for a vague promise. I'm a terrible spy, anyway. Two kings have made me spy for them, and I got one of them killed, so you want nothing to do with me. I'm sure you are a fine man, but I am here for my soul and for my children.'

'You spoke to the Grand Master of a lost father,' Miles said, a wry grin on his lips. 'Think about that if you hear anything in the order I might want to know about.'

'You will not bribe me into helping you,' Richard said, 'I'm sure that would have me cast out of the order. Please leave me and my family alone, I am not in the Holy Land to play games.'

'That is a shame,' Miles said, 'Guy is a bad man, and siding with the Templars makes him a bad man with powerful friends. If he gains the regency as he desires, remember that you will be in the kingdom when he does it. Any consequences of his rule will come down on all of us. Including your children.'

'He can do whatever he wants,' Richard said, 'and the Templars must have plenty of more stable options than Guy. He will insult them before he ever gets anywhere near the regency.'

'He is your friend,' Mile said, 'you are associated.'

'He is not my friend,' Richard said, 'I don't even think the

Marshal is my friend any longer, not now, but Guy is someone I never wish to see again.'

'Suit yourself,' Miles said, 'I will be here if you change your mind.'

'I'm not a spy,' Richard said, 'and I don't want to have anything to do with any spy ever again.'

Miles half grinned. 'I'm sorry, Richard, but there are spies everywhere.'

# MESSENGER OF GOD

Richard discovered what his first assignment as a Templar would be just as Bowman finished telling him about his visit to one of Jerusalem's public baths.

'Everyone bathes together?' Richard asked.

'Of course not,' Bowman said, 'I had to take Alexander and the other one into the men's baths, and Alice took Lora into the women's.'

'Whatever next,' Richard shook his head.

'You should try it after a day in the sun,' Bowman said. 'I feel lighter.'

'I haven't been outside all day, I've been through the initiation with the Marshal, Sarjeant, and Gerold, and that's been deep inside the darkness of the Temple Mount.'

'Rather you than me,' the blonde man said.

A lay brother of the order appeared in the dormitory and his eyes searched for Richard.

'Yes?'

'I have a message for Richard to report to the Grand Master at once,' the brother said, 'if you are Richard.'

'Don't keep him waiting,' Bowman shouted as Richard left his friend and worked his way through the underground labyrinth of the Templars.

The lay brother took him to the private chamber of Arnold and shut the door firmly behind him on his way out.

The chamber was sparsely furnished, but did have a chair and a table covered in piles of parchment. It had something else on it too, sheets like parchment but whiter and thinner, the brighter leaves also had ink scrawled across them.

'I like to get new members out into the world as soon as possible,' Arnold sat in the chair, four candles burning across the desk, for there was no window. 'And I also like to test new members early. You see, we have had knights come to us who cannot stand up to the conditions of the frontier. It is all very well swanning around Jerusalem in their new surcoats, but an entirely different matter amongst the dust and boulders further away from comfort.'

'I am happy to serve,' Richard said, although he had seen little in the Temple Mount he could describe as giving physical comfort.

'They all say that to begin with,' Arnold picked up a leather tube with a leather sling connected to each end. 'Some disturbing news came to me this morning and I need to respond to it. This tube is your mission. You are to be an envoy, deliver the message inside this to a fort in the disputed region to the southeast.'

'Disputed region?'

Arnold raised his eyebrows. 'Are you afraid?'

Richard shook his head. 'I just want to know where I'm going.'

'To a fort at an insignificant place called Qal'at. It is a fort to guard a water source. A fort not garrisoned by Templars or even Christians.'

'You want me to take a message to the Saracens?'

'Heavens, no,' Arnold said, 'I shall leave it to Count Raymond to cavort with the enemy.'

'Who is in the fort, then?'

The Grand Master drummed the table with his fingers. 'You have taken the oath, so I suppose I have to trust you.'

Richard felt mildly offended, but stood still and waited.

'Qal'at is currently occupied by the Assassins.'

'What?' Richard nearly fell over. 'Aren't they a suicidal Muslim sect?'

Arnold nodded. 'But they are mightily effective. Now, this information is not for other ears, do you understand?'

Richard nodded.

The Grand Master held out the leather container. 'Take this to Qal'at, and try to avoid trouble or attention.'

Richard took the leather cylinder and hung the strap over his shoulder. At least it wasn't heavy. 'I have a cart and mule which I would like to leave here for safekeeping if you would allow it?'

Arnold shrugged. 'There is space under the Mount's esplanade for a hundred carts. Guy has already made the same request, although seeing the manner in which your friend the Marshal delivered his fortune of silver to me yesterday, I believe I know what is in the carts.'

Richard watched the Grand Master. If he knew his cart was full of silver, leaving it behind in Jerusalem was a gamble. But he also knew that a Templar, permanent or not, was unable to refuse an order, so he would go on the mission as instructed. However, the cart could not possibly go with him. 'You trusted me, so I shall trust you,' he said.

'Fascinating,' Arnold said, 'but if news reaches me from the west that a vast quantity of silver has been stolen from the church and then vanished, the carts are mine.'

'That will not happen,' Richard said with as much confidence as he could muster. Then a thought struck him. 'But why did Guy ask to leave his cart here? He's not joining the order, is he?'

'No,' the Grand Master replied, 'he surely lacks the discipline to be a Templar.'

'Then why is his cart to be stored here?'

Arnold smiled. 'The order is testing Guy, too.'

Richard's shoulders slumped. 'Please tell me you're giving him a message to send to someone else.'

'I will not speak of his task,' Arnold said, 'but Guy's path shares much distance with yours. At a place named Khirbet you will separate.'

Richard fought back the urge to complain. Instead he bowed. 'As you wish.'

'Very good,' Arnold said, 'we might make a good Templar out of you yet.'

'But where is,' Richard struggled to remember the names, 'either of the places you mentioned? I will never find them.'

'Of course not, you shall have a guide.'

'Oh, I see. How unfriendly is the land? I ask not through fear, but because I have only two knights, a sarjeant, and a squire. Guy's company is not large, either.'

'The lands are in Christian hands until Khirbet, but the Assassins will not give you trouble. Guy will progress into more hostile terrain, but that is why you will proceed with a Templar escort, mostly of turcopoles.'

'Turco-what?'

'Christian natives, men whose ancestors lived in the Holy Land before the liberation. They are fiercely loyal to the kingdom and the order, which is their primary asset to us. They usually fight in our way, but they are capable of fighting in the manner of the Muslims, and that is how they shall be armed to accompany you.'

'How will they fight?'

'They will be horse archers for this expedition. They ride swift Arabian horses, who do not tire in the heat, and shoot bows that can defeat the enemy, who do not often wear metal armour.'

'Because of the heat?'

The Grand Master shrugged. 'I have never asked them. But the turcopoles will be the company's scouts and defence. The Muslims favour the arrow over the sword or lance, so we sometimes find it best to fight fire with fire.'

Richard frowned. 'So Templar knights do not charge the Saracens?'

'We do,' Arnold said, 'but only at the correct moment and only when ordered. The Saracens know when to draw us out in disorder and at a time of their choosing, and in such a way they defeat most new knights from the west. I'm telling you this so you don't become one of them.'

'Is Guy in command of the expedition?'

Arnold snorted. 'Even if he attains the regency, he will be in command of little, I assure you. The turcopoles will be commanded by a Templar knight, our seneschal no less, who is second in command after myself. He will lead. He is a good man, ever keen to take the fight to the enemy.'

'I thought you only charged when the time was right?'

'Yes, and the seneschal, Gerard of Ridefort, is always keen to do so. Missing the right moment is as dangerous as preempting it. Obey Gerard's commands as if they come from the Lord himself. If Guy fails in his mission, Gerard has been instructed to finish it. Gerard hates Count Raymond, you see, he insists Raymond stole his bride from him, which was the catalyst for Gerard taking his vows as a Templar.'

Richard sighed. 'What about my family? I know I cannot leave them here with the carts.'

'They are not the order's problem,' the Grand Master said. 'You can do what you wish with them. Personally, I would leave them in Jerusalem, although you have little time to find a friend in the city, for you leave at first light tomorrow.'

The only person Richard had met in the city so far was Miles the Syrian, and he had no intention of leaving his children in that man's slippery looking hands.

'They shall have to come with me,' Richard said.

Arnold tapped his fingers on his table, causing the candle flames to ripple. 'I do not care what you do, but if you care for them, I would strongly, very strongly, advise not to take them east.'

'They survived the journey to Jerusalem,' Richard remembered the mountain lion, and his confidence faltered.

'You are not departing on a two-day amble across green and pleasant lands.'

'I thought you said it would be a quiet winter?' Richard asked.

'That was yesterday,' the Grand Master's eyes narrowed. 'But do as you will.'

Richard did. He furnished Bowman with the news of his task and set about preparing for it.

Before the sun had even risen above the Mount of Olives the next morning, Gerard of Ridefort had marshalled everyone under his command and marched them out of Jerusalem. The east road led towards Jericho, and Brian excitedly spent the morning telling everyone everything he knew about it. The children and Alice were sent to ride in Guy's company, Richard having been forbidden by Arnold from fraternising with them while moving.

Richard went to the head of the company where Gerard rode next to a sarjeant bearing the piebald banner of the Templars. It struck him as odd that the order's banner was not white with a red cross, but he didn't want to ask about it. All the Templar horses wore white caparisons emblazoned with the red Templar cross. The Young King and other nobles in the west had been identifiable by their use of caparisons, but in the east they were commonplace. The single or double layer of linen or wool wicked sweat away from the horses and kept the direct sunlight from their bodies. This kept them cool as well as protecting them from biting insects, of which there were many.

The guide responded to Richard's greeting with only a terse nod. The man had olive-coloured skin and a white wrapping around his head. His Arab horse was a dark brown colour, but otherwise looked much like Solis. Richard rode the blue roan, who put his ears back at the Arab horse while Richard was near.

'How long until Qal'at?' Richard asked the guide.

The man, some ten years older than Richard, didn't look at him. 'A number of days. It depends if it rains.'

'What is your name?'

'Ishmael,' he replied in a thick accent. Richard did not think the man was from Jerusalem, but if he was to be a guide for the east, then he was not likely to be a native to the holy city.

'Don't bother talking to him,' Gerard of Ridefort told Richard.

The guide's face remained impassive, and Richard moved the blue roan nearer to his new commander.

Gerard was a gruff man, slightly short and with a face that Richard couldn't work out. His bronzed complexion made Richard think he was Sarjeant's age, but he did look impressive in his bright white surcoat. 'And do not speak to me, either,' Gerard said, 'Templars march in silence.'

A fleeting thought of regret crossed Richard's mind. 'I am just trying to be prepared for whatever we might face, I don't yet know the order's rules.'

Gerard's face remained to the front as they climbed a hill which gave a stunning view behind them of Jerusalem's white buildings. A view which Richard entirely missed.

'Do nothing unless instructed,' the seneschal said, 'do not saddle your horse, mount it, dismount it, raise or lower your lance, or speak unless told to do so. Do not even drink unless I've commanded it. It is this discipline which makes us far superior to you unholy knights.'

'I have joined the order, I am a Templar.'

'But not for life,' Gerard said. 'Keep your mouth shut and your ears open. When we charge, keep your family war-cries to yourself. You may sing the psalm of David as we attack the infidels, nothing else.'

Richard frowned. Otto was right, the Holy Land was constantly surprising. He would also have to ask Brian to remind him of the psalm of David.

'Very well,' Richard said.

'It is already time to stop and pray,' Gerard nodded to a sarjeant next to him, who held a trumpet up to his lips and blew a few long notes.

The Templars were supposed to stick to a very strict monastic prayer schedule, but an allowance was given to knights in the field, and they had to say a certain number of the Lord's Prayer instead. Gerard took it seriously enough to stop the march while they did so.

Except Maynard didn't stop, or more correctly couldn't, because Solis dragged him along by his rope towards a bush some way off the road. The palomino's head was twisted by Maynard's attempt to hang on to the rope, but nothing was going to stop the horse from reaching the bush.

Gerard groaned as he watched. 'Is that your squire?'

'No,' Richard said, 'well, I suppose so now.'

'If he joined the order by himself,' the seneschal said, 'you are not permitted to beat him. Although in this case I might be willing to grant an exception.'

Solis reached the bush and tore thin branches and modest leaves from it.

Richard listened to Gerard recite the Lord's prayer seven times and tried to copy him. He was going to get very fed up with doing it every hour.

Gerard finished his prayers and watched Solis. 'There are not many horses so ill disciplined as that one, although his colour is rarer in the west than it is here. I knew a horse just like him once before. He belonged to a minor knight who had clearly never beaten him as a colt. He was useful in battle, but at all other times was quite insufferable.'

Richard's heart skipped a beat. 'Who owned the horse?'

'Why should you care? And we should not be speaking, it is time to resume the march. That is, if your squire can drag that horse away from the bush.'

'My father brought a horse to the Holy Land with him, the father of that palomino,' Richard said, 'I do not know what became of him.'

'The horse I knew is still in the stables at the Temple Mount,' Gerard pushed his horse into a walk.

'I didn't mean the horse,' Richard asked the blue roan to follow, 'but is he still alive? The horse was called Stultus.'

'I remember,' Gerard said, 'it is hard to forget a horse named after the Latin word for idiot. He is part of the order's breeding program, although he is almost too old for it now.'

Richard wanted to see the horse, the urge blooming almost like an ache, but he knew that would have to wait. 'What of its owner? He was my father.'

The trumpet signalled the restart of the march.

'Your true father, our Lord, resides above us in heaven, you should forget your material father. But I met the owner of Stultus long ago, before I was a Templar.'

'You knew my father?' Richard's mind tunnelled in and his heart pounded under his black surcoat and black mantle.

The seneschal sniffed. 'He was badly wounded in battle and I escorted him and some others back to Jerusalem. He had been stripped of everything but his tunic, and was covered in blood. I assume he is buried in the city.'

'What battle? Where is he buried?'

'Your questions are tiresome,' Gerard shot him a stern look, 'and your self-indulgence is displeasing. Your father is with the Lord, his horse is with the order. There is nothing more to say. Return to your position.'

Richard started to speak, but pulled his words back in. Gerard did not seem like a man to push, and there was a long journey ahead of him to catch him at a better moment. But he knew Solis's sire was alive at least, and meeting the old horse again after so many years would mean a great deal. He would return to Jerusalem and scour the graveyards too, surely a record of the burial would have been kept by the Templar clerks. At last

Richard had a clue, and the vast blue sky above seemed to offer hope.

He hung back until Bowman and Otto caught up with him. The Hospitaller knight had been absent more often than not, but Richard assumed it was because he didn't like the Templars. 'I am not complaining,' Richard said to him, 'but why have you accompanied us?'

The German grinned. 'When our paths crossed in that forest in Lagny, it was no accident of chance. I believe you have a purpose in this world.'

'Come on,' Bowman said, 'that's nonsense.'

Otto shifted his lance. In his black Hospitaller surcoat, he was only identifiable as a non-Templar because his cross was white instead of red. 'Of course,' he showed a toothy smile, 'whatever adventure befalls you, it will be infinitely more interesting than escorting pilgrims around the Holy Land. Their season is over anyway, and I tire very quickly of garrison duty.'

Richard sympathised with that. 'Even with Gerard in command?'

Otto spat onto the side of the white road. 'He can only be rude to me, he cannot harm me, and I am not obligated to obey him.'

'Lucky for you,' Richard said.

'Me neither,' Bowman chuckled. The blonde man had invested a silver coin on a surcoat of light green, and bought himself a lance, too, as the Templars would not arm those who were not members. And it was in groups of allegiance that the company separated as it marched east towards the Dead Sea. The Templars rode in front with their turcopoles, their horses only had black caparisons as they were not full brothers. Richard rode behind them with Bowman and the others, but Guy brought up the rear with his blue and white banner above him. He had not yet had time for anyone to make caparisons for their horses, and their coats were already hot to the touch.

To Brian's dismay, the company did not ride as far as Jericho, instead it took a road south and descended from the hills and sighted the shimmering lake that was the Dead Sea.

Gerard sent the Marshal with a turcopole to ride ahead, which Richard took as a sign that the territory was not quite as secure as that through which they had already ridden. When he returned, the Marshal was sent to the back of the Templar column rather than the front, which he complained about.

The Dead Sea was a long body of water stretching southwards, and it was down the eastern shore that they went. Richard felt exposed with the sea between them and Jerusalem, as white rocks rose up on their left-hand side.

'Feels like Niort again,' Bowman grumbled as he gazed up at those rocks. 'If someone was up there, we'd have nowhere to go but forwards or backwards.'

Richard watched the turcopoles march silently ahead of them. 'They seem quite relaxed.' He liked their horses, which were slighter than the blue roan, and was envious of their lack of armour. His own two mail shirts were not a serious burden, but the horse archers wore none, and he thought briefly about taking one of his shirts off.

'Why do they call it the Dead Sea?' Richard asked no one in particular.

The Marshal shrugged. 'There are no trees growing around it,' he said, 'although there are boats over there sailing across it.'

Brian, a fresh Templar cross sewn onto his robes, spoke up. 'This is well known to be the site of Sodom, which the Lord destroyed for its wickedness. Its ruin is under the sea, and all good Muslims avoid this place.'

'I hope the bad ones avoid it too,' Bowman glanced up at the rocks again.

As they progressed south, and into a second day, the scenery remained the same. Sea to the right, crumbling white rocks to their left. A few caravans passed them by, and once they overtook some merchants who stood despondently next to a cart with a broken wheel. Even though they were Muslims, Gerard nodded in their direction and four turcopoles dismounted to help repair the cart. Richard thought about it for the rest of the long day, but still couldn't understand why Gerard had granted them assistance.

Small ships sailed north, taking corn and dates to Jericho, and during a prayer stop Gerard complained to Richard that the Hospitaller ships were exempt from paying a tax when they sailed the Dead Sea. He then sent Richard ahead to where a

Hospitaller tower stood tall atop the rocky cliff-side, to ensure that the inhabitants of it would not shoot crossbow bolts down at them.

Richard felt quite insulted as he stood alone below the tower, waiting to see if someone would shoot at him, peering up at the lone Hospitaller sarjeant who stood on its platform. He shifted the leather cylinder onto his other shoulder and rode back to Gerard to tell him the road ahead was safe.

'Surely the Hospitallers wouldn't attack a Templar company?' Richard asked the seneschal.

Gerard grimaced. 'Never trust them. It is bad enough you've brought one along with you. If you try that again, I shall speak to the Grand Master about it. If wagering was not a sin, I would lay down a sum of money that he will disappear as soon as he discovers our mission.'

Richard didn't bother replying. A few wisps of clouds gathered, and the very occasional shade they brought was welcome. What was less welcome was when Bowman pointed out a lone ride on the cliffs ahead.

'Does that not worry anyone else?' the blonde man asked.

The rider disappeared before they drew too close, and four turcopoles were sent out to scout the path ahead.

Another day later, and with the monotony of the unchanging landscape grating him, Richard spotted another horseman. Again the turcopoles rode out, but nothing seemed to come of it. When the cliffs gave out and the land to their left opened out into a great dusty plain, it wasn't long before they saw the peaks of distant mountains, yellow spires above the haze. The company turned towards the mountains and left the Dead Sea behind them.

'I'm feeling quite far from safety now,' Richard muttered as they climbed the first of many hills and the terrain became ever more desolate. Barely a green bush broke up the whites and bleached yellows of rock after rock, and as they wound their way between ever larger peaks, Richard said a prayer that their guide Ishmael could be trusted. And that the guide survived, because Richard would never find his own way back.

Word filtered down the company that Kerak was only a day away further up into the mountains, and Richard wondered why anyone was bothered enough to fight over so barren a land.

A bird of prey wheeled overhead, and Bowman identified it as a saker falcon, but Richard was thirsty and didn't listen. Bowman complained that riders were following them, but they turned out to be a fast moving trio of messengers on the Lord of Kerak's business.

Richard checked on the twins whenever they camped for the night, but Alexander was frightened and Lora looked more like her mother every day, and Richard found himself struggling to speak to either of them. When he viewed the Red Child, he saw the Little Lord's face and wondered if anyone would ever tell him how his real father had died. And who was responsible.

So when Kerak finally loomed into view, Richard felt a sense of relief. They left a shallow and stony valley which opened out onto a basin between more peaks that was dominated by a central mountain. On that mountain, gleaming in yellow stone, lay Kerak Castle. The mountain under it had perfectly smooth almost vertical sides, and Richard couldn't tell if the whole thing was man-made, or if the smoothing had been added to an existing mountain. It towered above them regardless, a long castle with many huge towers and a monumentally enormous keep. It was so high up and immense that Richard wondered how mortal men had been able to build it.

'It is larger than the Tower of London,' Bowman whistled in appreciation.

'I think it's more like three of them stuck together,' Richard said.

Patches of green surrounded the fortified mountain, field systems and orchards and groves filled the valley floor.

The mountain holding up the castle extended to the north, and a town was built on the causeway that joined the castle to the mountains. A strong wall kept Kerak separate from the town, and Richard decided that the wall would be the only way to consider attacking Kerak's castle itself, for the other three sheer sides were defended by the man-made mountain.

Gerard halted the company outside a Templar complex in the town. Four compact rectangular buildings formed a defensible courtyard between each other, making the structure look like a small castle.

'Your family should stay here,' Gerard said.

Two dogs in a nearby alleyway fought each other with snarls and barks, and the town was an assault on Richard's senses after their time in the wilderness. Something cooking smelled like it was ready to eat.

'Is it safe?' Richard pulled his attention back to the complex.

'You've seen the walls,' Gerard said, 'Kerak will never fall. Saladin tried last year and gave up, he knows there is no way inside.'

'The castle, yes,' Richard looked at the Templar building, 'but I'm not so sure about that.'

'Kerak is the last town on our route,' Gerard said, 'leave them here or your children will be going all the way.'

Richard frowned and remembered Arnold's warning about the east. But what choice did he have? Solis had been as slow as their twenty packhorses, and Judas had lost a lot of weight keeping up. The children were fearful and young. 'They should stay here,' Richard admitted.

Alice shepherded them inside the small castle. 'You never told me we would be travelling so far from society,' she scowled.

'I didn't know, but it looks safe here. I'll leave Gerold with you, he's travelled enough too.'

'Society will flood Kerak soon,' Gerard said, 'a royal wedding will take place here in only a few days. King Baldwin's half-sister will marry the stepson of Kerak's lord, and several of the kingdom's greatest men and women will attend. Tomorrow, Kerak will be more full of society than Jerusalem.'

Alice smiled for a moment, then brushed some of the thick dust which had caked her dress. The silver circlet had been packed away.

'Be gone, woman,' Gerard waved Alice inside. 'We have suffered you long enough.'

Her eyes blazed at him, then at Richard, but he could only shrug and say his goodbyes to his children. The Red Child hugged Guy and ignored Richard before he walked off into the Templar castle, his sword dragging a line in the dusty street.

Gerold led Solis in through the gates built into one of the buildings, and Richard said a prayer that they would all be safe when he returned for them.

'Perhaps we can move at a proper speed now,' Gerard said as the gates shut.

Richard took a deep breath and let it out. 'Do we enter the castle or continue on?'

'We do not have time to see the lord,' the seneschal said, 'although Reynald is a fine man. Earlier this year he led a fleet to try to sack Medina and Mecca, two of the infidel's most holy cities. Think of the achievement that this was, to sail so far from safety to bring the fight to the enemy. There can be no doubt that the Lord Himself shields Reynald of Chatillon.'

'Reynald is a friend to the Templars, then?' Richard asked.

'Indeed, and once he is bound to the king, then we can all work together to defeat Saladin and save the kingdom.'

The trumpet blared to signal the restart of the march.

'Is the kingdom in real danger?' Richard asked.

'If unchecked, Saladin would destroy us all,' Gerard said, 'but fortunately the Lord has provided the kingdom with the means with which to defeat him. He created us.'

Richard glanced back at the Templar mini-castle as they left, and Gerard rode to the head of the company.

'You can't do anything about it,' Bowman found Richard, 'not once you took that cross. It's too late for regrets, young lord, but I won't stop telling you I told you so.'

Richard ignored him as the slightly smaller company rode south away from Kerak. The road became slow going and more of a track as it wound around mountain sides and along dry valley floors. Shepherds moved herds of thin and bleating goats around the countryside, but after half a day they saw nothing but merchants going the other way. Horses stumbled on rocks on the track and the sun beat down relentlessly. The hourly stops for prayers sapped Richard's patience as quickly as the heat, and gave him far too much time to think.

Richard asked the guide how far away Khirbet was, and received only an answer of, 'soon.'

The constant ups and downs depleted the blue roan's energy, and Richard took to swapping between it and his riding horse, the one taken from a Tancarville rider outside a small chapel in the woods in Normandy. How he longed for those woods now, the shade and coolness, the constant nearness to a stream or river. Clouds.

Grit wormed its way into his clothing and to his body, rubbing him almost raw. His face became hot to the touch, and all the newcomers in Guy's company sported bright red and pink faces. The Marshal was the exception, his swarthy skin not changing in colour at all as he diligently complied with every order he was given.

They stopped to pray at the most desolate and empty place Richard had ever seen. All around was white stone, white boulders, white dirt, white mountains. The only colour brought to the scene was the shadows the mountains themselves cast. The sky was pure blue, empty of clouds or breeze, and Richard wondered what he was doing. Why was he out in the emptiness, thirsty, tired, and hot?

They rode on, Khirbet apparently just over two more mountains, and they entered another valley system. The beds looked like riverbeds, just without the water.

'There must have been an actual river here once,' he said to Otto.

The German nodded. 'Maybe for a few days a year when it rains, which could be in a few weeks. Until then, nothing but scorpions.'

'What's a scorpion?'

'A creature you do not disturb,' Otto grinned.

Bowman turned his head right and then left. 'How long has it been since we met anyone else on the road?'

'I don't know,' Richard said.

Otto's face, tanned and weathered, lost its grin. He peered up to their right, where a steep hill flanked them, and then ahead where the valley turned sharply around that hill. The dry riverbed, which was quite wide, ran along the road to their left, a steep slope on the far side punctuated by ravines. 'He has a point.'

Richard strained his hearing, but he could only hear the sound of a hundred horses and their metal bits jangling. Occasionally, one snorted. 'I can't hear anything other than us.'

Otto sighed. 'You should ride ahead and see if our glorious leader will send out the turcopoles,'

'Why?' Richard asked.

He was answered by an arrow.

Richard noticed it sail up from their right, because he heard its fletchings whistle.

'On, no,' Bowman said and shifted his shield around to his front, but the arrow had come from their right, the side from which no shield would be of any help.

Richard looked forwards for instruction while Bowman unpacked his bow and strung it.

'You are not allowed to act with orders,' Otto said, 'but the rest of us should turn back, for that is the best option to survive.'

The arrow hit a stone and its iron head flew off harmlessly, but everyone looked right as other missiles followed it from along the length of the ridge. Richard saw human heads bobbing about on top of it.

The volley of arrows was not well-aimed or numerous, and most overshot the company. One horse was hit in the flank, but its turcopole rider stayed in formation as it hopped a step and then carried on as if nothing had happened.

Bowman swore. 'You're all looking the wrong way.'

Richard snapped his head to their left and across the dry riverbed.

'Mount warhorses,' Guy shouted behind and squires milled about to swap horses for those who travelled on palfreys or amblers. The blue roan was back with Maynard, and Richard remembered how Earl Patrick had been killed because he'd gone to mount his proper warhorse in the Niort ambush. But Richard didn't know the quality of the horse under him, and that made him nervous.

He had no time to think further as the enemy poured out of three ravines. They spread out into a long loose wave, swiftly passing around rocks and yelling war-cries that curdled Richard's blood. They were unarmoured and dressed in a range of colours, and between their horses ran foals. Richard found himself surreally marvelling at the wisdom of acclimatising foals to battle instead of preparing for battle himself.

Horses in the column fidgeted, sensing the approaching danger, and some spun around to face it.

'What do we do?' Richard asked.

The trumpet blared out some notes.

'Is that the attack?'

'No,' Sarjeant said, 'that's for the turcopoles.'

Bowman nocked an arrow as his horse pawed the ground. 'Stop it,' the blonde man drew back the bowstring but hadn't shot from horseback before.

The attackers also had bows, bows which curved the wrong way at the ends. They shot before Bowman thought they were in range.

The arrows curved through the air and peppered the company as the turcopoles turned to face them. Horses were hit.

Bowman loosed. His arrow spiralled through the air and landed between two enemies. 'No, no,' he shouted. His horse spun around and kicked out at Richard's, but luckily missed.

'Just bad luck,' Richard said.

'I've lost it,' the blonde man cried.

The turcopoles surged forwards and loosed arrows as they moved. Their horsemanship impressed Richard as they rode without reins, and their arrows felled many attackers.

The Muslims turned about in a moment, throwing up a cloud of dust, and rode back the way they'd come, but still they let arrows fly towards the pursuing turcopoles.

The trumpet sounded again.

'That's us,' Sarjeant said, 'follow the piebald banner.'

Richard's eyes found it at the head of the column, which was now only Gerard, his bannerman, and the trumpeter. He spurred the Tancarville horse to catch up, everyone else behind moving him.

Gerard cantered his horse along the road which curved to the right.

'He's trying to flank the ambush,' Bowman shouted from next to Richard, his black horse seemingly happy to extend its stride and gather speed for the first time since their sea voyage.

The air rushed over Richard's face as he caught up with Gerard, and Guy's company closed in behind.

The Marshal shot in front of the banner for a stride, but hauled himself back before he could be reprimanded. Richard remembered when he had not been so aware of himself. Arrows sailed over from the cliff, but now the horses moved too fast to be hit.

Horses thundered on the white earth and dust flew up all around. They rounded the bend in the road and turned off it, curling back to climb the ridge and find whoever was shooting the arrows.

The slope was steep but the cantering horses bounded up it, sometimes leaping and jerking their riders in the saddle as they dislodged stones which rolled down behind them. One of Guy's squires fell off.

Richard was right behind Gerard as they reached the top of the slope and could see out over the plateau that ran alongside the road.

Boulders the size of houses littered the summit, and enemy archers on foot rushed to congregate together. They were not far away.

The banner waved and the trumpet blared out three shot notes.

'Form the line,' Sarjeant shouted, but he was out of breath.

Richard wasn't, he gripped his lance and gritted his teeth. His horse felt steady enough beneath him, but he had no idea if it was experienced in battle.

Gerard and his two Templar companions picked up their battle-song. 'Not to us, O Lord,' they sang, 'not to us, but to your name give the glory.'

Bowman cried something unintelligible to one side, but the Templar's calmness was more terrifying.

The archers had nowhere to run. The large boulders were too far away to use as cover, so they took aim and shot from wherever they stood.

An arrow whirled over Richard's head, and another put a hole in the piebald banner, but when Gerard lowered his unpainted lance, Richard did the same.

The ground rushed by, a blur of white, and Richard aimed his weapon at an archer who stood up and turned to run. Richard's lance caught his shoulder before he could flee, and the man

63

spun around as his shoulder was torn apart.

Gerard had aimed for the largest group of archers, maybe twenty of them, and he cut through them all, his horse a ship ploughing through the waves of the enemy.

The charge swept over the ambushers and turned back to finish them off.

Bowman loosed an arrow from horseback. 'I'm going to hit one,' he cried.

The arrow landed between an archer's legs and the blonde man howled in frustration.

Richard chased a fleeing man and brought him down as his lance sliced into the man's unprotected back.

An arrow hit Richard's side and tangled in his layers of mail, and he thanked himself for having resisted the temptation to remove it.

Gerard flashed his sword at the group of routed archers as he and his Templars chased them along the ridge.

'Over there,' Sarjeant shouted, pulling his horse up and pointing his blood-red spear over to the sea of enormous boulders.

The archers had not been alone.

A wall of spearmen advanced, more archers mixed into their ranks, loosing arrows at Richard and Guy's company, who had arrived too late to charge the archers.

Bowman loosed an arrow at the mass but it sailed over them. He grunted, slung the bow over his shoulder, and retrieved the lance which he had tied awkwardly to his saddle.

'Where's Maynard?' Richard looked around as Otto joined them.

Guy shouted at his company and they wheeled left in a well-drilled line to approach the enemy spearmen.

'He's going to attack,' Sarjeant said, 'and now we're Templars, we are obliged to attack too, regardless of the opposition.'

'Are you regretting it yet?' Bowman pointed his horse towards where Guy's blue and white knights gathered themselves up and lowered their lances.

'Maybe a little bit,' Richard urged his horse on, 'form our own line on me.'

Bowman, Sarjeant, and Otto obliged, and they rode around a

boulder to get behind the enemy.

Guy charged them head on. Richard missed watching their charge as they rounded a boulder the size of his old castle at Yvetot, but when he emerged from behind it, the blue and white company was on the far side of the enemy.

Spearmen lay scattered on the ground, but two Lusignan squires and one knight lay with them. Guy's men turned around, some left, and some right, and the battle broke up as the Muslims re-formed in small clusters.

Richard aimed his small formation at the nearest cluster, who were concentrating on Guy's men, and charged them from behind. All ten men were flattened and torn apart, although Bowman's lance broke as it jammed into the ground.

'I can't afford more,' the blonde man cried as he drew his sword and they targeted another band.

Richard's company split that cluster in two, some of the surviving spearmen ran to a boulder for protection and Richard decided to leave them alone.

The Lusignan company rode through the field once more and then gathered itself up, pairs of squires and separated knights flocked back to the blue and white striped banner.

The Saracens regrouped, too. Half of their number was dead or scattered, but the survivors bunched together in search of safety. Except that one knight still fought in their midst.

The Marshal, his black mantle torn in two and his black surcoat stained even darker with blood, rode in the centre of the enemy, slashing with a sword in one hand and mace in the other. His reins hooked onto his belt, his stallion leapt in a small circle as he battered down at spearmen all around him.

'Damned peacock,' Bowman muttered.

'We need to save him,' Richard cantered over to Guy, whose men had stopped to catch their breath.

'Attack now,' Richard said, 'the Marshal won't last for long.'

'He shouldn't have let himself get caught up in there, should he?' Guy rested his lance on the ground and drank from a wineskin. The red liquid oozed down his chin as he gulped it.

'What are you doing?' Richard shouted.

Guy plugged the wineskin. 'What does it look like I'm doing?'

'We're charging, with or without you,' Richard said, 'but you can't leave a fellow Christian to die like this.'

The Marshal took an arrow to the helmet, Richard heard the clang of iron on iron.

Guy picked up his lance. 'He will murder me in two years, he said so himself. Why would I go and rescue him now?'

'Because he's a Christian and he's about to die.'

A spear grazed the Marshal's horse, but most of the Saracens hesitated to commit themselves and kept just out of reach of the horseman who pirouetted around again and again.

'We need every man if we are ambushed again,' Richard said, 'and we need every man to defeat these Saracens.'

Guy shrugged. 'I'm catching my breath.'

'What will the nobles of Jerusalem think of you when they hear you failed to protect a Christian from the Saracens?' Richard asked. 'Do you think they will want a coward for regent?'

'Coward?' Guy roared. 'Come closer and dare to say that again.'

Richard spun his horse around and foam flew from its mouth. 'Come and get me, then, you coward,' he shouted back and spurred the Tancarville horse towards the Marshal.

Bowman was right beside him as they raced towards the Saracens. Otto bellowed a war-cry that seemed to comprise swear words rather than psalms, and Sarjeant wasn't far behind. Maynard was still nowhere to be seen.

Richard felt sweat sting one of his eyes as his horse put its head down and surged on. He supposed it knew battle, after all. His body was red hot inside his mail and layers of wool and linen, but he clenched his teeth again and lowered his lance.

The Saracens were so transfixed by the Marshal and his evasions that they turned to face Richard and his companions far too late.

Richard's horse barged two spearmen down to the ground as his lance sliced across a face, stabbed right through the throat of another, and buried itself in the chest of a third man. His horse slowed as it pushed against the mass of bodies it charged, and when it punched through to the Marshal it had dropped to a walk.

The Marshal grinned and crunched a spearman's head with

his mace. 'You took your time.'

Richard's lance was wrenched from his hands when it caught in a ribcage, and he drew Durendal, Roland's sword, and used it to cut a spear shaft almost in two.

Otto's horse slammed to a halt and the German half fell and half threw himself to the floor, where he rolled and set about the Saracens with his mace. A spear glanced his arm and severed some mail rings, but then, just as the enemy realised the horsemen had stopped moving and were easy targets, Guy's company crashed into them like a lightning bolt.

The wave of Lusignans rolled over the Saracens, trampling those with hooves who didn't succumb to lance or sword.

Guy's horse collided with Richard's and their feet tangled up, Richard's foot being wrenched from his stirrup. 'Careful,' Richard shouted.

'Get out of my way,' Guy punched Richard's shield with the pommel of his sword.

Richard stepped his horse aside and looked for targets, but the battle was already over.

Unable to flee from the mounted victors, a dozen Saracens threw themselves to their knees and wailed in their native tongue, bowing towards the Christians.

The Marshal cantered his horse straight into Guy's, the chest of his beast almost barging Guy's mount over. 'You left me to die,' the English knight yelled, 'I'll cut you down.'

Guy's horse recovered its balance and took itself away from the Marshal. 'Don't think so much of yourself,' Guy said, 'you survived, didn't you?'

'But it was no thanks to you,' the Marshal chased Guy and swung his sword at him. Guy raised his shoulder to bring his shield up to take the blow, when a shout echoed off the boulders.

'Enough,' Gerard bellowed, his face red with anger. 'One more blow and you will be cast out of the order and excommunicated. Sent back to Jerusalem on foot.'

It was the last sentence that stunned the Marshal back to his senses, and although still seething, he backed away.

Some of Guy's men cantered off in various directions to chase down those Saracens who elected to flee, and none would escape the flat plateau alive.

Gerard rounded on Guy. 'We saw your delay. No fighting man should delay for a moment when a Christian is in danger. That is the single circumstance when a Templar is allowed to attack without orders, that is how important it is. Do you not understand the purpose of knights in the Holy Land?'

Guy simmered, deciding how far to push Gerard.

The Templar's breathing was rapid, his eyes shining with fury. 'When you hear the order to charge, you charge. That means you follow me. Not ride off on your own, this isn't Normandy or wherever you came from. You listen to me, do you understand?'

Richard waited for Guy's response, and when it came it was a meek nod.

'We would have waited here for the turcopoles to return,' Gerard pointed down at the spearmen, 'who would have filled these men with arrows and saved your men from dying. We cannot afford to lose those you have lost here. You do not know best.'

Guy looked away.

The turcopoles galloped up the slope as if on cue and slowed when they saw the battle was finished.

'See?' Gerard wasn't done. 'You've lost a tenth of your strength because of your hot-headedness, your arrogance. You obey me now, do you understand?'

'Yes,' Guy mumbled.

The surrendered Muslims knelt or prostrated and begged for their lives, oblivious to the argument which raged around them.

'Will they fetch a ransom?' Bowman sheathed his sword after wiping it clean on his saddlecloth.

'We do not take captives in the Holy Land as we do at home,' Sarjeant said.

Richard found it within himself to chuckle. 'I've only just realised, for the first time in my life I have enough silver to actually ransom myself if I needed to.'

'And now,' Bowman said, 'you've come to a land where no enemies will ransom you.'

'It's almost funny,' Richard said, 'so what is done with

prisoners we capture?'

Gerard glanced over at the turcopoles.

Otto stood by the prisoners, his chest still heaving from his exertion, and three arrows hanging out of his surcoat. None had gone through to his skin.

Gerard turned to Richard. 'No Templar captured by the Saracens is ever allowed to live,' he said.

'Oh,' Richard replied.

'That is why we always fight to the very last man. To the death,' Gerard looked down at Otto. He closed his eyes as if summoning the energy to forget he was a Hospitaller, then nodded.

Otto brought his mace around with an almighty heave and it caved in the top of a Saracen's skull. It came away with blood-stained hair attached to it, and the other captives howled.

The turcopoles rode over them, cutting them with their swords until the white earth ran red and the screams ceased.

None of the horse archers showed the slightest emotion at the execution they had conducted, some dismounted to loot the bodies while others merely scanned the horizon for danger.

'This place makes men hard,' Richard whispered.

Sarjeant nodded. 'Or it breaks them.'

Richard frowned and watched as the turcopoles untied leather armour from fallen foes and claimed a few iron helmets.

'Were they bandits?' Richard asked. 'They were more numerous than a mercenary company in the west, and they are not as poorly armed as they first looked.'

Gerard grunted. 'The bowels of hell are full with the infidel, they spill into this world and their teeming masses never seem to be exhausted.'

Ishmael the guide seemed nonplussed about the death around him, but the seneschal spotted him. 'You, did the turcopoles destroy the horse archers?'

The guide watched the horizon and didn't return Gerard's gaze. 'We trapped a few in the ravines,' he said slowly, 'chased the others out. They are scattered and will not regroup too quickly. They will not bother us after this death here.'

'It matters little either way,' Gerard said, 'if they return we will see them off again as we did here. Despite the impetuousness of the western knights.'

Guy rode back to his knights, where he ordered them to reform, but he snatched angry glances back towards Gerard.

The guide rode his Arabian horse to the pile of trampled and lacerated prisoners. 'Check the bodies,' he said, 'check for freshly minted coins. Saladin is freer with his wealth than any lord in the Kingdom of Jerusalem. His coffers are always empty, so he has to pay with new coins.'

Gerard nodded with little interest and some more of the turcopoles dismounted to check for coins.

Richard peered down and watched, partly to give his head time to cool down. Under his nasal helm, his scalp pulsed as if some red-hot coals had been placed on it. He knew the heat would fade, but until it did his thoughts would be slowed and his reactions dulled. On the edge of his mind there was an urge to throw the helmet off and pour water over it.

Bowman unlaced his own helmet and sighed as the sweat on his hair helped to cool it. 'That's better,' he said, 'it is wonderful being able to do that without someone else's permission.'

Richard suspected Gerard would not order anything of the sort, so instead he focused on the bodies. Plenty had impressive beards, but some were clearly quite young men.

No hoard of freshly minted coins were discovered, and Gerard chided the guide for wasting his time. He did send out the turcopoles to look for a camp or baggage train, but they returned some time later empty-handed.

Bowman spent the time searching amongst the boulders, and he came back with news of footprints and some strange hoofprints. They were confirmed by the guide to be camel tracks once he'd looked for himself.

'Camels?' Gerard asked the guide when he reported back.

'That is what I said,' the guide replied.

Gerard sighed and signalled the trumpeter to sound a recall, and as the notes blasted over the plateau, turcopoles and Guy's men assembled. Maynard was with them, but he didn't look quite as overheated as everyone else.

'These were no bandits,' Otto remounted his horse. 'They were too well armed.'

Gerard frowned at him. 'We do not need a Hospitaller to tell us that.'

'Is it Saladin?' Richard asked.

Gerard laughed. 'His name is spoken in Jerusalem to cow the masses. He is but one man, not everything in this desert is his doing.'

The company reformed, although it didn't bury Guy's lost men because the ground was too hard to dig.

Brian complained but was given a stern order to be quiet. They left the plateau and rejoined the road. Some of the turcopole horses walked with arrow shafts snapped from their bodies, but the hardy beasts seemed uninterested. Richard did think there were not as many horses as before.

Bowman laced his helmet back on as they rode and turned his eyes to the ravines. 'They are coming back,' he said.

Gerard snapped his head back to look, but the enemy horse archers followed only at a walk, and in small numbers here and there.

'There's only a handful of them,' Gerard said.

'They're shadowing us,' Bowman said, 'which is not going to be very relaxing.'

'Do bandits normally do that?' Richard asked.

'No,' Gerard said, 'they don't.'

# DECIDUOUS TEETH

Khirbet, it transpired, was not much further on than the ambush site. Ishmael the guide led the company along a sandy track which snaked between towering pillars of rock, and then through gorges which sometimes had traces of plant life at their bottom. The final gorge led to the foot of yet another yellow rise in the ground, which they climbed and climbed. At the top of the hill, with flagging horses and weary men, they spied a tall mountain which pointed up towards the setting sun.

'Khirbet,' Ishmael said as he led Gerard towards the peak.

'Khirbet is a mountain?' Richard was too exhausted to appreciate the view, but as they rose and the air cooled, he could see for tens of miles all around. Mountains and hills dropped below as the air thinned and it became harder to breathe.

The summit was a flat but small area, completely covered with large chunks of masonry. Big square building blocks lay fallen all around as if a bucket of them had been tipped out from the sky.

'They remind me of the Roman ruins at Lillebonne,' Richard said.

Sarjeant shrugged. 'The Romans ruled in the Holy Land too, this could be more of theirs.'

The guide watched them with unmoving eyes, then told Gerard they could camp here safe from attack from the Saracens that had followed them as far as the base of the mountain.

There was no grazing area, or anywhere to release the horses, so they would spend the night all tied together. Some turcopoles distributed barley to their mounts, for Templars did not feed horsebread, while others pitched canvas tents and made beds. There was no wood for fires, for they were far above the treeline. Which was a shame, because the air bordered on cold and a stiff breeze swept over the ancient stonework, stonework that barely left enough space for a man to make his bed.

Richard soon had to pray with the Templars, but Ishmael stood on the edge of the summit and sniffed the air. 'Change soon,' he told Gerard once the evening prayer was complete.

'Rain?' the seneschal asked.

The guide nodded. 'But the wind is low.'

Richard left them to find somewhere to sleep. He found Bowman had already taken a spot under a short stretch of waist-high wall, which was far more intact than the rest of the site.

'We should put the shelter up in case of rain,' Richard told him.

Bowman rummaged around in the gaps of stone. He popped his head up. 'Rain? We haven't seen rain since we left the Italian States.'

'Trust me,' Richard felt the air cool now that he thought about it. 'What are you doing?'

Bowman stepped over a square building block which had long since split in half. 'I'm looking for treasure.'

'We already have treasure.'

'More treasure wouldn't hurt,' the blonde man looked down at a chunk of masonry. 'That's something, but it's too big to carry.'

Richard clambered over the wall to see. Bowman had found a large statue of an eagle wrestling with a serpent. It was the size of his son, but one side had sunk somehow into the ground so it sat at a forlorn angle.

The head of the serpent was missing.

'Probably not valuable, though,' Bowman said. He left the statue alone as Gerard noticed where Guy's company had placed itself.

The Lusignans had moved as far away from the Templars as possible, at the far edge of the summit, but right where the wind hit the mountaintop.

Ishmael made his way towards them, the area so small that all conversations could be heard.

'That is a poor choice,' the guide said, 'camp next to us.'

Guy stared at the dark-skinned man and then turned away and continued whatever he'd been doing.

Ishmael shook his head and returned to the turcopoles, just as the sun dipped behind a distant mountain range.

Bowman watched the orange disc sink. 'This place should be beautiful,' he said, 'but it's just so empty.'

'It reminds me of the Wicklow Mountains,' Richard said, 'just yellow and white instead of green and boggy.'

'So nothing like it, then,' the blonde man grinned.

Richard returned to their shelter, which Maynard was securing to the rocks, and found Sarjeant holding a cup of wine which he must have filled himself from one of the many barrels carried by the packhorses

Richard could smell some herbs or spices coming from it, but Sarjeant wasn't drinking it.

The large man sat on a square stone next to their low wall and turned the cup around in his large hands. He was hunched over as if protecting it, and then he sniffed it and groaned.

Richard stepped softly closer. There was no harm in Sarjeant drinking wine, indeed it was what everyone was mixing with water they found to make it safe to drink. Although from the strength of the smell, Richard thought ginger and cloves, Sarjeant's cup had little water in it.

Richard moved to sit down next to his old steward, but before he did, Sarjeant hurled the wooden cup against the ground where it snapped in two and showered the yellow stones with red droplets. It looked like someone had been killed.

Sarjeant put his head in his hands and cried.

Richard bent down next to him and put his arm around him while Maynard tiptoed away.

'What happened?' Richard asked.

'Cloves,' Sarjeant said, 'it's the cloves.'

'What is?'

Sarjeant wiped his now puffy eyes and looked up. 'Don't you see? It's the cloves in the wine I shouldn't drink.'

'Why not?' Richard's own throat was dry and he looked with longing at the red liquid that ran down the stones and pooled on the sandy earth.

'Clove wine was my weakness,' Sarjeant said, 'once I tasted it, I could never stop. And now it is the only spice we have left, the ginger mixed wine is all gone.'

'Then you'll have to drink the clove wine,' Richard said, 'but we can help you to not drink too much.'

'It's humiliating,' Sarjeant said, 'I'm worse than a child because a child does not know better. We should not have come. I knew I shouldn't have come back.'

Richard looked around for support but Bowman scratched his neck and looked the other way. 'Look,' Richard said, 'we are where we are. I will help you through this. You will conquer the clove wine and it will all be forgotten.'

'That sounds ridiculous,' Sarjeant sniffed.

'Come on,' Richard said, 'Gerard is lighting a fire, I suppose the seneschal is grand enough for wood to be carried around for him. We'll sit by that fire and you can sip the clove wine and overcome the temptations of it.'

Sarjeant needed Richard to haul him up to his feet, but reluctantly trudged over to the small fire a turcopole lit for Gerard.

The sun was gone now and the clear sky made Richard think it could be a sharp night. There was no sign of rain clouds, but the breeze remained steady.

Richard sat down next to Sarjeant and shared a new cup of wine with him. Richard kept a hold of the cup.

Gerard removed his helmet at long last and stretched his arms out.

Richard waited a moment, but then his patience ran out. 'Do you remember anything else about my father?'

'Who was your father?'

'William Keynes,' Richard said, 'the wounded man with the idiot yellow horse.'

'Ah, yes,' the seneschal watched the fire crack and pop, the bone-dry wood burning quickly but brightly. 'He was in poor condition when I left him at the infirmary within the Temple Mount. He bled too much and mumbled words incoherently during the journey, which is always a bad sign. He begged the Lord for his life more than once, I sensed he was a weak man, in both body and mind. He blamed somebody for the unfortunate end to his life.'

'Who?' Richard sat up.

Gerard shrugged. 'I do not recall if he even said, but then I was not very interested in his pathetic mumblings.'

Despite himself, Richard frowned.

Gerard watched Richard. 'Templars should not take offence so easily. You should pray on that. Your father was not important and even then I had better things to do than ferry wounded men around. Your father is dead. You should think about the situation in which you find yourself, because you may not end up any different to him. Forget him.'

Brian pulled his new Templar mantle around his robes and drew it tightly around his neck. 'This land makes you feel close to heaven. Don't you feel it, Richard?'

Richard didn't.

The monk smiled. 'I lost my family too, but the manner and reason behind their deaths made my suffering neither greater nor smaller. I found a cause greater than myself instead, and the pain faded.'

'And now you have your cause,' Gerard said to Richard.

Richard hoped so, he hoped he could forget, but Gerard hadn't given him enough to satisfy his burning curiosity. He'd just teased him with more questions, questions Richard couldn't answer while he was stuck out on the edge of the desert.

A spot of rain landed on the stone next to Richard and he glanced up at the night sky. He couldn't see the stars anymore, clouds had advanced quickly.

Brian followed his gaze and shivered. 'The wind is strengthening.'

More rain fell and the fire seemed to hiss back at it.

'The fire won't last the night now,' Gerard grabbed his own mantle and hid under it.

Richard had to go back towards their wall and shelter to find his own. Bowman lay under his bedding in the dark while the fresh wind ruffled the canvas above him. Otto had joined them but was buried under blankets and his Hospitaller cloak. The other shelters that covered the ruins made snapping noises as the rushing air caught them and tested their tethers.

Richard huddled next to the blonde man, who groaned under his blanket as the rain turned into a howling storm.

Gerard's fire spluttered and died, and the last flickers of its pale light extinguished and left the summit in total darkness.

Sheets of rain blanketed the mountain and Richard watched the canvas above him jump and pull and nearly tear.

Shouts and a scream erupted from Guy's end of the camp, the end where the wind was strongest.

Richard waited a moment in the hope the noise would go away. 'Are we under attack?' he asked Bowman.

The blonde man, only his hair showing, had to shout above the sound of the weather. 'The mountain slope was sheer, no one climbed that in this storm.'

The shouts didn't cease, instead they grew louder and more urgent.

A piercing shriek cut through the buffeting wind and some ran washed under the shelter and splashed Richard's face.

He pushed himself to his feet and wrapped his cloak around him.

'Where are you going?' Bowman asked.

'I'm wet and awake,' Richard said, 'so I'm seeing what's happening.'

Bowman didn't respond or move, so Richard left the partial safety of their shelter and was immediately almost pushed over by the wind. A strong gust blew the air from his mouth so he couldn't breathe, and he had to use his hands to make his way towards the edge of the ruins where more screams and shouts fought against the noise of the torrent of rain that lashed Khirbet.

Guy's camp was a mess. Shelters flew in the air, attached to the ground by some ties while others flapped helplessly in the sky and one blew away entirely. Squires tried to catch the loose ends to re-tie them, but the wind was so powerful that some were taken off their feet. Guy stood in the middle barking commands, but no one could really hear him.

The shelter closest to the mountain's edge ripped up a corner and the canvas shot up as the wind caught it. The Lusignan squire who huddled under it was smacked in the face and knocked backwards. He rolled past a block of stone he tried to cling on to, but missed, and tumbled from sight as he rolled off the edge of the summit.

Richard pushed against the storm, passed Guy, to reach the shelter. He dropped to his belly and crawled to the edge of the mountain and tried to look down it. Gusts tried to topple him off, but Richard clung to the earth and the ruins. Down the mountainside he saw little, it was pitch black more than a few feet below, and the squire was not there. He wouldn't have survived his fall.

Richard crawled backwards while the Lusignans tried to repair their camp around Guy. The rain soaked into their mantles and surcoats, rusted their mail, but eventually the storm eased and the company spent a miserable night shivering in sodden clothing.

Richard returned to Bowman's shelter where Maynard had also taken refuge, and they huddled together as the night wore on and the wind mercifully died. Richard thought of the falling squire and heard his scream over and over again, but at some point, and despite the numb feeling in his fingers and toes, he fell asleep.

The dawn sun illuminated a scene of abject misery.

Water pooled in puddles between the ruins, puddles yellowed with the sand mixed in, although that didn't stop the tired horses from drinking from them. The animals had been so crammed together they had resisted the wind, but none had slept and many were wide-eyed and angry.

The canvas shelters were sodden and were folded away wet, adding a considerable amount of weight to the already grumpy pack horses.

Richard felt sorry for his pack animal as he tied their dripping shelter over everything else it carried in the hope it would dry as they went.

Mantles and surcoats were draped over stones in a futile

attempt to air them. Water stained from black dye dripped down the yellow stones, leaving trails like tear marks down to the ground.

'I'm not drinking from that,' Bowman considered a puddle, 'not with any amount of wine mixed in.'

Richard agreed, but he had to join Gerard for their next set of prayers. Brian led them, the seneschal having accepted that the monk knew his prayers well enough.

Ishmael saddled his horse even though Gerard hadn't yet given the order. The guide studied the path which led down from the summit, although still not yet fully lit by the morning sun. 'The path down is clear,' he said.

Richard looked around the vast and distant mountain ranges as rainwater trickled down from his hair and into an eye. He wiped it away, then pointed to a hill beyond the road. 'The Saracens are still here.'

The guide nodded. 'They wish us to leave this place,' he said, 'they leave the path down the mountain open for us.'

'We can't just stay here because they want us to leave,' Gerard tied on his helmet after completing the prayers, 'and I have said before, I care little for what they might do.'

Richard remembered his conversation with Arnold. 'Are we to separate from Guy now?' he asked. 'As he has a different task to mine.'

Ishmael shook his head. 'The foolish knight does not leave us here.'

'I thought the Grand Master said we would leave him after Khirbet.'

'Other Khirbet,' the guide said.

'What?'

'This is Khirbet temple. South is Khirbet town. It once was a great town, now it has goat herds and an olive grove. We reach it before midday.'

Richard didn't tell Sarjeant or Otto about the two Khirbets because he didn't want to be told how surprising the Holy Land was again. Instead he rang out his tunic, swore at the orange tinge on his mail, and remounted his Tancarville horse as the trumpet blared and they all left the ancient ruins on the mountain. Everyone was glad to be gone.

The company descended, and the air warmed as the sun rose in the cloudy sky. Puffy white clouds floated lower down, and larger grey ones higher up.

'It could rain again,' Sarjeant said, his lips cracked from a lack of drink.

Richard agreed. They rejoined the road and travelled south along the banks of a river valley, the same riverbed as before, but now it was brought to life by a real river of fresh rainwater.

Ishmael gestured across the river. 'That way is east. Khirbet town is across the river. If it rains more, the wadi will swell and we will not cross.'

Gerard nodded. 'But if it rains more after we have crossed, the infidels will be stuck on the wrong side. We will cross, then pray for rain, the Lord will surely see fit to protect us and send a torrent.'

Spots of rain fell on the sandy road and covered the horses in dark spots.

'We should push on,' the guide said, 'cross the river quickly.'

Gerard shook his head. 'The Lord will delay the swelling of the river until we cross, and Templars always preserve the strength of their horses.'

Richard thought that wise, although he was sure some horses were skinnier than before. He could see ribs through the coats of the turcopole horses, but then, he wasn't sure if that hadn't always been the case. The blue roan he sensed was angry at the lack of food, and he was the bulkiest horse in the company, so the most bothered by hunger. That was why Richard didn't want to ride him.

Gerard was proved right when they reached a bend in the river that ran around a hill. On that hill across the river, yellow but with a sparse covering of dull-green grass, were more bleached ruins. The town of Khirbet sat on a causeway between two plateaus, and was set against the backdrop of a huge mountain that ran tall into the distance. Layers of darker and lighter colours ran across the whole length of it, from north to south, and made the mountain range seem all the more huge.

'It's not much of a town,' Bowman said when they left the road and entered the riverbed.

'It's the size of a castle. A small castle,' Richard reached the new river and let his reins down so his horse could drink. The whole company did the same, and refilled every container they could before preparing to cross.

The horses easily waded through the river, the water only up to their knees and hocks, but they splashed so much their riders came out wet again.

A shepherd on one of the plateaus watched the company approach the ruins and drove his flock in the other direction. A few small patches of crops grew here and there, and a few columns of smoke rose from the ruins.

'We shall all pray for rain,' Gerard said, 'and if answered, we can allow the horses to graze for a day in safety.'

The rains had already refreshed the land, tiny shoots of grass appeared and tufts which had been yellowed before grew brighter.

The seneschal looked back towards the road. 'The company should rest after such a night, and the horses would become sour if we push them on today. Make camp, the ruins are perfectly defensible.'

The Marshal approached and gazed over the river. 'The ruins are too small for us and our horses to fit in,' he said, 'the Saracens could surround us and kill whoever is left outside the town. We should not stay here.'

Gerard growled as they reached the ruins. 'What do you know of war? Especially here?'

'I don't need to know much to know they will shoot our horses if we leave them outside the walls.'

'The river will rise,' the seneschal looked to the skies as the occasional drop of rain turned into a steady flow. He glanced back at the Marshal and raised his eyebrows. 'You see? The Saracens will be stuck on the west bank.'

'Isn't that still our way home?' Richard asked Bowman quietly.

'Aye, it is,' the blonde man replied, 'we'll still have to get through them when we want to go back.'

The rain fell harder and Gerard ordered the shelters to be put up to cover the ruins, which looked small enough that they should be able to turn the whole place into one covered area. As they laboured to accomplish it, the rain ran off the mountains and swelled the river little by little.

The few locals were evicted from Khirbet, which at least had a well, and their modest stocks of firewood and food were commandeered.

Richard left Maynard and Sarjeant to add their shelter to the canvas roof being built when he heard Gerard's voice across the ruins. The town was far more intact than the temple on the mountain, with walls taller than men, and distinct rooms and buildings still all connected and usable.

Richard entered one such room and found the seneschal arguing with two old men. One was Richard's height, the other taller, but both were dressed in old and faded white cloaks. To his surprise, they spoke as clearly as any English or Frenchman.

'There is no room for you here,' Gerard pointed outside the walls, 'leave or we shall throw you out.'

'We are Christian men,' the shorter man said, a great beard covering half his face, 'Templars never cast men of the true faith aside.'

'The survival of the kingdom depends on our mission,' Gerard said, 'it is regrettable but unavoidable that you must leave. There is not enough space within the walls as it is, let alone with two more people.'

'We have a cart to move and no beast to pull it,' the bearded man said, 'we cannot leave.'

'Then leave the cart here,' Gerard said, 'we must quarter as many men and horses inside the ruins as we can.'

'Why?'

'The infidels are on our heels,' Gerard replied, 'if they attack we must husband our forces. You are in our way.'

The two old men looked at each other. 'Infidels are coming?'

Gerard nodded. 'The rising river should keep them away, but if God deems to test us through combat, then we must prepare.'

'You cannot allow any infidels here,' the shorter man said, his voice almost pleading.

'Why should you care?' the seneschal asked. 'You look to have been living here for some time unmolested.'

'That is not your concern,' the shorter man said with more force than Richard expected.

'Everything here is my concern, I am the seneschal of the

Knights of the Temple.'

'The Lord and your order wish you to leave us in peace,' the man said.

Gerard laughed, a sound Richard hadn't heard before. But it wasn't a happy laugh, it was a cruel laugh.

'You are unfit to speak to me,' Gerard said, 'much less order me.'

'We cannot abandon our cart,' the bearded man said, 'but if you lend us a horse broken to drive, we could be on our way.'

'Even if I had one, I would not give it to you,' Gerard snarled, 'your lack of respect is galling. I do not care for your cart.'

Richard noticed it in the next chamber, where six turcopole horses were already packed in around it. It was four–wheeled, the wheels cracked and worn, and was a platform with no sides to hold cargo. It had a square hole in the middle of it.

The increasing rain made Richard wipe it away from his eyes as a squall swept over Khirbet town.

A cry rang out and Richard gulped.

'Saracens,' a squire in Guy's company shouted.

Richard went to the west of the town to look over the river they'd crossed, where he was joined by everyone else, including Gerard.

The enemy horse archers rode along the road in an unhurried column.

'They have all regrouped,' Bowman walked up next to Richard and leant on the stone wall. 'They outnumber us again.'

'See how the Lord watches over us,' Gerard shouted so all could hear.

The reborn river billowed with water, the riverbed now obscured by a torrent of rushing and swirling runoff from the rains.

Some of the Lusignans cheered and Guy's face, one which had been full of tension since the storm, broke into a tired smile.

Otto tapped the wall next to Bowman. 'See how the turcopoles react?'

Richard didn't, because the native Christians had already gone back to erecting shelters and using loose stones to make the outer ruins taller.

Bowman groaned. 'I wouldn't cross that. Would they?'

The cheers subsided when the Saracens turned to the river and went down to the edge of the water. Their horses drank for a while, a hundred or more stretched out along its length, foals drinking and following their mothers, before their leader walked his horse into the river one step at a time.

Guy's men fell silent.

Richard snatched a glance at Gerard, who had whitened ever so slightly.

The Saracen's horse kept walking, the water washing onto it but not carrying it away in the current.

'I'm going to get my bow,' the blonde knight left.

Gerard made the sign of the cross. 'O Lord, tempt the infidel across and sweep him away. Let the glory be yours.'

The Saracen's horse suddenly dropped into the water with only its head above it and the rider held his bow high and dry with one hand.

The horse didn't float away though, it swam.

One of Guy's squires went to run, but Guy caught him by his thick fabric collar and hurled him back to the wall. 'See if they can cross before you panic like children,' he snarled.

Richard said a silent prayer in thanks of the decision to leave his own children at Kerak.

Other horse archers entered the river, followed by their foals and spare mounts.

'They're going to make it, aren't they,' Richard whispered.

Otto nodded. 'But death will not come to us quickly.'

'Oh,' Richard replied, 'everything's fine then.'

The German shot him a glance. 'The English, always quick to joke when it is least appropriate.'

'It wasn't a joke,' Richard ran his fingers along the wall, the sand coming off and sticking to his damp hands.

Gerard kicked the ground in frustration. 'Turcopoles to the walls, everyone else, unpack all the spare arrows from the baggage and hand them out.'

The lead Saracen's horse found hard footing again and started to walk out of the river. The rest of the horse archers were not far behind, and soon the enemy stood on the east bank. They let out a cheer, a chilling sort of yell that Richard didn't appreciate.

The Marshal walked away from Gerard, on his way past Richard he put a hand on his shoulder. 'I told him, we're stuck now.'

Richard didn't reply because he watched the horse archers split into two groups. One began to make a camp on the plateau they were already on, and the others rode the long way around the town.

'They're going to camp on the other plateau,' Otto said, 'so that we have no way to leave the town. They are fresh and they can fetch fodder for their horses. We are tired and will not be able to feed our horses in four or five days when we run out of barley. Then we shall have to start eating them.'

'Eating the horses?' Richard felt sick.

The German nodded. 'That is how the very first crusaders survived, horse flesh is not so bad.'

'I swear I will never eat it,' Richard shook his head.

Otto shrugged. 'This is now a siege. See how you feel in six days.'

Gerard gave some more orders, then found Richard. 'Your message needs to reach its destination soon, we shall break out tomorrow once the horses have slept and eaten.'

Ishmael stood in the old doorway to a chamber, leaning on a yellow stone indented with carved patterns smoothed by centuries of weather. 'The Grand Master was clear,' he said, 'the Saracens cannot know of the mission. The envoy must reach Qal'at without the awareness that we have travelled that way.'

Gerard sighed as Guy's men led their horses into rooms and tied two layers of canvas above them to protect from arrows.

Richard thought it was probably the most sensible command Guy had ever given.

Gerard watched the enemy skirting around their camp. 'Indeed. Richard cannot break out during daylight.'

The Marshal carried a large square stone, brushed past Gerard's nose, and placed it on top of the crumbling outer wall. 'He can sneak out,' the Marshal said, 'Richard is very good at sneaking around at night.'

Gerard frowned at Richard.

The guide shook his head. 'The enemy is at home in this land.

This is their land.'

'It is our land,' Gerard said.

Ishmael almost looked annoyed. 'They have been here longer than you. They will see a westerner who tries to evade them. I could go alone if you give me the message.'

The seneschal laughed. 'I don't think so, you think me a fool?'

The guide didn't reply.

'I could have your head for that.'

Ishmael's dark eyes stared unblinkingly at Gerard.

The Marshal groaned. 'Richard is good at sneaking, but I'm also good at diversions.'

'Diversions?' Gerard asked.

The Marshal nodded. 'If the Saracens are under attack in the dark, they won't notice a few riders heading east, will they?'

'Not if the attack is strong enough,' Gerard smiled. 'The lord will cover Richard's escape.'

'Like he stopped the Saracens fording the river?' Richard asked.

Gerard's face reddened. 'You overstep, boy.'

'Allow me to lead the diversion,' the Marshal said, 'tie blankets around my horse and I shall charge out. The turcopoles can follow to shower the enemy with arrows. They will flee for a moment and Richard can leave unseen.'

'If Ishmael can guide me,' Richard said.

Gerard's face twitched. 'This is not how the Templars conduct themselves.'

'This way,' the Marshal said, 'The enemy need not know of Richard's direction, and you will have obeyed the Grand Master. Isn't that why we are here?'

The guide stepped out of his doorway. 'This plan could work. It is what the enemy would do. I will lead Richard to Qal'at.'

'After dusk then,' Gerard turned to Richard. 'Make your peace with God, give your confession to our priest.'

Richard frowned. 'Who is our priest?'

'Your monk,' Gerard replied. 'And ensure the men you take with you do the same. But take no more than three of them.'

Richard dragged Sarjeant over to Brian first, the monk just as surprised as everyone else that he was to hear their confessions.

Richard left them together in a room crammed to the brim with horses, the blue roan snapping his teeth at others and swishing his tail in their faces in frustration at his confinement.

'I've never heard a confession before,' he heard Brian say.

'But you've given your own?' Sarjeant asked him.

The monk had. 'I suppose just speak and you'll feel better.'

'I know how it works. And I have little I wish to tell you.'

'Just pretend you don't know me,' Brian said.

'I don't,' Sarjeant replied, 'and I am sure you already know of my problem with clove wine, for I've seen how everyone looks at me when Richard hands me the drink. I have long ago confessed my old sins in the Holy Land, not much is left unsaid.'

Richard left them to it and went to tell Bowman he was next.

The blonde man laughed. 'I don't think so, young lord,' he left their cramped room and went to explore the rest of the ruins.

Richard returned to the confession room as Sarjeant left it. The large man shook his head. 'I don't feel any better.'

The canvas sheets flapped overhead and the sound of rain pattering down on them almost sounded like hailstones.

'At least it's done,' Richard said, 'we're leaving once it's dark. We'll each take one spare horse, so best to start packing now.'

Sarjeant nodded and went to do so.

Richard stepped into the confession chamber as the blue roan bit another horse on the neck because he was bored.

'I think you make the horses misbehave,' Brian said.

'He's just a stallion,' Richard said, 'and we shouldn't be squeezing them all in so close together, so it's hardly his fault.'

'At least you get to leave,' the monk said, 'I'll be stuck in here getting shot at while you're free in the desert.'

'I wouldn't call it free,' Richard said, 'it isn't Christian land we'll be riding through.'

'You better say your confession, then.'

Richard moved close to Brian and lowered his voice. 'You

know almost every bad thing I've done,' he said, 'do I need to repeat myself?'

'Only if you feel the need to,' Brian shrugged, 'but I don't really know how this works.'

Richard sighed. 'I have killed priests and monks, watched many innocents die, and killed at least two kings. What's the point in confessing? Heaven is far, far away for the likes of me.'

'God forgives all,' Brian said solemnly.

'Really?'

'Well,' Brian said, 'that's the response I know I'm supposed to give. But no, it sounds like you're on the way to hell.'

'Thanks.'

'But all your evil deeds were done for good reasons,' Brian said, 'I think, anyway. And God may choose to welcome you. You have taken the cross and joined the Templars, which everyone keeps saying will erase all sins.'

'But what if I die before I complete my two years? What if I die before I return to my children? Then I'm no better than my father.'

Brian rubbed his chin. 'The Temple will find them homes until Alexander is old enough to join the order, then his soul will be saved. Lora, I suspect, will find Alice a caring guardian.'

'You really think that?'

Brian nodded. 'I believe so. She is almost too old to marry now, and might never have children of her own. She likes yours, and even though she's a Lusignan, I think being around the young ones has tamed her.'

'I don't know about tamed,' Richard thought about it. 'And I don't know if I want Alexander to be a Templar. He would miss out on so much.'

'It seems to be good enough for you,' Brian said.

'Fine,' Richard said, 'although my opinions matter little if I die, events will unfold however they will regardless of what I want. But what of my father? He is why I am in the Holy Land in the first place. I surely cannot leave or die before finding his grave? I still need to learn his story.'

'Did we not already deal with that?' the monk asked. 'I thought you have moved on?'

Richard sighed. 'It was easier to say the words than believe them.'

'You will meet your father in heaven, you can ask him then.'

'I still don't think I'll get there.'

Brian groaned. 'You're a Templar, heaven is assured.'

'So you say,' Richard replied, 'but on what authority? How does anyone know?'

'Bernard of Clairvaux was very sure,' Brian said, 'and every archbishop in Christendom agrees. What more do you want?'

'I'm struggling to have confidence in any of that.'

Brian grinned. 'I think you need to take a leap of faith.'

'I'm not ready to leap anywhere,' Richard said, 'and I intend to survive this mission.'

Brian nodded. 'I would be very sad if you were lost,' he said, 'but just to be safe, you must make peace with yourself and let go of the attachments of the material world. Your father is one of those.'

'How did you do it?' Richard asked.

'Do what?'

'How did you let go of your sin when you went to poison the well in Waterford?'

Brian's eyes dropped to the yellow ground and the canvas sheets blew around loudly under a heavy gust. 'I don't want to speak of that.'

'Why not?' Richard asked. 'You're supposed to be helping me overcome things, so why not tell me how you overcame your guilt?'

The monk pursed his lips and looked up. 'I didn't. I just forgot about it. It was the unfounded faith you had in me afterwards that helped me through the worst time. That unearned trust which you had no right to show me, that helped me to move on. I can be a better man now, and you helped me get there. Is that the answer you wanted to hear?'

Richard softened. 'I'm sorry, I wasn't trying to upset you.'

'I should be thanking you,' Brian said, 'you saved me without even trying.'

'There is no need to thank me,' Richard said, 'I am only struggling to come to terms with the loss of my father. When I was young he was the constant in my life. He was always there to tell me how to do things. How do I accept him not being here?'

Brian's eyes eased and he let out a heavy breath. 'We are all born and we all die. None of our deeds in between will be remembered by future generations, no matter how great or glorious they were. Your great, great grandchildren will not know your name, and if they do, they won't know anything else about you. How much do you know of your great, great grandfather?'

'I don't even know his name,' Richard said.

'You see? Everything is ethereal, only your faith is eternal. Death is not a defeat, Richard. Your father's death was not his defeat, nor yours a loss. It is not an end, and it is not to be feared. It is just another step on the journey of life.'

Richard sniffed. He thought about it. 'That is rather bleak, Brian.'

'Is it?' the Monk asked. 'I think it is rather freeing. Bowman would agree, I'm sure, and see it as an excuse to do whatever he wanted. Which is why you shouldn't share this with him, by the way.'

'I agree,' Richard half grinned. 'But you are right. My children still matter, but I am so small and insignificant that my sufferings do not.'

'Spoken like a true Templar,' Brian said.

Richard sighed deeply. Twice. 'I think I can let my father go. I feel lighter already. It is of no benefit to me or my children if I discover if he caused his own death or was wronged by someone else. No matter at all. I can live my life, Brian, thank you. I can be a Templar for two years and then build a home for my children.'

'Amen,' the monk placed his hands together and bowed.

The rain lightened and the canvas sheets were able to settle down at last. Richard felt a sense of relief, maybe the confession had worked even though he hadn't confessed anything. The dampness which had weighed him down felt less burdensome, and his tiredness had been banished. He even started to believe the Marshal's typically self-centred plan might work.

Bowman's exclamation broke this trail of thought. The blonde man cried out as if in triumph and burst through the ruins until he ran into Richard. In one hand he held a wooden cross, and in the other a gleaming golden box with enamelled figures decorating it. 'I found something,' he shouted, his eyes excited.

Gerard ran through a doorway with his sword drawn, looking for the source of the alarm, and stopped dead when he saw Bowman. The seneschal's eyes squinted at the box and the cross. 'Is that?' he whispered. 'Did that simple wooden cross come out of that box?'

Bowman. 'It did, seems strange to put a bit of wood in it, but I'm not questioning it.'

The Templar's eyes fixed on the small cross. 'I was expecting it to be larger, but it must be.'

Bowman peered at the box. 'I don't know what you're talking about, but this box is actual gold.'

Gerard dropped his sword and it clattered on the stone-covered earth, but he wasn't looking at the golden box. Then he dropped to his knees and water filled his eyes. He stretched his hands forwards. 'The lost cross,' he cried.

Bowman looked at the wooden cross in his other hand. 'What, this? It's just a piece of wood. I'm talking about the box, it's beautiful. Look at it, it must be worth a fortune.'

'You can keep the box for all I care,' Gerard said, 'but that cross you hold in your hand is the one true cross. The cross which has been lost to us. I have found it.'

Bowman scrutinised the cross, but his eyes drew him back to the golden box. He rattled it around and popped the lid open. 'There's something else in here,' the blonde man held up an old pouch, cracks in the creases of the dried leather.

Gerard pulled himself to his feet as a crowd gathered around them to see what the fuss was about. The seneschal snatched the pouch from Bowman's hands.

'God's teeth, you're rude,' Bowman snapped.

'No,' Gerard poured the contents into his hand. 'Christ's teeth.'

In the Templar's palm were six small white teeth.

'What is happening?' Richard asked.

'A double miracle,' Gerard held the teeth up to his eyes.

Brian edged up next to Richard. 'Are they deciduous teeth?'

'What are deciduous teeth?' Richard asked.

'Milk teeth,' the monk replied, 'baby teeth.'

'Yes,' Gerard's voice was in awe. 'They are so small. It is hard to imagine they came from the very body of Christ himself.'

'Very hard to imagine, indeed,' Bowman locked eyes with Richard.

Brian fell to his knees and gazed up at the ceiling of canvas. 'We have found Christ's deciduous teeth. One of the most holy relics, a part of Christ's own body. This is a great blessing and a sign that our mission is righteous.'

The two white-robed old men pushed their way into the now packed chamber, the shorter one's eyes were furious. 'Those are not yours,' he raged, 'you are not worthy to even touch them. Put them back and return them to us. You risk much with your tampering.'

Gerard poured the teeth back into their pouch. 'Who are you?' he asked. 'Relics of such power should be nowhere else but Jerusalem. Why do you claim them to be yours?'

'We are the keepers of the true cross.'

'You mean thieves,' Gerard snarled, 'you stole them from the church, from the kingdom. I'll have your heads for it.'

The shorter man threw back his hood. He had a straight nose on a very weathered and darkened face. His beard was long, dark at the roots but greying and white flecked.

'We were tasked with keeping the true cross safe when it was being hunted by the infidels. Their agents roamed the kingdom, killing those who stood in their way. Do you not remember?'

'By the look of the two of you,' Gerard said, 'that must have been a decade ago. You look as if you've been wandering the desert without food or water, like common brigands.'

'Not quite a decade,' the man said, 'and not long enough for the danger to have passed.'

'The true cross will be perfectly safe in Jerusalem,' the seneschal said, 'but I was told it had been stolen only recently from the order?'

'Do we look like we have only arrived here recently?'

Gerard had seen the cart, the cart which clearly hadn't moved for years.

The man shook his head, his face angry. 'You do not understand. You bring these enemies upon us and risk the true cross. You must return it to our keeping and leave this place.'

Guy barged through a cluster of awestruck turcopoles. 'What's going on?' he gazed at the golden box. 'We will share all spoils equally,' he said.

'It is the true cross,' Richard said. 'And some teeth.'

Guy snorted. 'That's a piece of wood. Anyone could have made that.'

'Heresy,' the robed man cried and whirled around at Guy.

'Calm down,' the Lusignan said, 'but maybe I should look after it anyway. If I take that back to Jerusalem, it will be a bigger trophy than this Sibylla woman.'

'The true cross belongs to the church,' Gerard stepped forwards. 'If you try to take it, I'll kill you myself.'

Guy hesitated.

Gerard bent down and picked up his sandy blade. 'How long will you last out here on your own?'

Guy watched him. 'Fine,' he folded his arms. 'You keep it, it's just kindling, anyway.'

Gerard spun around to the bearded man. 'The cart,' he said, 'that cart was built to hold a large cross, is your cart the cart which once wheeled the true cross into battle? The true cross was fixed to the centre of the large hole, am I right?'

The man scowled but nodded. 'You are correct. It belongs here with us.'

'Here?' Gerard chuckled. 'It doesn't belong here, it belongs at the head of the army of Jerusalem. With the true cross, we will sweep Saladin before us.'

The man shook his head. 'The time has not yet come, our victory has been foretold, but only if we avoid a confrontation with the infidels for several more years.'

'On whose authority?' the seneschal asked. 'You could be anyone. Or more likely, no one.'

The man shook his head, his hair long and unkempt. 'You force us to reveal ourselves, you undo all our work. We are knights of the Temple, just as you are. We have been the wardens of the cross for years, keeping it safe from the hunters. The Grand Master himself gave us this mission himself.'

Gerard choked in disbelief. 'Arnold did not give you this mission, why else would he have me out in the desert looking for it?'

Richard hadn't been aware that the true cross was part of their mission, but he supposed he hadn't needed to know.

'Arnold?' the man asked. 'I don't know who that is. The Grand Master, Bertrand de Blanchefort, set us our holy task.'

'Bertrand has been dead for years,' Gerard stood back for a moment. 'We have had two Grand Masters between Bertrand and Arnold, and Arnold has been searching for the cross. So either Bertrand never passed on word of your mission to any other Templar, or you are fabricating your entire story.'

'Do not call me a liar.'

'It is time to bring the cross home,' Gerard said. 'It is fitting to have recovered it, and my name will be forever known as the man who recovered our most holy relic.'

'I thought we acted to give the glory to God,' Brian pointed out, but Gerard ignored him.

'Who are you then?' the man asked. 'Who is the man who shall bring down the Kingdom of Jerusalem?'

'I am Gerard of Ridefort, seneschal of the Knights Templar.'

'Gerard?' the man said with surprise. 'Of Ridefort?' He narrowed his eyes at the seneschal and shook his head. 'It cannot be.'

Richard blinked. 'What?' he muttered to himself, his mind confused as a possibility dawned on him.

The man walked up to Gerard so close that he could smell the wet linen of his mantle. 'It is. My God. You took me to safety after I was wounded, you saved my life.'

Gerard stared blankly back at the man. 'I have never saved someone like you, you look like an old hermit.'

The man bowed. 'I owe you my life so I will acquiesce here,' he said, 'as is only proper.'

Richard shook his head and stepped forwards. 'This can't be real, can it?'

Gerard looked at him. 'What is wrong with you? You can't have caught the sun in this weather?'

Richard stood close to the old Templar with his long beard, straight nose, and unwashed hair. 'William?' he mumbled faintly. 'William Keynes?'

The man turned a pale white, the colour draining from his tanned face. He squinted at Richard. 'How do you know that name?'

A gust of wind lifted the canvas sheets up and smacked them back down again, sending a shower of droplets down to those standing beneath. They landed on Richard's face as if they were tears.

Gerard threw the pouch of deciduous teeth back into the golden box with a thud.

Richard looked back at the old man whose expression matched his own.

'Because you are my father.'

# THE SINS OF THE FATHER

William Keynes's eyes widened and he gasped and struggled with the realisation that it was his son who stood before him.

Richard did not gasp.

Instead he punched his father in the face.

The old man reeled backwards clutching his nose, and a splatter of blood soiled his white robes.

The turcopoles and knights all around cried out, but Gerard held his arm up to signal silence. 'What is the meaning of this violence? Striking a Templar, which I now believe this man to be, is enough for you to lose your mantle.'

Richard did not care about his Templar mantle. 'What are you doing here? You're supposed to be dead.'

'I'm alive,' William looked down at the crimson on his hands.

'I know you're alive,' Richard said, 'but that makes it worse. Until today I thought you had just left your family behind, then died. Now, it turns out that as well as leaving us behind, you survived and just never bothered to tell us, which is far worse. You never came back. Before this, I thought you'd just made a bad decision, now I know you've actively neglected us.'

William forgot about his bleeding nose and his eyes watered, but not from the punch.

'A letter,' Richard cried, 'you could have written a letter. Just one, even if it was a goodbye letter, it would have been better than us thinking you were dead.'

William Keynes was stunned. 'I,' he stammered, 'I thought you all to be dead. I knew what my brother and Eustace planned, and it was weeks before I had recovered enough to even speak. All letters sent by Templars or from their infirmary are read by the Grand Master, so I could not bring myself to write of such a humiliation. But I thought you were dead.'

'Well,' Richard said, 'I'm not. I survived, and Adela survived too, she's in Ireland now, probably with hundreds of nuns in her care the way she was going.'

'Ireland?'

'Don't ask,' Bowman mumbled.

William glanced at Bowman, unsure of his involvement with his son. 'What happened? To my wife, to my brother?'

Richard's hands were fists and he thought about answering with them, but a man keeping watch on the north wall shouted. 'Saracens, Saracens are coming.'

'This family nonsense can wait,' Gerard said.

Everyone except William rushed through the ruins to the north wall, Richard barged past his father on his way, his veins pulsing and his mind enraged.

He reached the north edge of the town, a low wall between waist and shoulder height, with arrows laid along its length and turcopoles readying their bows.

Except it was a lone Saracen who approached, holding his hands out flat before him.

'I think he wants to talk,' Richard said.

'Shoot him,' Guy said, 'it'll be one less we have to kill later.'

Ishmael the guide watched the man as he walked slowly over the plateau towards them. 'That is their leader.'

'Even better,' Guy cried, 'cut the head from the snake.'

Ishmael sighed.

'Let's hear him,' Gerard said, 'we might learn something which is to our advantage.'

The Saracen wore a robe which crossed over at the front, right over left, decorated with bands of golden trim along the neckline and down the front.

'Ghulam,' the guide sneered. 'Unfree warrior.'

'He looks pretty rich to me with all that gold,' Bowman said.

Ishmael shook his head. 'You do not understand.'

The ghulam halted and gazed at the bows ready to be drawn in his direction. He spoke in his own tongue for a while, after which Ishmael coughed and sighed.

'The ghulam is their leader, he says. He is offering us terms for surrender.'

Gerard snorted. 'We are not in as desperate a situation as they think we are. We can charge and scatter them at any time we please. Why would we even speak of surrender?'

'Because,' Ishmael answered, 'Saladin has launched his invasion.'

'His what?' Guy froze. 'Where is he? He's not coming here, is he?'

Everyone looked to the guide. Who shook his head. 'No, not here, but close by. Saladin has attacked the only castle which blocks armies and caravans moving between Egypt and Syria.'

Gerard rubbed his chin. 'We shall have to take another way back to Jerusalem, then.'

Richard tried to catch their attention. 'Why would we have to go back to Jerusalem another way?'

'Because the castle Saladin is attacking is Kerak.'

'No,' Richard whispered.

Bowman put a hand on his shoulder and squeezed. 'You saw Kerak,' the blonde man said, 'no one is climbing those walls, or digging under that mountain.'

Gerard nodded. 'Indeed. Kerak is impregnable. Reynald has been using it as a base to raid the trade routes the guide mentioned. Saladin tried to take it last year but was chased away. This year's attack will be no different.'

'I need to get back there,' Richard said.

'Yes, I know,' Gerard kept his eyes on the Saracen, 'your family. But you do not go where you wish anymore, you are a Templar now and go where I command.'

Guy had a long look at the Saracen camp on the plateau. 'Perhaps we should break out sooner rather than later. Just in case Saladin sends men this way. We are not very far from Kerak.'

'I know exactly where we are,' Gerard said, 'and you will also follow my orders. There will be no talk of changing plans or surrendering. Guide, why do the Saracens bother offering terms to us? They can plainly see that Templars are here.'

Ishmael relayed the question to the ghulam. He almost smiled and relayed the reply. 'They are not offering terms to you, only to the knights from the west. He says that this war is not their war. This land is not their land. The knights from far away will one day go back home anyway, so they should simply do so now. If they leave, the Saracens will not trouble them.'

Guy tilted his head from side to side. 'That sounds relatively fair to me. It would allow me to return the true cross to Jerusalem.'

'My children are in Kerak,' Richard said, 'we shouldn't be running away to Jerusalem, but defeating these Saracens and riding to Kerak.'

'What do you want to do?' Gerard sneered. 'Lift the siege on your own?' He glanced at Guy. 'And we do not surrender, ever, as is written in our Rule. We have the stronger force here, and God on our side.'

'They infidels also believe God to be on their side,' Ishmael added.

'I didn't ask you about it,' Gerard snapped and looked back at Guy, 'and I didn't ask anyone else. I am in command here and no Templar knight has ever been as rudely treated as I am being here and now. How dare anyone question me?'

'We should at least hear them out,' Guy said, 'there is no reason not to. We can keep the true cross and those teeth and return home with a greater prize than we set out for. It would be a historic triumph.'

The Marshal pushed through the crowded turcopoles. 'You must be the most dishonest man I've ever met. I told the Young King he shouldn't deal with you, and I was right. Now you're betraying the Templars the very first time you're tested. If you accept their offer and leave, you'd be leaving us behind here to fight alone. And without your men we would no longer be the strongest side.'

Guy shrugged. 'There's only really Gerard here who would be a loss, the rest of you are nobodies. I am especially sick and tired of listening to you complaining, I'd be glad to be rid of you.'

'Enough,' Gerard shouted so loudly even the ghulam outside of Khirbet flinched. 'We do not make deals with Saracens. Anyone who does will be punished.'

Guy rolled his eyes, but there was little defiance in them.

Gerard continued. 'Our plan has not changed. Tonight we launch the diversion and the envoy and his message shall sneak off to Qal'at. With a change of horses, the message will be delivered by midday tomorrow, and the envoy can sneak back into Khirbet the following night, under the cover of a second diversionary attack. Then we all leave together, before the food runs out.'

'Sneak back in?' Richard asked. 'What if they are waiting for us?'

'I do think a second diversion is too predictable,' the Marshal said, 'although I volunteer to lead it anyway.'

'Aren't you the hero,' Guy muttered.

Gerard faced the Marshal. 'The second attack is only foolish if the Saracens know Richard left in the first place, as well as his destination and likely time of return. They will know none of these things. God willing.'

Richard wasn't all that comfortable leaving that to God, and he didn't want to get stuck outside of Khirbet with enemy horse archers roaming around.

Ishmael had watched the arguments quietly. 'The Assassins hate Saladin,' he spoke slowly. 'You would not understand why, but the hate is so strong that they may lend aid against his siege of Kerak. All that matters is that the envoy reaches them.'

Gerard laughed his cruel laugh again. 'Don't be absurd, the Assassins will not aid us. I don't know why we're even bothering to send them a message, they hate us as much as we despise them.'

The guide went to look at Richard but held himself still.

Guy shrugged. 'If anyone is willing to help us, then we should consider it.'

Gerard put his head into his hands before he addressed Guy. 'We agree on many things, but you have the backbone of a worm. Our plan is set. Once the envoy has returned with whatever reply comes from Qal'at, we shall all continue our mission south and aid you in the task the Grand Master gave to you. We shall not be waylaid by Saracens, Assassins, or anyone else.'

Guy frowned but didn't dare push his case for surrendering any further.

'Templars fulfil their duties because they are difficult, we do not wilt under the threat of danger,' Gerard told him, 'this is not some lush Norman knightly manor.'

'I'm not from Normandy,' the Lusignan replied.

'I don't care,' the seneschal snapped. 'You will obey me, now and forever. We will sit inside this fort of ours until Richard returns.'

'What if he doesn't return tomorrow night?' Guy asked.

Gerard stared at Richard. 'We'll give him one more day and then leave.'

Richard didn't think that was a particularly generous window. For all he knew, the recent rains would lengthen the journey he needed to make. Or he'd have to evade more Saracens. Or lose a horse.

'You should prepare,' Gerard told him and the guide, 'pack lightly, but pack enough. Choose your horses with care and try to sleep before evening. Oh, and Richard, try not to waste all your energy speaking with your father.'

Richard had forgotten about that.

William stood at the back of the press of men who watched the ghulam wait for an answer to his message.

Gerard turned to Guy. 'You may be changeable and weak, but we do agree on some things,' Gerard raised his voice to his turcopoles. 'Loose your arrows.'

The turcopoles had been waiting for such a command, and a dozen arrows spiralled through the warm air to the horror of the ghulam. Half struck him, dappling his robe with shafts, and pushed him over with their force. The Saracen's eyes bulged in disbelief as he lay on the ground, knowing there was no use in trying to return to his feet. Cries of shock and horror rang out from the Saracen camp and the turcopoles settled down to wait in case the Saracens launched a revenge-fuelled attack. Everyone else went back to their part of the ruins and waited for whatever was going to happen next.

Richard didn't go anywhere because William Keynes still stood in one of the stone doorways.

William's eyes were red. 'I see that I wronged you, my son. Will you ever be able to accept my forgiveness?'

Richard's anger bubbled under the surface. 'You don't know

how much suffering you've caused. And you're in a white mantle, so I suppose you're a full brother of the Temple now? Which means you can't leave the order and right any of the wrongs you've caused.'

'I swore a promise on what I thought was my deathbed,' William replied, 'I thought I would be a full brother for a day, then meet my end. I never expected to recover, and then when I did, I was bound by my oaths to the order.'

'Young lord,' Bowman still carried the golden box and true cross, 'we sailed all the way to this godforsaken place to find out what happened to him, maybe you should at least ask about that while you still can.'

'You came here for me?'

'Yes,' Richard replied, 'I wanted to find out how you died. Why you died. If you were betrayed or did it to yourself.'

'Both,' his father answered, 'I failed to see the danger Eustace posed until there was nothing I could do to stop things. He found my weaknesses and turned them against me. He gave me the choice of giving in or him killing my family.'

'Ah,' Bowman said, 'Eustace did like to do that.'

William didn't hear Bowman. 'During the battle we chased the Turks off and into a marsh, but their retreat was not a true flight, instead it was a trap. They circled us and wore us down, drawing our charges in and chipping away at our numbers. The result was inevitable, and I was fortunate to be dragged away rather than being captured. Many great men were taken, Raymond of Tripoli, the Prince of Antioch and even men from the west such as Hugh of Lusignan.'

'You knew him?' Guy had remained to watch the Saracen camp. 'Geoffrey Martel refused to tell me much when I confronted him at Corbie.'

Bowman looked at Richard but luckily kept his mouth shut.

William's eyes burned at Geoffrey's name. 'The elder Martel is a far greater one than his son, but he is still devoid of the grace of God. Are you a son of Hugh of Lusignan?'

'I am,' Guy said. 'What happened to him?'

'He was one of the first to surrender to the Turks,' William said calmly, 'and from your recent words here, that streak seems to run through your blood.'

Richard's anger was too much to allow him to laugh, but Bowman did.

Guy drew his sword.

'And brandishing your blade at an old and unarmed man is supposed to make me think you are not a coward?' William asked.

Bowman put the cross in the golden box and drew his sword. 'Just so you know, I'm not attacking anyone,' he said, 'I'm just helping you to put your sword away, Guy.'

Richard's hand moved to Durendal and Guy backed down.

William sneered ever so slightly at him. Then his face relaxed. 'Your father died after years in captivity, I never met him but he was not known to be a bad man. He did not deserve his fate.'

'For years I never even knew he'd been captured,' Guy said, 'between us, my brothers would have found a ransom for him.'

Richard almost felt something for Guy, almost.

'The army was full of great men, men who did not deserve their imprisonment following that battle. Raymond of Tripoli was confined for almost a full decade. Some who deserved it avoided it, such as Eustace Martel, who is one of the sorriest men I have ever met. May God curse him.'

'I don't think you're allowed to say that,' Bowman put his own sword away. 'But don't worry, Eustace is dead now.'

'Dead?' William said. 'How is that possible? The man was beyond the reach of mortal men, he was strong and surrounded by his company everywhere he went.'

Bowman yawned. 'I ripped his jaw bone off, and I can assure you that I am quite mortal.'

'You did what?'

'I was going to feed it to my dog, but instead I laid it to rest in the grave of my brother, who Eustace had killed.'

William looked at Richard. 'Who is this man you seem to travel with?'

Richard grinned. 'My friend. And we put an end to Eustace together.'

'And my horse's hooves,' Bowman added, 'that's what actually killed him in the end.'

'Hooves? That is barbaric. Although if anyone deserved it, it

103

was him.'

'I never liked him,' Guy said.

Richard groaned. 'We don't care, no one gets what they deserve. I didn't deserve what happened to me, neither did Bowman. I'm sure Raymond of Tripoli didn't deserve to be locked up for ten years just for fighting for his faith.'

'Raymond is one of the better men in the kingdom today,' William said, 'he knows of our mission to hide the true cross.'

'He's not popular with the Templars,' Richard said, 'they think he's an agent of the Saracens.'

'He is more sensible than the Templars give him credit for,' William said. 'Raymond favours diplomacy and negotiation. Which, when the enemy is larger than we are, must be the correct path. The warmongering of some in the order is wrong, but they are the minority.'

'Maybe when you were last in Jerusalem that was true,' Richard said, 'but now all the Templars sound like Gerard here, or even Guy. Except for the urge to surrender, that is.'

'I'm standing right here,' Guy said, 'and we can't negotiate with the infidel, we are here to clear them from the Holy Land, are we not?'

'You were happy to negotiate when you thought it would save your life,' Richard said, 'and you're here just to carve out lands for yourself, or have you forgotten I was with you when the Young King died? Don't pretend to be pious now.'

'This sounds a petty matter,' William said. 'What are you doing in the Holy Land, Richard? It is not safe here.'

'Don't you presume to preach to me on what is safe,' Richard said, 'you sailed here just as I did, except that you left your family behind, not knowing if you'd return, and not leaving any method for them to look after themselves if you didn't.'

'But I did not die.'

'We thought you had, which is the same thing,' Richard remembered the day his uncle had come. 'Luke told us you were dead. Then he killed my mother.'

The colour drained from William's face, and he shook.

'Uncle Luke tried to take her,' Richard said, 'and then he killed her. Then I ran away. If it wasn't for this man, he's called Bowman, Eustace's men would have caught me. You were wrong to leave us, and without that one piece of luck when I met Bowman, me and my sister would also be dead.'

Two tears streaked down William's face. 'I expected to return, most who leave on pilgrimages return.'

'And plenty do not. You should be ashamed of yourself.'

'I am,' William's face grew red. 'I allowed Eustace to intimidate me and allowed Luke an opportunity to think himself able to usurp me. What do you think I have spent my time in this wilderness thinking about? My guilt has never left me, no amount of prayers have been able to shift it.'

Richard took a breath and went to lean on the wall, but it was so covered in waiting arrows he couldn't. He sighed and turned back to his father. He told him about Adela, and then his own children, although he left out all the bad things he'd done. Which felt like a lot.

It also took most of the day, and as the sun threatened to drop below the mountain range to the west, Gerard returned looking for Richard. 'You have had enough time to settle matters here,' he said, 'dusk is upon us. Dress for the mission the Grand Master placed in your hands. Leave all your armour behind, as well as anything you do not need. Speed and faith shall be your armour.'

Bowman groaned.

The Marshal's horse was barely visible beneath its new armour. Cloaks and blankets had been tied all over it so only its legs and the sides of its head could be identifiable as a horse. The animal shook its head and tried to dislodge the blanket tied over it, but the Marshal had spent all day preparing and his knots were strong.

The Marshal himself wore his black Templar surcoat over a large robe one turcopole had leant him, the native Christians approving of his courage and willingly lending their assistance. Two dozen of them stood by their horses under the canvas covers of the ruins as the last vestiges of the day drained behind the mountains to the west and left the plateau covered in darkness. This was the second plateau, the one where a ghulam did not lie dead, and it spread out to the southeast until its rim sloped down and the land turned into a maze of gullies and ravines.

Richard couldn't see those as he rubbed his hair and wished he was allowed to lace on his helmet. Richard and Sarjeant's horses did not wear their white Templar caparisons because of the brightness of them, although Bowman had been allowed to keep his green one.

Otto had been forbidden to join them by Gerard due to the secret nature of the mission, and the German stood next to Maynard to watch the diversion and escape unfold.

The guide mounted his horse, small enough not to hit the canvas roof over the ruins, and rode forwards away from safety.

No fire had been lit in Khirbet, so that the eyes of those who would be fighting or riding through the night would already be adjusted to the dark.

Richard could see a way along the plateau, but not the enemy, apart from some fires which flickered away as spots in the gloom.

Gerard spoke quietly to the Marshal and made the sign of the cross.

The Marshal nodded and mounted his horse outside. Richard wondered if the knight just wanted to die so he could join his fallen master in the afterlife. But he had himself to worry about as the turcopoles filed through the gap in the wall which served as a gateway, then fanned out in an irregular line facing the Saracen camp.

'May the Lord be with you,' Gerard said to each of the envoy party.

Richard only nodded a reply, then led his Tancarville horse out of Khirbet. He would lead an Arab horse as his remount, but wanted a horse he knew for this most critical part of the plan.

The turcopoles cantered off along the plateau once they had formed their line, although Richard could only see half of them until even they vanished into the black. He could see when they crossed in front of the lights of the enemy fires, blocking their light here and there, but he couldn't make out their shapes.

Richard felt no nerves for himself. He ached with worry for his children if he was killed, but the thought of the act itself no longer brought fear. It was inevitable, he thought, and it had to happen, so why worry about it?

The Marshal cantered off next, his horse excited by whatever it thought was about to happen, and its speed was unhindered by the layers of fabric which flapped up and down on its body and neck.

The Marshal's horse disappeared, and Ishmael turned his horse to face Richard. 'It is time.'

Richard pulled the Arab horse along with him, Bowman and Sarjeant close behind each towing their own spare horses.

A bow twanged out in the night. Richard squinted to see but saw nothing other than occasionally more shapes blocking out the enemy fires as the turcopoles advanced and the sounds of their bows loosing echoed over the plateau.

Ishmael put his whip to his horse and it bounded off to the left of the southerly direction taken by the turcopoles. Richard's route lay east, but to go that way they had to ride a way along the plateau and then find a path down from it.

Richard's Arab horse pulled back when he cantered, but soon realised it was being led and it caught up with the Tancarville horse. Their hooves thundered on the hard ground so loudly Richard thought their ride couldn't possibly be achieved with any level of stealth.

He caught up with the guide, for the Tancarville horse had grown up on green pastures and rich horsebread, and had more power than the guide's did.

Cries of alarm rose from the Saracen camp and Richard heard a war cry that sounded very much like Dex Aie the Marshal.

'He doesn't learn,' Bowman said beside him, the hooves of his green-clad horse pounding the stony ground.

'There are watch fires,' Richard said as cool air whipped past his face. 'They will have watch men.'

Lone fires blazed away around the plateau, fires small enough that they hadn't been visible from Khirbet, but now, some way away, they formed a ring of sentry posts which they would have to negotiate.

A great clamour rose from the camp, Richard heard at least

one clash of iron on iron, and shouts and screams filled the air. But not near Richard, near Richard he could really only hear their horses as their metal shoes kicked stones and sent them flying noisily over the ground.

'We must ride quicker,' Ishmael said, 'we have no choice.'

Richard apologised to his horse, then applied his spurs.

The guide adjusted the direction of his horse as it lowered its head and entered a full gallop. He aimed between two of the watch fires.

Richard's horse stumbled on a stone but whirled its legs around quickly enough to catch itself, and Richard didn't fall.

The watch fires drew nearer and larger. Then a shout called out from one of them. Richard couldn't hear anything else, he sped along and air buffeted loudly in his ears. He urged the Tancarville horse on and snatched a glance behind to check Bowman and Sarjeant were still there.

They were.

The guide charged between the fires, Richard wondered if arrows were shot at them as he followed, but his horse was too loud to hear any missiles, and if shot, none hit.

Once through, Ishmael slowed his horse, but only because he couldn't tell how far away the edge of the plateau was.

Richard felt a sudden fear of tumbling down a cliff and held his horse up. The Arab horse on its rope surged ahead and Richard had to brace himself against his saddle and lock his arm to catch it when it ran too far ahead and pulled the rope taut to nearly unseat him.

The rim of the plateau arrived with only a moment's warning.

Richard applied his spurs sharply to make his horse stop, thanking his father for having taught him the method, and skidded a horse's length along the stone-covered ground.

The guide and his spare horse cantered down the slope, the two Arab horses at home despite the steepness, a steepness that made Richard's stomach heave.

The Tancarville horse slid down the scree slope instead of cantering, it threw its head up in fear but they reached the bottom of the long cliff with a jolt and in one piece.

Sarjeant's spare Arab burst past them, its long rope trailing behind it.

Sarjeant himself followed, wide-eyed and cursing the Arab.

Richard didn't have time to worry about the loose horse, he followed the guide, who broke into a gallop again and entered a narrow rock-lined gulley. The gully was a jagged scar in the yellow earth, zigzagging left and right with sharp turns that made Richard's pulse quicken and tested his nerves. Their horse's hooves splashed through the small amount of water that trickled through the gulleys, which Richard thought would probably mean they would leave very obvious tracks for anyone who came after them.

Richard overtook Sarjeant's loose horse, which stopped to drink from the water, then rounded a bend and caught up with Ishmael at a fork in the ravine, and stopped because the guide had stopped.

All four horses gulped down air. Although the Tancarville horse rasped more strongly than the Arabs, for his power came at a price.

'Stay still,' Ishmael said when Sarjeant and Bowman joined them. 'We listen for pursuers.'

Richard swallowed and wanted to reach for his water but didn't have a free hand.

Bowman tied his spare horse's rope to his saddle and swung his already strung bow from his shoulders. He nocked an arrow as everyone watched the exit from the ravine and caught their breath.

Silence.

One of their horses snorted loudly, and when that sound evaporated, in the distance Richard could hear something.

Bowman raised his bow.

The guide slowly pulled his own short recurve bow from the back of his saddle and laid an arrow on its string.

Richard realised he'd need to tie his Arab horse to the Tancarville one if he was going to have to fight and started to try to find the best place to tie it.

The distant thumping started to echo with splashes.

'There better not be many of them,' Sarjeant drew his sword.

Bowman drew his arrow back to his chin.

Richard fumbled to tie a knot in the rope he'd looped around his tall wooden pommel, but his fingers shook and couldn't complete the delicate work. This hadn't happened before.

Sarjeant moved his horse away to spread out from the others.

Richard pushed the rope through a loop in itself, but he rushed and when he let go it fell back out. He swore.

Ishmael drew back his arrow. Whoever was chasing them was close.

The more Richard tried to tie the rope in the dark, the more his fingers seemed too big and clumsy. He wasn't going to secure the horse in time.

A horse galloped out of the ravine, its front legs bounding so fast they blurred together in the non–existent light.

Bowman loosed. The arrow flew straight, but straight past the enemy and into the rocks behind him. Bowman howled.

The rider realised his danger and pulled his horse around to go back the way he'd come. Except that Sarjeant's loose horse had wandered along the narrow ravine and blocked his path.

Richard dropped his rope, he'd have to worry about spare horses later. He drew Roland's blade and the Tancarville horse leapt at the Saracen.

The enemy horseman flapped his legs on his horse to urge it to push Sarjeant's Arab aside, but the Arab itself stood firm and squealed at the Saracen's mount.

Richard reached him, flashed his sword, caught him on the arm and felt the blade bite into flesh.

The Saracen cried out, his hand half severed, and Sarjeant appeared on his other side and cut down onto the man's shoulder. The blow cut through his robe and dug deeper. He swayed almost out of the saddle, which dragged his horse off to one side, frightened it, and caused it to bolt. The jolt of the sudden leap of the horse threw the Saracen out of his saddle and he crashed into the ground, but still with one foot in a stirrup. That only spooked the horse more, and it bolted back up the ravine, Sarjeant's Arab fleeing behind it with its tail stuck straight up in the air.

Richard noticed Ishmael's arrow sticking out of the Saracen's back as he was dragged back towards his camp.

'A lucky shot,' Bowman mumbled.

The guide strained his hearing. 'He was not alone. We should go.'

Richard agreed, put his sword away, and thought about how best to retrieve his spare horse.

'No time,' Ishmael said and galloped off down one of the forks.

Richard groaned and followed.

An arrow cut through the air above him, hit a rock, and the separated arrowhead spiralled down in front of him so that the Tancarville horse felt he had to jump it. The leap caught Richard unawares and threw his body into the pommel of his saddle and winded him.

As he gasped for air, he felt a thud on his back. He reached behind him with his free hand and felt the smooth shaft of an arrow caught in his mantle.

'Go faster,' Bowman shouted behind him.

They turned a corner, galloped up a ravine with a steep incline, then around another corner which opened out onto a dry riverbed. The moon shone through the clouds above and gave the stony ground a silvery glow.

'We can't outrun them,' Richard shouted, 'Bowman, go left, I'll go right. We need to fight.'

Bowman turned sharply left out of the ravine and jerked to a halt a little way from its exit. His spare horse whirled around and pulled on the blonde man's saddle, but both the saddle and his knot held.

Sarjeant rode on behind the guide, the bait in Richard's trap. He just hoped both men would turn around at the right moment to come back and help.

Richard himself moved to the other side of the ravine to Bowman and drew his sword. He fought to control his breathing and flexed his fingers on the handle of the old blade. Richard might not be able to tie a knot, he thought, but he could still hack down with the weapon on men who were not wearing mail.

He heard horses thundering through the ravine, their hoofbeats echoing off the tall and stony sides.

With the quantity of arrows which had pelted him, Richard expected at least two riders to burst forth, but in the end, it was another lone Saracen.

Bowman had forgone his bow and charged with Richard, the two of them coming together perfectly so their enemy couldn't squeeze his horse away between them.

The Saracen cried out, and with a bow in his hand and an arrow in the other, could only try to stab Richard with the arrow.

Richard ignored it and cut with Durendal. Except he was for once without his armour and the arrowhead sank into his chest.

Bowman's sword snapped the Saracen's bow and kept going to carve a chunk out of his arm.

Richard pressed his attack home and the old sword was still sharp enough to slice into his foe's body.

All three horses had come together in a clash and tangle of legs, and the Tancarville horse lashed out at the Saracen's mount, causing it to pull itself backwards in an attempt to flee its ambush.

Bowman expected it, stepped his horse sideways to track the enemy's movement, and crashed into it. He hooked his sword arm around the Saracen's head, locked it in, and dragged him to the ground.

The blonde knight let go and allowed the wounded archer to smash down head first onto the silvery riverbed.

His horse spun around on its back legs, saw open space, and ran off.

Richard looked down at the stunned man, who moaned faintly, not yet aware of the pain about to sweep his body.

Ishmael arrived in a cloud of dust and peered down at their fallen opponent. 'You learn quicker than others from the west,' he nodded.

'This isn't the first time we've been chased,' Richard said.

Bowman grinned. Then he glanced at Richard's chest. 'You forgot we'd taken our armour off, didn't you?'

Richard replaced his sword and suddenly felt a stinging sensation on the right side of his body. His black surcoat had a rip in it, and he put his finger into the hole. The finger slid through the tunic underneath, and came out wet. Under the moonlight the liquid was black. 'It's more of a graze,' Richard said. 'It was only an arrow.'

'Your God watches you this night,' the guide said.

'He could have let us pass between the watch fires unnoticed,' Richard murmured.

Bowman watched the ravine. 'I don't hear anything else. They can't track us until dawn, so I think we're safe.'

'Don't say that,' Richard said, 'every time you say something like that, an enemy company appears on a hill or bursts out of a wood.'

'I think that's you,' the blonde man grinned.

The fallen Saracen's eyes opened and he turned his head to his badly wounded arm.

'What do we do with him?' Richard asked.

'Templars do not take prisoners,' the guide said, 'and he is an infidel. Your enemy.'

'You want me to kill him?' Richard asked. 'I'm not sure I want to. No, I am sure, I'm not killing him, look at him. He can't harm us anymore. Leave him with some water and we can go.'

'Are you sure you are a Templar?' Ishmael asked, the moon behind him shrouding his face in shadow.

Richard nodded. 'I have been through the initiation. Which was boring. But that does not mean I need to blindly agree with them. I wear the black mantle, not the white.'

Ishmael patted his horse on the neck, who snorted and shook his head at the sweat which itched it, and dismounted.

'You are a very odd Templar,' the guide said. Then he crouched down over the Saracen, said some words in a foreign tongue, and cut the man's throat.

A very brief hiss of air escaped from the man and his body relaxed as his head rolled back onto the earth.

'Did you do that for mercy?' Richard asked.

Ishmael wiped his blade clean on the Saracen's robe, looted his arrows, and stood up. 'No,' the guide said, 'he was my enemy too, and like the Templars, I do not take prisoners.'


The dawn brought much needed warmth, for Richard's fingers, ears, nose, and toes had all gone numb during the night. They'd ridden along canyons, and then through a pass in the sweeping mountain which had been visible in the distance from the ruins of Khirbet. The glow of the rising sun lit their path as they rode directly towards it, which made Richard squint, then try riding with his eyes closed. He didn't do that for long. The only saving grace of their escape was that the guide didn't force them to say prayers every hour, and if Sarjeant had thought about it, he didn't mention it.

Once Richard could feel his right hand, he reached down into the food bag slung around the back of his saddle and started to eat a handful of dates. He liked dates.

Bowman did the same, but only reluctantly. 'I miss real food,' he said.

'I think the food here is better,' Richard said.

The blonde knight snorted.

'Did you see the spices in Jerusalem?' Richard asked. 'There were sacks of cinnamon. Do you remember the tiny handful I gave Sophie?'

Bowman's eyes softened. 'Aye, young lord.'

'She would have liked Jerusalem,' Richard gazed at the sun as it started to burn through the clouds on the horizon.

'I'll concede it smells better than London,' Bowman said, 'and the weather is better.'

'I'm not so sure,' Sarjeant shook his cold hands to warm them. 'These nights are as cold as any in the west.'

'You all complain like children,' the guide said from the head of their small group.

The white stony ground gave way to a valley, through which a river ran, fast and swirling, they heard its rumble before they saw it.

'It looks angry,' Bowman said, 'I suppose it's too much to ask to presume there's a bridge over it?'

'When did you last see a bridge?' Ishmael asked.

'Not since before the Dead Sea,' Richard replied. 'Surely you don't want us to cross that?'

The guide shook his head. 'It is too fast and too deep.'

'Thank the Lord above,' Bowman said, 'for a moment there I thought you were going to make us ford it. Best case, we'd lose a horse or two and all our supplies.'

114

The guide halted his horse and studied the foaming water as it rushed around huge boulders. 'I said it is too fast and too deep, not that we didn't have to cross it.'

'What?' the blonde knight cried. 'We'll be swept to our deaths.'

'Do you fear a little water?' Ishmael almost smiled.

Bowman gritted his teeth and blew air out through his nose.

Richard didn't like it any better. 'I suppose if we try to go around, we can't possibly return to Khirbet in time?'

The guide remained still.

'I suppose that's a yes,' Richard sighed and asked the Tancarville horse to walk on. He descended the gentle slope that was really part of the riverbed and marvelled at how big the river must have once been.

But even now it was an obstacle. Standing at the water's edge, it rushed and spat, water was thrown up and onto the bank and his horse lowered his head and snorted at it.

The guide joined him. 'Your big horse is like all the horses from the west, brave in combat but terrified of things it doesn't know.'

'It knows rivers,' Richard said.

'Have you ever crossed one other than the stream outside Khirbet?'

Richard frowned. He gently asked the horse to walk a step into the river but it braced and snorted again. 'No,' he replied.

'Smack him across his rump with the flat of your sword,' Bowman said, 'we don't have time for niceties.'

Richard shook his head. 'You're right, that will work today, but what about when we come back on our return journey? Then he will see the river and only remember being beaten. I'll be stuck on the other side.'

The blonde man rolled his eyes. 'Suit yourself, I'll show you how it's done,' he growled loudly at his Arab horse but the animal seemed at peace with the river and walked into it without concern.

The flowing water reached its hocks and then its belly. Bowmen yelped as the freezing water washed over his feet and then his legs.

Ishmael followed. 'You must cross now,' he said as his own

horse entered the river without complaint.

Richard's horse waved a front hoof at the water, touched it, and jumped back. It tried to spin away but Richard faced it back to the river. 'You can watch it as long as you like,' he told the animal, 'but you can't run away. You have to go into the river, or at least be trying to go into the river.'

Sarjeant waited beside him. 'Do you want me to wait with you?'

'No,' Richard said, 'if all the other horses are on the far bank, it will make him want to cross all the more.'

Richard's spare horse, although loose after they'd ambushed the Saracen, had followed its friends this far by its own accord. The now frayed rope dangling between its legs, it followed Sarjeant into the river.

'Why can't you be like that one?' Richard asked. 'Everything Tancarville is cursed, isn't it?'

He watched Bowman reach the middle of the river, the force of the water had already pushed him several paces downstream, but now it took hold of him as the river deepened and his horse had to swim. The sudden drop caught Bowman by surprise, and everything other than his own and the horse's head were submerged under water.

'That's going to ruin our swords,' Richard mumbled.

The Tancarville horse weaved from left to right as its friends grew further and further away, a battle in its mind between its fear of the river and its fear of being alone.

'Come on,' Richard said, 'you're a horse, you can't be on your own. Don't make me take Bowman's advice.'

The horse reared up and tried to spin away from the river again. Richard had to pull it back to face it. 'No,' he said firmly, 'face your fear. The way forward is good. Just go forward.'

Sarjeant cried out from the shock of the water as he too was dunked into the river, except his entire head went under for a moment and he gasped when it popped back out.

The Tancarville horse snorted. It went to sniff the water so Richard gave it full reins, allowing it to reach. 'Come on,' he said, 'you can do it. I'm more stubborn than you are.'

A huge sigh escaped the horse. Richard felt its back lower beneath him, and without having to ask it, the animal stepped into the raging waterway.

It pushed through the water as it grew deeper and Richard braced for the cold. When it came it chilled him, saturated his clothing, and made his breathing short and sharp.

Bowman left the river ahead, still towing his spare horse, but all his food and water bags had been washed away.

The guide emerged unscathed, but Sarjeant drifted some way down river, shouting and flailing his non-rein hand. Eventually his horse struggled out, but he'd also lost everything other than his saddle. His scabbard was still belted to him, but the sword was gone.

The Tancarville horse was a strong swimmer. It flexed its grass-fed muscles and pushed through the water, its head held high and its nostrils flaring, and carried Richard through the water, having drifted less far downriver than anyone else.

When he was able to walk again, and the water only up to his hocks, the horse shook. It was a great shake, water droplets flew everywhere and the saddle itself vibrated like an earthquake had hit it. The shaking dislodged Richard's saddlebag and his supply of dates and water fell into the river and were carried away.

He sighed.

Bowman's face was dark. 'I told you. I told all of you. What are we going to eat now? We have one man's supplies between four, and Sarjeant doesn't have a horse to change to.'

The guide nodded. 'And now is the time to change mounts. We must gallop to Qal'at.'

'Why?' Bowman asked. 'Because you want us to be as uncomfortable as possible, galloping in soaking clothes?'

'No,' Ishmael faced back the way they'd come. 'Because of them.'

Richard dropped his mantle and went to see what the guide meant.

Bowman swore. 'We won't have been hard to track since sunrise.'

'How many of them are there?' Richard asked.

'Hopefully less than four,' Sarjeant said, 'as I have no weapon.'

'More than four,' Bowman said, 'can't you see the dust rising?'

'No, I think I still have water in my eyes,' Sarjeant said.

'There is no time to waste,' the guide said, 'change horses and ride.'

Richard's spare Arab was nearby, trying to tease a piece of long and almost green grass out of a crack in a rock. Richard lifted himself out of his saddle, and weighing almost as much as he did in armour, lowered himself to the ground with a wet squelch. As he walked towards the Arab horse, he left watery footprints behind him. Fortunately the horse wasn't interested in running away, and Richard swapped the bridle from the Tancarville horse and put in on his new steed. The Arab's head was smaller and the bridle didn't really fit, but Richard had neither thought of it in advance, nor had time to do anything about it.

The Arab chewed at the bit in its mouth, playing with it because it was too loose.

Sarjeant watched him. 'You won't leave me behind, will you?'

Richard shook his head as he swung himself up into the saddle. 'No, but that won't save you if your horse tires.'

They rode east again, with the sun now high and to the south, the landscape of yellow stone, sand, and dust repeating itself again and again as they traversed ridges and skirted empty valleys. Richard wished to see green fields again, or even just an olive grove or the pomegranate orchards around Jaffa.

Richard's new horse was thinner than the Tancarville one, but he quickly got used to it. The Arab ran and ran and ran in a steady rhythm, but Sarjeant's horse was not as fresh.

Richard pulled ahead of him, only slightly at first, but as the sun swept overhead and began its descent, the large man and his jaded animal were too far behind to shout at.

'We have to slow down,' Richard called to the guide.

Ishmael turned his head. 'We are already holding back. The enemy will not. Your man should peel away, take some of the enemy with him, so that his death has meaning.'

Richard spat out some dust which had flown into his mouth. 'I can't leave him.'

'Can't or won't?'

Richard scowled.

'Hand me the cylinder,' Ishmael offered, 'I can take the message on. At least we do not have to fail our task.'

'Gerard would kill me,' Richard said, 'he wouldn't even let Otto come along, so I can't hand it over to a non-Christian. I'm sorry, but we can both keep together with Sarjeant and do what we are here to do.'

'That's more like it,' Bowman shouted from where his Arab flew across the earth so elegantly the blonde man thought he was riding a cloud. 'Remember in Castle Tancarville when you chose not to try to save Edith at the same time as your family?'

Richard did, and he'd still lost Sophie.

'This is more like the old you,' Bowman said, 'the one who thinks he can fix everything.'

'If you say so,' Richard replied.

'It is, however,' the blonde man said, 'the sort of sentiment that gets us into trouble.'

'We're slowing down so Sarjeant can catch up.'

'Exactly, young lord, and we'll probably get killed.'

Richard sat back a little in his saddle and the horse instantly slowed down to a slow canter. When Sarjeant had nearly caught up, Richard looked back and could see specks of black behind them.

'It is not far,' Ishmael had to hold his horse back.

'It had better be,' Bowman said. 'They'll be able to shoot at us soon.'

Richard licked his lips but his throat was dry and swallowing was hard. He cursed the river for having washed away their water, and the guide had not offered any of his to anyone else.

'Through that valley,' Ishmael veered his horse towards a gap in a cliff, 'we will find Qal'at.'

'We're nearly there,' Richard shouted back to Sarjeant, whose horse bobbed its head and was drenched in sweat. Richard could smell his own horse and would have let Sarjeant swap to the Tancarville stallion had they the time to.

And they didn't have much longer, because the Saracens were gaining on them. Richard didn't want to look hard enough to see how many chased them because he didn't want his neck to be jerked around if his horse tripped on a stone, but it was clearly more than five horses who pursued them.

They charged into the valley, its sides reached up and grew taller as they ploughed deeper in. The ground became more sandy and a huge dust cloud from their hooves enveloped Sarjeant and obscured the Saracens who gained on him.

'We need to wait for him,' Richard slowed his horse and Bowman copied.

The guide turned around and shouted at them, but carried on.

'I like the man as much as you do,' Bowman said, 'but are you sure you're really willing to wait around here for him?'

Richard grimaced at Bowman as their own dust cloud drifted over them, obscuring even the valley sides for a moment.

Ishmael realised Richard was serious and stopped his horse. 'Are you mad?' he shouted back.

'That's a good question,' Bowman said. 'They could run right into us.'

'I'm not leaving someone behind. I'm not my father.'

'No, you're not,' the blonde man said, 'look, there's your man, can we carry on now?'

Sarjeant appeared first as a shadow in the dust cloud, but then as a man riding a horse. A horse which wasn't going very fast.

'He stumbled,' Sarjeant reached them, 'because he couldn't see where he was going in your dust cloud.'

Richard cursed himself for allowing the three of them to pull even slightly ahead of Sarjeant. 'You'll have to push him on,' Richard said, 'it could be a case of you or the horse.'

Richard let Sarjeant, who didn't need telling twice, get ahead of him before following. They caught up with the guide, who muttered some words in his own tongue and then raced off on his swift horse. The valley gradually rose and the sandy footing gave way to harder stone, almost rock.

That at least meant they no longer generated dust, but as Bowman's horse went to avoid a man-sized boulder, it slipped on the ice-like surface.

The Arab's back feet both violently skidded to the side and the horse's body came crashing down onto the hard stone. There was a crack as the wooden saddle impacted and part of it snapped, and a cry from Bowman as his leg did a poor job of cushioning his horse's fall.

Bowman stayed on the ground as the startled horse threw

its legs in every direction in order to get back onto its feet. It hauled itself up and snorted.

The blonde man stayed down, his moans bounced around the valley in a great echo.

Richard halted beside him and jumped down.

'Leave him,' Ishmael shouted from ahead of them, 'you have only moments to live.'

Richard, his horse's reins in one hand, held out his other to Bowman. 'You better be able to get up,' he said.

Bowman swore and rubbed his leg. He tried to move it and although it obeyed, it did so sluggishly.

Sarjeant's horse limped onwards but it wasn't getting too much of a lead.

'Where are you going? I waited for you,' Bowman shouted after him. 'Ungrateful bore.'

Richard pulled the blonde man up, and Bowman put weight on the squashed leg. 'It'll be fine.'

'Hurry up,' Richard said, 'you can feel sorry for yourself later. I'll hold your stirrup for you.'

'I'm more worried about my shoulder,' Bowman brought his horse around and Richard held the right stirrup firmly to help Bowman remount.

'You fools,' Ishmael cried and cantered over. His horse almost slipped on the stone too. 'Throw me the case, you are done for.'

'I'm sure we've got time,' Richard said as he placed his own foot in his stirrup to remount.

'I'm not sure we do,' Bowman spun his horse around, 'I hope they're not good shots.'

Eight horses with six riders emerged from the dust cloud and clattered onto the slippery stones. They rode with drawn bows, but clearly thought they had the advantage, for instead of shooting, when they neared they spoke.

Richard settled himself in his saddle but didn't dare draw his sword.

Bowman thought about preparing his bow, then decided he'd miss his shot anyway and didn't bother.

'At least Sarjeant might get away,' Richard said as the Saracens fanned out in a semicircle.

'Good for him,' Bowman rubbed his neck.

121

Ishmael thought about running, but he knew he'd unlikely evade all the enemy's arrows.

A Saracen spoke to the guide, his words angry and short, although addressed to Richard.

'They wish for us to surrender,' Ishmael relayed.

'If anyone has any ideas to avoid that,' Richard said, 'don't hold back.'

Bowman sighed. 'If we wore our mail, young lord.'

'I know, blame Gerard.'

'Oh, I am certainly blaming that self righteous fool,' Bowman replied.

'I don't think this is helpful talk,' Ishmael said, 'they are impatient.'

'I can see that,' Richard also knew the more time they wasted, the less likely the Saracens would go after Sarjeant.

'They order you to throw down your swords.'

'Are they really afraid of two unarmoured men with swords?' Bowman asked.

'Three men, they mean mine, too,' the guide said.

Bowman shrugged. 'I'll throw my bow down, I might as well get rid of it anyway as it's no use to me.'

The Saracen barked more words, and Ishmael frowned. 'Drop swords now or they take you. They care not whether alive or dead.'

A stone bounced and rolled down the valley side, Richard turned to watch it but there was no one there. The dust clouds from both parties settled, except for a small cloud which remained around the mouth of the valley.

Ishmael seemed to look through the Saracens and at the cloud. Then he looked up and around. He smiled. He said something to the Saracen, and all six of them burst into laughter, white teeth from their grins flashing in the sunlight.

'What did you tell them?' Richard asked.

'I asked for their surrender,' Ishmael said.

Bowman nodded. 'I like you. I think. I suppose we're going down fighting, then?'

Ishmael shook his head and the laughing Saracen coughed and spoke. Ishmael snapped back a terse reply and grinned a grin of menace.

'What did they say?' Richard asked.

'They asked us to surrender again,' Ishmael said, 'and I told them to yield or die. They think I am mad, but now there is uncertainty in this dog's voice.'

'I think they're right about you being mad,' Bowman said, 'but very well, draw swords on the count of three and we'll get this over and done with?'

Richard let his hand slip in the direction of Durendal. If some arrows missed, this might even work, he thought. For sure, not all three of them would survive, but maybe one of them would, and that was better than nothing.

Ishmael shook his head. 'There is no need. You western knights always look for ways to die. Like your friend.'

'He's a peacock,' Bowman said, 'we're not like him.'

'So you say. Be patient.'

'Patient?' Richard said. 'I'm not sitting around waiting for my death, I'm riding towards it.'

'Wait,' the guide said sternly.

'Why?'

'Because Allah is the one true god, and he favours neither these enemies nor you. He favours us.'

'Us?'

'Oh,' Bowman noticed the dust cloud at the entrance to the valley hadn't dissipated. It had advanced.

The six Saracens also realised that someone approached and spoke between each other with hurried words and fleeting eyes.

Richard looked down the valley to Qal'at, and there were horsemen approaching from there too, because he could dimly hear their hooves on the harder stone.

Ishmael reeled off a long burst of words at the Saracens, it sounded more like a sermon than a discussion.

'What's happening?' Richard asked. 'Are these your people coming?'

'These dogs grew too excited by the hunt. Too arrogant. They entered the valley and therefore entered land which they are not welcome in.'

Two of the Saracens turned their horses to confront the impending dust cloud, but it was bigger than theirs had been.

'Who is coming?' Richard asked.

'Answer us, guide,' Bowman cried. 'Do we need to worry about them more than these Saracens?'

Richard realised that the riders approaching on the hard stone would already have met Sarjeant. He swallowed down his worry, or at least tried to, because between thirst and nerves, his swallow got stuck and he could only cough.

The leading Saracen implored the guide with desperate words, Richard assumed for some agreement, but Ishmael mocked him and spat on the ground.

A moment later, arrows flew out of the dust cloud and the two Saracens who had turned towards it fell peppered with arrows.

Richard watched the horsemen charging from the other end of the valley. Only a few they might have been, but now the remaining Saracens realised they were outnumbered and trapped.

'I see,' Bowman swung his bow into position and whipped out an arrow. 'The enemy of my enemy, as they say.'

While the Saracen leader gawped at his fallen comrades, Ishmael shot him in the back.

Bowman let his arrow fly at the same man, but it sailed by his target. 'God's eyes,' he roared, 'how?'

A group of horsemen surged out of the dust cloud as swiftly as their arrows. They were dressed in much the same way as the Saracens, but brought down the rest of them with a flurry of missiles shot from their bows quicker than Richard thought possible.

'Plenty of them missed,' Richard said to Bowman, 'you don't see them complaining about it.'

'But when do I ever miss?' the blonde man moaned and slung his bow over his shoulder.

Richard glanced at Ishmael, who even though his face was impassive, somehow looked pleased.

'So if these are your people,' Richard said, 'and we're just outside Qal'at, does that make them the Assassins?'

Ishmael's head turned to face Richard. 'That is but your name for us, it is not correct.'

'Oh,' Richard said, 'so you are one of them?'

The guide's lips curled into a full smile. 'Evidently.'

# THE OLD MAN OF THE MOUNTAIN

The fortification at Qal'at might as well have been a castle. It was a squat square building made from perfectly cut rectangular blocks of stone, which was the only feature in the flat and yellowly landscape the Assassins led Richard to. It was not a large fort, and the four sides were really buildings surrounding a small courtyard with a stone well at its centre.

Ishmael barked orders at the guards and attendants, of whom there were few, and led Richard with Bowman and Sarjeant through a large stone arch from the courtyard into one of the chambers within the walls. A fabric curtain across the arch acted as a door, and inside Richard found the yellow walls coated in tapestries of alien designs and patterns.

But at the back of the chamber, sitting on a fine carpet, was a man. He was probably the same age as Richard's father, but he had an even longer beard. Dressed no more finely than the other Assassins, and in a long and flowing green robe, Ishmael bowed to him and spoke for a long time.

'Do we just stand here?' Bowman asked.

Richard nodded.

A young man brought in water and offered it to them from a jug, and all three of them gulped it down with relief.

'I swear I'll be tasting the dust and sand for the rest of my life,' Bowman said.

'I'd forgotten how bad it was,' Sarjeant said, 'and I wish

already to forget again. When those men rode at me, me without so much as my sword, I said my prayers and waited for my end. I have never felt as sure it was coming, not even when I saw the smoke rise above Yvetot.'

'Every moment you get from now,' Richard said, 'is extra time from God. Make the most of it.'

Bowman rolled his eyes. 'Don't let this place get to your head, young lord.'

'I've had a lot to think about,' Richard said, 'I don't know if you've noticed.'

Bowmen went to reply, but noticed that the old man and Ishmael were both staring at them in patient silence.

'Are you finished?' the old man said.

He spoke in French, with an accent more like Guy's than Richard's, but still with words Richard could understand.

'You look surprised?' the old man asked.

'We told him that would happen,' Sarjeant said, 'I don't think he quite realised how much.'

Richard bowed to the old man because it seemed like a good idea. 'My apologies, I am new to the Holy Land and have not yet come to terms with it. I assumed you would not speak our language.'

'A polite Frank,' the old man looked at the guide.

Ishmael stared at Richard for a while. 'As I said, not like most of the others. Maybe in time he could adjust as Raymond has. If he is still a Templar, that could prove useful.'

The guide shifted his gaze to Bowman and said something not in French.

The old man laughed with Ishmael.

'This is about the archery, isn't it?' he crossed his arms. 'Haven't we got better things to talk about?'

'We probably should talk about it at some point,' Richard said. 'Something is wrong with you.'

'I don't want to. I want to know who this old man is. In the baths men spoke about the Old Man of the Mountain. Is that you?'

'Our lands are very, very far from here,' the man replied, 'the leader of our order would be reckless if he ventured here and made himself so vulnerable. These men here are few, the head of our order has much to do, you would not likely find him here.'

'Is that a no?' Bowman asked. 'Or just a way of saying yes but sounding mystical?'

'Maybe he is not as stunted in the head as I thought,' Ishmael said to the old man.

Richard put a hand on the blonde man's arm and gripped. 'Not now.'

Bowman pulled his arm away. 'Fine, but he's just avoiding my question.'

'It does not matter who I am,' the old man said, 'only that I have the authority to deal with your message.'

'Oh,' Richard slung the cylinder off his shoulder. The leather had dark stains from the river crossing, but he assumed it would be dry inside. He hadn't thought to check.

'Shouldn't we be sure he is the right man to deliver it to before you hand it over?' Sarjeant asked.

Richard shook his head. 'He said he is, and he is at Qal'at. That is good enough for me.' He pulled off the lid of the cylinder and poured the message out.

Except that it was not a simple roll of parchment. There was a leaf of white paper with a message, and then some rolled up parchment which, as it scattered all over the carpet on the floor, looked like the pages from Eric and Enid. Richard's copy was in Kerak, he thought mournfully.

Sarjeant picked some of the parchment pages up. 'These are either the gospels or the new testament.'

'Good,' the old man said, 'then the Grand Master is taking us seriously.'

'What?' Richard handed over the message while the young man who had offered them water picked up the rest of the parchment and stacked it up. Probably not in the right order.

'It should be the new testament,' the old man said, 'we requested it for the betterment of our order. The Christ you base your lives around to us is one of a cast of prophets and we wish to learn more about him. But he is but one among many.'

'That's blasphemy,' Sarjeant said.

'Indeed,' the old man replied, 'but as a prophet, we still value his words and his message.'

'I thought you hated us?' Bowman asked.

The old man rubbed his forehead and sighed. 'Do not paint everyone in this land who is not Christian with a single brush. There are many different peoples here, and ten years ago we attempted to learn more about your faith. Our leader at the time even wanted to convert to it. He asked the Kingdom of Jerusalem to send him the gospels and any other Christian works they could. The kingdom was very happy to oblige, happy that perhaps we could ally with them against our common enemies. Our messenger arrived in the kingdom to collect a set of gospels under royal protection. Royal protection.'

Richard felt a sinking feeling for where the story was heading, but he was also acutely aware that between him and their horses were a dozen Assassins and a very thick stone wall.

'Our envoy,' the only man continued, 'was murdered. By a one-eyed Templar.'

Sarjeant groaned.

'Your king at the time, King Amalric, had to arrest the Templar himself after your order tried to protect him, and then he tried again to deliver the holy works to us. Amalric, may peace be upon him, was a good king. True to his word and his friends. Our leader received the works with pleasure, and sent back a man who in your world would be called a priest, into the kingdom. He was to be baptised, receive your holy sacrament, and return to baptise the rest of the order. Do you know what became of our priest?'

Richard sighed. 'I think we have a pretty good idea.'

'The Templars,' the old man frowned, 'your order. Again they killed a man under royal protection. These unprovoked killings, of envoys...'

Richard, aware of exactly his role, shuddered at the emphasis on the word.

The old man cut short his sentence and shook his head. 'What can men do when trust is broken?'

Richard said nothing because he didn't think the old man was really asking him.

'For ten years we have kept our distance. But now, our common enemy has a new face and we have tried again for a third time to join with the Franks. Your message should contain the new testament as a sign that the Knights of the Temple can now be dealt with more honourably than before. That they will not kill our envoys.'

Richard frowned, for from what he'd seen himself, it seemed unlikely the Templars would really cooperate with the Assassins. Although, even Gerard had helped the Muslim merchants with the broken cart, so who could know the truth of it?

'Your Grand Master sent us what we requested,' the old man said, 'so we can proceed now with some hope.'

'I'm very sorry for what the Templars did to your envoy and priest,' Richard said, 'and I am aware that I myself am their envoy now. Are we in danger here?'

'Your directness is uncourtly,' Ishmael snapped. 'Speak with more respect.'

'I thought I was.'

'It is not your mistake,' the old man used his eyes to silence the guide, 'it takes time to learn the customs of others.'

Richard relaxed, although not fully.

The old man read the message and then read it again. 'Your Grand Master's message is intriguing. He has made us an offer so good it would be foolish not to accept. I will need you to return word of our agreement back to him.'

'What is the offer?' Bowman asked.

'And some men,' the old man's lips tightened into a line, 'take longer to master new customs than others.'

'He's not going to tell us,' Richard said.

'I was just curious,' the blonde man said, 'and I was curious about another thing.'

'Whatever it is,' Richard said, 'don't ask it.'

'Do you really murder people while drugged?'

Richard thought he felt the chamber cool. 'Why? Why would you ask that?'

'Calm down, young lord,' Bowman took a step towards the old man, and Ishmael, who had been sitting, stood up and put a hand on his sword.

'My horse fell badly on me,' the blonde man said, 'the guide saw it. I heard in the public baths that the Assassins are

130

named after the hashish they smoke before they run off to die heroically on the Old Man of the Mountain's bidding. My shoulder and leg hurt quite a lot from my fall, and I could do with feeling heroic for a while. Especially if we're about to ride straight back through that wasteland again.'

'That wasteland is our home,' Ishmael said.

'I thought you said the Assassins were based far away from here,' Richard said.

A burst of laughter escaped the old man and he slapped the guide heartily on the shoulder. 'This Frank is as sharp as one of our knives, nothing escapes him.'

'We're moving away from the subject of pain-soothing drugs,' Bowman said.

The old man rubbed his eye. 'The order's castles are far north or east of here, but Ishmael is from these parts. He would hardly be a useful guide if he were not. True believers find a home with us wherever they are from.'

Bowman shrugged. 'That is all well and good, but I am still in pain.'

'We are not named after hashish,' the old man said. 'We are Allah's principle people, the *Asas*. From that word, you foolish westerners have imagined for us a whole new name and ridiculous legend.'

'Oh,' Bowman's face dropped, 'so there are no drugs for me?'

'It's for the best, men become addicted to it,' Sarjeant scratched his neck where the mountain lion had sunk its teeth.

Richard noticed the large man's face turned a slight shade of pink as he said it, but it could have been sunburn.

'On the contrary,' the old man said to Bowman, 'we have things here which would ease your pain if you are not man enough to endure it.'

Bowman paused for a moment then shrugged. 'I will gladly take whatever you will give me.'

The old man said something to the young man, who beckoned Bowman to follow him out of the chamber.

The blonde man grinned at Richard and followed closely. 'You have to ask,' he said, 'or you don't get anything.'

Richard didn't mind, it might stop the blonde man moaning about his shoulder. He turned back to the old man. 'Thank you for helping him.'

'Despite his rudeness,' the old man replied.

'Yes,' Richard said, 'people do call him rude. We will happily deliver your message to the Grand Master, will you lend us fresh horses and some water for the journey?'

'Of course,' the old man said, 'and I will do better. Ishmael says your camp at the old town of Khirbet is surrounded, so some of our order will ride with you. The Saracens cannot be allowed to intercept your message, so our men will ensure that you return to your comrades.'

'Why is the message so important?'

'You will not prise secrets from me, and do not try a third time, because there will not be a fourth.'

Richard bowed his head. 'I will not. You are not what I expected.'

'What did you expect?'

'From what we've heard of the Assassins,' Richard started, but realised he had no real idea, 'I do not know, but something else. I didn't really think about it, but all the Christians are wary of you and the Templars do not seem to like you.'

The old man watched impassively. 'It only matters what the Grand Master does and thinks, the other Templars will obey him regardless of his orders. We will work with Christians because Saladin and his kind are our mortal enemy just as they are yours. More so than your people or your faith. We are few, the Sunnis are many.'

'Sunnis?'

'A different branch of the true faith.'

'You mean your true faith, not our true faith.' Richard frowned, he needed Brian to navigate this conversation.

'Be careful,' the old man said, 'our courtesy only extends only so far to those who question our beliefs. But the real threat to us is Saladin, who will destroy us in the way he intends to destroy you. He will take his time, but we should not mistake that for weakness or lack of purpose. Others already have, and it has been to their great cost.'

Richard nodded. He didn't understand how the Templars and the Assassins could work together in any way, but that wasn't his job. His job was to take a message back to Arnold in

Jerusalem. Even if he would rather go to Kerak.

Ishmael left to fetch writing materials.

'A question is written on your face,' the old man said, 'what is it?'

'If your order acts by assassinating their enemies, why did you not assassinate the Grand Master of the Templars after they killed your envoy? That would have sent a message not to act against you. It might have saved your priest.'

The old man sighed. 'We have killed the heads of Christian kingdoms before, but the Templars are not a kingdom. If we strike down a Grand Master, then another man will step up and take his place. All the officers are replaceable, you see. Killing any of them makes no difference and we cannot predict who will be elected to replace them. Kingdoms have heirs, they are predictable. The Templars were made for war, so a war they must have. For us, we must ensure their enemy is Saladin and not us. We seek more information on Christianity to build bridges with them, and so that we are less of an infidel than the Saracens.'

'Did the Old Man of the Mountain ten years ago actually want to convert to our faith?'

The old man's eyes twinkled. 'I Cannot speak for him. I do not seek conversion, but if I can speak through converted men I trust, then the Templars might be convinced to at least leave us and our envoys alone. Until then, those who wish to speak to use must send men like you. Although in the north it is easier, for we are very alone here in Qal'at. This is not our land either, this is a place we hold because Saladin does not know we are here. To his men we are simply some guards of a water-fort. When they arrive we pretend to be like them. In this way, we are able to communicate with Christians in the south.'

'How many Templar envoys have visited here?'

The old man half snorted. 'Secular knights, a few. Templars, none have completed the journey alive. One made it here dead, still on the back of his horse. We were able to read his message and respond, which is why you are here.'

'I'm surprised anyone wants to talk to you,' Richard said, 'Count Raymond is the most conciliatory of all the leaders, and Count Raymond's father is one of few Christians to be murdered by Assassins, so he hates you.'

'The world is complicated,' the old man said as Ishmael returned and laid out his materials in preparation to scribe their reply to Arnold's message.

The old man watched for a while. 'Your Grand Master and Raymond are enemies,' he said, 'our talks with him are part of a strategy of peace. It will not come to fruition quickly. Your mission is part of the first offering of an olive branch.'

Richard sighed. 'So I'm just a very expendable dove.'

'So long as a falcon is not hunting the dove, it can live a very good life.'

Richard had no idea what that meant.

The old man told Ishmael something to write. 'Envoy, all men will bend when something they want is more attractive than the hate they harbour within themselves. Count Raymond wants peace more than vengeance, because if he fails he will lose his life. But even so, our deal is not with him, but with the Templars, and no one outside of the order must know of it. You will deliver your cylinder, unopened, to the Grand Master himself.'

'I will,' Richard said.

Bowman arrived after Ishmael had completed the letter and the guide waved the paper around to dry the ink.

The blonde man walked a not entirely straight line through the curtain and into the chamber. 'This place is great, Richard,' he said, 'what was it called again? Chalad?'

The guide looked up with a scowl. 'No, Qal'at.'

'That's what I said,' Bowman reached Richard and put a hand on his shoulder to steady himself.

'I assure you it was not,' the old man grinned. 'Ishmael is very proud of his land, and you did mangle the name.'

'Mangle?' Bowman's pupils were dilated. 'Don't mock me for not being able to say your strange words. You try to say Yquebeuf, go on.'

The old man almost fell into Bowman's trap but stopped himself from attempting the name. 'Now that your man is no longer in any pain, it is time for you to leave. Ishmael suggested that your safe return depended on speed.'

'I knew they wouldn't be able to say it,' Bowman grinned and spun around quicker than his senses could really cope with. He nearly overbalanced, caught himself, and strode out of the chamber.

'We will provide you with food to eat during your return journey,' the old man said, 'our men will already be ready and waiting for you in the courtyard.'

'Thank you,' Richard slid the message into the cylinder and closed it. He nodded to Sarjeant. 'Right. Let's do it all again.'

A dense cloud of flies hid the bodies of the Saracens in the valley with a buzzing and moving shroud made from their black bodies. The vultures had already left, birds Richard had only seen from a distance and immediately disliked.

'Ride far around them,' Ishmael said, 'or the flies will follow us.'

They started their journey at a walk so they could eat the bread and dates provided by the Assassins, but Richard knew it wouldn't be long until they picked up the pace. The Tancarville horse followed on a long rope, but all the other horses were fresh from Qal'at's stable and paddocks. Although paddocks was probably not the right word for the roped off square of sand and stone beneath the fort's walls.

Bowman watched the swollen bodies as the reinforced party gave them a wide berth. 'Death is swift here and life is consumed just as swiftly,' he said grandly.

'Whatever they gave you,' Richard said, 'it is making you unusually poetic.'

'I think it's the landscape,' the blonde knight said, his green surcoat lighter now due to the ingrained sand that was now almost woven into its fibres.

'I don't think it is just that,' Richard replied.

Bowman sang for a while, and although Sarjeant complained he wailed like a cat, he didn't stop until they'd left the valley.

'At least the sun is behind us now,' Sarjeant said, 'my face is throbbing from riding towards it yesterday.'

'That's the last thing I'm worried about,' Richard said, 'there are so many other worries I'd happily swap for a painfully red face.'

'It must be hard for you,' Sarjeant said, 'we all thought your father lost. I still cannot quite believe he lives.'

Richard shook his head. 'All that time I yearned so badly for him, I wished so strongly I could have had more time with him. And now I can, I am furious with him.'

'His story is as sad as yours, my lord,' Sarjeant said, 'and he was a victim of fortune and circumstance just as you.'

'Not really,' Richard said, 'he was a grown man who made choices. I was a child who was given none.'

'From what I can see,' Bowman started.

'I don't care what you think at the moment,' Richard said.

'And you call me rude?' the blonde man threw a date up for his mouth to catch, but it missed and fell to the sand.

'I will forgive him,' Richard said, 'in time.'

'Do it sooner, young lord,' Bowman yawned, 'before a cloud of flies surrounds either him or you.'

'Can you not say things like that?'

Bowman shrugged, then grinned. 'Shrugging doesn't hurt now. I liked that place, whatever it was called, do you think we could go back?'

Richard glanced at Sarjeant. 'Do you know what he's been given? Or how long until it wears off?'

'I am afraid not. They could have plied him with anything. If he is like this when we reach Khirbet, I am worried he will do something stupid and alert the enemy.'

'We've got a lot of riding to do before that,' Richard said.

Bowman sang again. A song about a hare who became a lord and did something inappropriate to a nun. Richard wished he wouldn't sing rude songs about nuns, and apparently the Assassins didn't either, because they slowly edged ahead until they couldn't hear him.

'Don't they like my songs?' Bowman asked.

'No one likes your songs.'

'If they talked to me, then I wouldn't have to sing,' the blonde man said. 'I just want to ask them what it is that we are doing all this for.'

'How would they know?' Sarjeant asked. 'When we have not the slightest idea ourselves.'

'Our answer is in this cylinder,' Richard patted the leather container slung from his shoulder across his body.

'Well, what's in it?'

'Their message.'

'What does it say?'

Richard groaned. 'They wouldn't tell us. It's probably best that way, too, because it will probably not be something I like. Not while my children are under attack in Kerak and I'm out here doing nothing about it.'

'They'll be fine,' Bowman rolled his head around his neck.

'Like my wife was?' Richard asked.

'Probably,' the blonde man burped.

'Ignore him,' Sarjeant said, 'his words are not really his own.'

'They never are,' Richard mumbled to himself.

'Open it,' Bowman said, 'there is no seal on the leather.'

'I can't do that,' Richard said, 'I've given my oath and joined the Templars, I can't rightly go against them already. It is not a trivial matter to break promises and oaths made under Christ, not within sight of his own holy tomb.'

'Young lord,' Bowman replied, 'you're always so good. Why are you always so good?'

Richard took in a deep breath and tried to hold for as long as he could. 'I'm trying to get into heaven, not accrue more sins.'

'What if I opened it?' Bowman said with a gleeful face.

'You're not.'

'But you'd be free from sin,' the blonde knight smiled and rode his horse closer and closer. 'Come on, pass it to me.'

'Stop it.'

'Don't you want to know what it says?' Bowman rode knee to knee on Richard's left.

'Of course I do,' he replied, 'but I have duty, and the messenger's duty is sacred. In all lands and among all peoples.'

'Prude,' the blonde man reached out and wrapped his fingers around the leather tube. He pulled it so hard the leather strap snapped on Richard's neck, although not before it jerked him painfully half out of his saddle.

Bowman held his prize. 'Ha, see, now it isn't your problem.'

'Give it back,' Richard rubbed his neck but could feel it would hurt a lot more quite soon.

Bowman moved his horse away and tore off the leather cover. He pulled the paper out and tried to hold it up to his eyes. 'I think I can read it, but the words are magic,' he said, 'the ink moves on the page. What sorcery is this?'

Richard swore. 'They'll kill us for opening that.'

'Probably,' the blonde knight giggled, then held the paper out to Richard. 'So you might as well die knowing what it said.'

Richard was torn between punching his friend once in the face, or punching him twice. Instead he shook his head and snatched the paper back. It was written in French so that the Templars could read it. 'No, I can't. Sarjeant, you read it,' Richard held the paper over to where the big man rode.

'I'm a Templar, too,' Sarjeant said.

'But I'm the envoy,' Richard almost threw him the message, 'I cannot be the one to read it.'

Sarjeant took it. 'I don't think, when you're being judged, that your reasoning here will be enough to clear you of breaching your promise.'

'Just read the damned letter,' Bowman said.

Sarjeant read it. 'Oh, my.'

'What? What does it say?' Richard asked.

'Are you sure you wish to know?' Sarjeant asked. 'What with your high-minded views on your role as envoy.'

'Just tell me.'

'Hurry up,' Bowman said, 'before the Assassins come back because I'm not singing anymore.'

Sarjeant checked how far away their escorts were. 'It might be best that we seal the paper away quickly.'

'Why?'

'Because if the guide knows what it says, then he will not want us to have read it.'

'He does know what it says,' Richard said, 'because he wrote it.'

'Ah,' Sarjeant rode closer and gave the letter to Richard, 'quickly, seal it back up. Bowman, give the cylinder back.'

The blonde man returned it to Richard, who put the letter back inside. With the strap broken, he was going to have to hold it for the rest of the day.

'Well, then?'

Sarjeant sighed. 'It is very bad.'

'You've made that quite clear,' Richard said.

'It appears to be an agreement between the Templars and the Assassins.'

Bowman threw a date at the large man. It hit him on the arm. 'How come I can do that but not shoot an arrow?'

'We know there's an agreement,' Richard said. 'What is the agreement?'

'The Assassins have agreed to kill someone, from the wording I think the Grand Master suggested it.'

'The Templars are trying to order assassinations now?' Richard said. 'That does not seem very pious.'

'Who is the target?' Bowman asked. 'Please let it be Guy.'

'It's not Guy,' Sarjeant said.

'Or the peacock,' Bowman said, 'we don't need him prancing around.'

Sarjeant's face wasn't pink anymore, if anything it was a shade of white. 'The Assassins are going to kill Saladin.'

'What?' Richard cried. 'Saladin? This is big. This is very big, and very bad. We can't get caught up in this.'

'You wanted to read it,' Sarjeant shrugged. 'I did warn you.'

'What is the price?' Richard asked. 'Saladin must be the hardest man to kill east of Rome. What are the Templars giving the Old Man of the Mountain for it? Heaps of gold?'

Sarjeant licked his lips. 'You see,' he said, 'Saladin's name isn't the worst bit. The price is the worst bit.'

'What can be worse than a plan to kill Saladin?' Richard asked. 'If it fails and he finds out, he'll want revenge. And we're involved.'

'True, my lord,' Sarjeant said, 'but the price isn't gold. It's a place.'

'So?' Bowman asked. 'It's not going to be Jerusalem is it? Does any other place matter?'

'It does to us,' Sarjeant said.

Richard's heart iced up and he missed a breath. 'It's Kerak, isn't it?'

Sarjeant didn't reply. Instead he nodded. 'I'm sorry.'

'Why does it have to be Kerak?' Richard groaned. 'How many other castles must there be to bargain with?'

'Well,' Bowman said, 'everyone's been saying Kerak is important.'

'He's right,' Sarjeant said, 'Kerak breaks Saladin's link between his two territories, Egypt and Syria. Caravans going between the two need an army escort because Reynald can sally out into their routes and run back to Kerak before anyone catches him. It is a thorn in Saladin's side, which is probably why he tried to take it last year.'

'It doesn't matter why,' Richard said, 'only what we can do about it.'

'I don't think there is much,' Sarjeant said, 'if this letter were to say, be washed down a river, the Assassins have already decided to take action, and the Templars have already made their offer.'

'I'd say stopping the Assassins killing Saladin might work,' Bowman said.

'How?' Richard snapped. 'And we can't do that, can we? Are we going to ride up to Saladin and warn him?'

'The Assassins might fail on their own,' Bowman said, 'then this all comes to nothing.'

'A failed attempt might still scare Saladin off,' Sarjeant said.

'How do we ensure that happens?' Richard said. 'And what if it just makes Saladin more determined?' He sighed. This was making his head hurt. 'So the important thing is to make sure the Saracens lift the siege, then my family inside will be safe?'

'I do not think so,' Sarjeant said slowly. 'The wording was quite clear.'

'What do you mean?'

'Kerak is not a Templar castle, so it is not theirs to give away, but the old man's reply mentions Kerak being a place for only the faithful, and that no witness to their agreement or their takeover can exist.'

'We're already witnesses,' Richard said.

'But only because we read the message,' Bowman added.

'And whose fault was that?'

Sarjeant coughed to interrupt. 'You are both missing the point. I think the agreement allows the Assassins to take Kerak and kill everyone in it. Which makes sense, because Reynald of Chatillon is hardly going to agree to stepping aside while he is still alive.'

Richard swallowed. 'Do you really think that's what it means?

My children are in Kerak. Gerold is too, not to mention my horse.' He almost mentioned Alice, but knew Bowman would only chide him.

'So what are we going to do about it?' the blonde man asked.

'Not talking about this with anyone else would be my first suggestion,' Sarjeant said.

'Certainly,' Richard said, 'but we can't do anything here, the matter will be decided in Saladin's siege camp around Kerak, or on the walls of the castle. The Assassins might be on their way to carry their attack out already. We can only save Kerak if we are there.'

'Good luck with that,' Bowman swatted at an insect that landed on his arm. It flew away and he swore. 'Your problem, young lord, is that you're a Templar now, as you keep mentioning, and can therefore only go where Gerard orders you. So you're not going to Kerak.'

Richard sighed. 'You know what? Now I regret joining them.'


The river that had washed away all of their provisions was now even higher. It almost filled its previously only half-filled channel, and this time everyone stopped and re-tied everything their horses carried down carefully.

The Tancarville horse snorted at the rushing torrent, but this time Richard just had to growl a harsh word at it for it to wade in.

All the horses swam the river, and Richard was happy for the chance to wash some of the sand out of his clothing and his hair. It had got right into his hair, down to his scalp, and itched. It was under his fingernails and in his eyes, too, but the cold water saw to all of it.

Richard emerged refreshed, physically at least, for he could think of little else than the fact his family were in danger and he couldn't help them. The parallel to his father was obvious, and it grated Richard, but Sarjeant was right, what could he do at Kerak anyway, without an army or at least a viable plan?

When they arrived at the cliffs which signalled the start of the ravines, Ishmael sent one of his men ahead to scout for Saracen lookouts. As the sun was still high, they settled down to wait on foot, stretching out their riding muscles and giving their new horses a rest.

Except for Ishmael, who stayed on his horse, his gaze intent on the ravine through which his scout had ridden. He waited as the sun arced across the sky and then dropped.

'He's been there so long you should have prayed at least three times,' Bowman said to Richard.

'If you tell Gerard I haven't been doing it,' Richard said, 'I'll punch your shoulder.'

'I don't care,' the blonde man said, 'I'm more interested in how our guide can sit there on his horse for so long like a statue. He hasn't even shifted himself around once, it's unnatural.'

Ishmael turned his head. 'You have no discipline, no self control. Even before you gave in to the temptation of pain relief.'

'How do you do it?' Bowman asked.

'Training,' the guide answered, 'and practice.'

'It looks boring,' the blonde man said, 'is that how you kill your enemies? Through boredom?'

Ishmael drew a short but sharp knife. Its hilt was golden. 'We kill our enemies with these. Poison can be taken by the wrong person. Arrows, as you know, can miss.'

'And you called me rude,' Bowman frowned.

'Poison is a woman's weapon in the west,' Richard said.

Ishmael nodded. 'We kill with the blade because we can be sure our work is completed. Many stabs will kill. We come so close to the target we can be sure of success.'

'You think you can just walk up to powerful people you want to kill?' Richard asked. 'Won't they have guards?'

'Again, we use patience,' the guide said, 'which the two of you are testing. We disguise ourselves or infiltrate the enemy. Joining the guard of a king or sultan, for example, is a very good way of getting close to such men.'

'It would take years to be trusted enough to join a king's guard,' Richard glanced at Sarjeant, 'or a sultan's.'

'I will say it again,' Ishmael said. 'Patience. But planning too, our order does not stay inside our secluded castles in the mountains. We have members in armies and orders across the land. When called upon, they strike with their knife and their duty is fulfilled. This is why we are feared, we cannot be stopped and are always ready. Our attacks are usually carried out in public, to further the terror which follows the whispering of our name.'

'That all sounds barbaric,' Richard said.

'But quite effective,' Bowman nodded. 'Although for my taste, it seems like a lot of sneaking around and stabbing people in the back. I think I like it, and I think I do like you.'

Ishmael groaned. 'Your pain will return soon, which I will be glad of.'

'Again he's rude to me,' Bowman said to Richard.

Richard ignored his friend. 'So once it's dark, will we follow Gerard's plan? Or sneak around and stab the Saracens at the watch fires?'

Ishmael turned back to the ravine. 'It depends on what my companion finds. I favour killing the entire camp.'

Bowman coughed. 'There were dozens of them.'

'And the dark is a very confusing place,' the guide grinned. 'We will kill their sentries before your peacock knight begins his diversion.'

'I like it,' Bowman nodded, 'it's all the better because it takes his glory away.'

'Glory has no use,' Ishmael said.

Richard was inclined to believe him.


The scout returned with unsettling news. The enemy camp had been reinforced by Saracens from the other camp on the far side of Khirbet.

'They expect us to try to return,' Ishmael frowned when he'd been told, but that hadn't changed his mind. In the half-light of the evening, with the moon large and round in the stubbornly cloudless sky, they rode along the ravines and gullies until the scout said they were behind the enemy camp. Richard had asked Bowman to stay behind with their horses, but the blonde man had insisted he couldn't feel his injuries and refused to stay behind, so Sarjeant had done so instead. Bowman had promised not to sing.

The Assassins simply tied their horses together and left them, but Richard wasn't going to risk losing theirs, and Sarjeant didn't complain when he realised he wouldn't have to take part in the attack.

Without their horses, they had to walk the last part of the way, which only served to remind Richard why horses were so important. He could feel even the smaller stones through the leather soles of his shoes, and the muscles on the front of his upper legs grew tired from stepping over boulders and picking his way through the ravines, which were wetter now and sometimes slippery.

Ishmael made them wait at the bottom of the cliff that surrounded the plateau until it was dark. Richard wasn't sure it was dark enough, but they had to make their move before the Marshal struck, and the guide assured him the enemy would be looking the other way.

Richard checked Sir John's dagger still hung around his waist and said a prayer in thanks that it hadn't been washed away in either river crossing.

Ishmael nodded at everyone and pointed up the cliff. It wasn't a sheer cliff, instead a jumble of large boulders with patches of sand filling crevices. Richard climbed up behind the guide, his party of Assassins spread out and made their own way to the top.

Bowman followed Richard and once grabbed his ankle by mistake. Richard nearly kicked him in the face trying to shake the hand off.

At the top of the slope, Richard followed the guide, who crawled very slowly on his belly. His Templar surcoat caught on stones as they went, and more than once he heard a tear, but it was better than being spotted.

So low to the ground, Richard couldn't see the camp, only the moon above as the stars came out, and once when he took a breath, he inhaled sand and had to stifle a cough. The air cooled, but he didn't notice as he heated up from the effort of crawling. His hands grew dustier and sand got under his fingernails again. Richard's knees were sore too, sharp stones dug into them and grazed the skin. It felt like an age before Ishmael stopped and Richard crawled up next to him.

He could hear voices. Unconcerned voices with the occasional laugh. If they expected Richard to return, he thought, they did not expect it so soon. Gerard had been right about that.

But then Gerard had not planned for them to attack the camp on their way back, and Richard sniffed the air when he smelled something cooking on the almost non-existent breeze. He thought it was probably rabbit.

A scuttling sound came from beside him, and Richard searched for the source of the noise. A small creature, black with a shiny body that reflected the moonlight, scurried between two stones right in front of Richard's face. It was small, like a giant beetle, but with black pincers and a tail which it carried up and over its body. Richard instinctively didn't like it.

Ishmael pointed at it. 'Stay away. Sting painful.'

'What is it?'

'Scorpion.'

Richard shuffled to his side away from it. He pointed at it and turned back to Bowman. 'Stay away from that,' he whispered.

Ishmael crawled on and Richard followed.

A moment later Bowman yelped and Richard spun around. The blonde man was where the scorpion had been and shook his hand in the air.

'What did you do?'

'It attacked me,' the blonde man crawled away from it and shook his hand again.

'I told you to stay away from it,' Richard hissed.

'It looked friendly,' the blonde knight's face, hard to make out in the dark now, looked offended.

A noise from the camp stole Richard's attention. Footsteps approached. Richard drew his dagger and cursed himself for having given in to Bowman's request to come along.

Ishmael lay as still as the stones around him. He lay in a shallow depression in the ground, worn down by a thousand years of occasional rainwater, and Richard hoped the Saracen who he heard approaching wouldn't see either of them.

Lying still behind the guide, Richard made out the shadow of the man walking towards them. He stopped and looked around, a sword visible in his hands. The man shouted something back to his comrades then put his sword away.

He arranged his robes and the sound of urine splashing on the stones filled the air along with the telltale smell.

Ishmael advanced. He was not far from the man but he moved with patience. Richard decided not to follow, because Bowman would be behind him and he didn't want the man to make any more noise than he already had.

The guide slithered up behind the Saracen and rose from the earth silently. Ishmael's left hand covered the enemy's mouth and pulled him backwards as his right hand plunged the dagger into his chest. Not once, but a flurry of strikes shattered the Saracen's body as he was dragged down.

The man tried to shout but the guide's hand was tight around his face and his breath failed him before he could alert the camp.

Richard let out his own breath, then crawled up to Ishmael.

The guide laid down the body quietly.

Richard put his head up. He saw a trio of fires up ahead, spaced throughout the camp he thought, being used for cooking and light.

His hands still on the ground, Richard felt something through them. A rumble. The turcopoles and their horses were on the way.

Ishmael heard them and waved at Richard and Bowman, then jogged towards the camp as the rumble grew audible.

Richard pushed himself up and followed. He shifted Sir John's dagger to his left hand and drew Durendal in his right. He'd never fought like that before, but the enemy wore little armour and was unprepared.

Bowman scuffed the stone behind him. 'My hand hurts,' he grumbled.

The still unseen turcopoles yelled war-cries in the distance. They were usually supposed to advance in silence just as Templar knights did, but now they rode out to create as much noise as possible.

Richard had to run to keep up with the guide, who was far more nimble than he looked.

Ishmael met a Saracen at the edge of the camp who thought he was the man who had just been stabbed to death. He greeted Ishmael and never understood why his friend drove a knife into his throat.

The Saracens picked up bows and rushed to fend off the turcopoles. The earlier sound of laughter and conversation was gone, now the sounds that filled the plateau were of war and horse's hooves.

Richard wondered if the plan might work, maybe their timing was perfect, because as the Saracens faced the attack of the horse archers, they were not looking behind them.

A Saracen cried out in pain to their left, presumably falling to an Assassin's blade. Richard charged the camp, ran past one campfire with two rabbits cooking over it, and threw himself into the loose archery line the Saracens had formed.

Sir John's dagger slid into the neck of an archer who had just loosed an arrow into the night and fumbled for another. Richard put his leg behind the archer's and pulled him backwards, throwing him down to the ground.

'Dex Aie the Marshal,' echoed over the plateau. It sent a shiver down Richard's spine, and he wasn't even the enemy.

'Damned peacock,' Bowman was already to Richard's right and killed a man with his sword.

'Shut up,' Richard ran at a Saracen who glanced around in confusion as their foreign words. Durendal ended his confusion.

'My shoulder hurts again,' Bowman looked for someone to attack, but Ishmael killed the man nearest to him and in the dark it was hard to see anyone else.

An arrow whizzed past Bowman and he realised he should be quiet.

Arrows flew into the camp, too. The turcopoles were well within range and their shafts skimmed over the earth, and some found Saracens.

The Marshal's war-cry rang out again, but very close now, and Richard could hear the hooves of his charging horse drumming on the hard ground.

A Saracen deep in the gloom aimed his bow at Richard, who raised his left arm as if it had a shield strapped to it. He jumped to one side and the arrow grazed his arm and tore a hole in his tunic as it sailed away.

The Marshal's horse trampled the archer, who screamed as he was knocked to the ground.

Richard ran and pounced on him and finished him off, for a man could be trampled by a horse and die, or suffer nothing more than some bruises, and he didn't want to take any chances.

The hail of arrows from the turcopoles ceased. The Christian horse archers however, did not leave the Marshal to fight alone, instead Richard heard their hooves approach. His heart dropped.

'We need to tell them we're friendly,' he shouted. 'Shout at them, they'll recognise our language.'

Bowman obliged by singing his song about the nuns. Richard rejoined him as horses rushed through the enemy skirmishing line and swords flashed in the inadequate firelight. Ishmael bumped into them and added his voice to the air, shouting at the turcopoles as one rushed by with a confused look on his face.

The Marshal charged back, his sword raised, and cantered towards Richard.

'It's me,' Richard cried, 'we're in the camp, don't attack us.'

The knight swung his sword down at Richard and his horse nearly knocked him over. Richard blocked the attack but the force of it sent him reeling to the ground.

'You?' the Marshal stopped his horse with its layers of protective blankets. 'You aren't supposed to be here.'

'We've brought friends,' Richard said.

'What do you want me to do about it? It's dark and they turcopole have got carried away and joined in. Everyone on foot will be killed.'

A man ran towards them and the Marshal spun his horse to face him.

'He is one of mine,' Ishmael shouted and the Marshal hesitated.

The noise all around was mostly hooves, no Saracen shouts cut through the carnage.

Another Assassin joined them, but Ishmael looked almost upset when no one else came. 'You have killed my men.'

The Marshal put his sword away. 'What were you thinking? Your men look like the enemy, and you knew we'd attack.'

'The turcopoles were not supposed to charge,' the guide said.

Richard wiped his sword clean on a dead Saracen's robe. 'What's done is done, can we just get back to the camp?'

Bowman tried to look at his hand but it was too dark. 'Do those little black things with the sharp tails have venom like snakes? Am I going to die?'

The guide nodded.

The blonde man groaned. 'Of all things, I can't believe I'm going to be killed by a sting.'

'No,' Ishmael said, 'that scorpion is not deadly to adults. You will die because you are annoying me.'

Richard ignored them because the battle was over, and the turcopoles busied themselves with looting the enemy. He left them and trudged in the direction of the ruins.

Gerard shouted at the turcopoles before they'd reentered Khirbet. His voice boomed over the plateau, condemning them for disobeying him and charging without orders.

'A Christian was in danger,' one shrugged as he dismounted and led his horse into the ancient town.

Even in the dark, Gerard's eyes shone with fury.

'He's just upset they didn't do what he told them to,' Bowman said, 'even though they have done us all a great favour by killing so many Saracens. Our marching will be less stressful now.'

The Templar seneschal's face soothed when he saw Richard. 'Praise the Lord,' he said, 'I never doubted He would bring you back, but it is still a surprise to see you. Do you have a reply?'

'It is with our horses,' Richard said. 'We should send someone back for Sarjeant, he's holding them all on his own beyond the plateau.'

Gerard sent the lead turcopole who had answered back to him out to fetch Sarjeant.

'You look terrible,' the seneschal looked Richard up and

down.

'I feel it,' Bowman rubbed his neck.

'We were followed and attacked by some of the Saracens,' Richard said, 'and nearly drowned in a river.'

'Did any of the Saracens escape?' Gerard asked.

Richard shook his head. 'Thanks to Ishmael and his friends, no.'

Gerard raised his eyebrows at the two Assassins next to the guide. 'And who are they?'

'My friends from Qal'at,' Ishmael said, 'they accompanied us to ensure the reply reached you.'

'If they are Assassins,' Gerard said, 'I'll kill them myself.'

Richard shrugged. 'I don't know who anyone is, but they saved our lives on the way to Qal'at, and made sure we got back here, so I think they are our friends. They are on our side and many of their comrades were just killed by the turcopoles, so I would be less harsh to them.'

Gerard watched deep in thought as the last of the turcopoles returned to the ruins.

The Marshal dismounted his horse, arrows hanging out of the blankets which protected it, and pulled one from his own surcoat. 'I prefer tournaments to this, although fighting in the firelight had a certain charm to it.'

Gerard rolled his eyes. 'Despite the ill-discipline, this is a fine outcome,' he said, 'now we can push on south to the castle at Sela and rescue Sibylla from Count Raymond. Then we can finally get back to Jerusalem, with both the true cross and the king's sister.'

'We should return to Kerak,' Richard said, the words slipping out before he was aware of them.

The seneschal frowned. 'Should we?'

'I just think we should help if they are under siege.'

Gerard sighed. 'Your keenness to fight the infidel is commendable, but Saladin has an army. We will muster one of our own to face him, it is more useful for us to do that, isn't it?'

'I can't wait for that,' Richard said, 'I need to know if my children are alive.'

'We have all heard quite enough about your children,' Gerard said. 'Thanks to Count Raymond, I will never have any, so do not push me. If you obey me, you will see them again. And be alive to see them again.'

Guy walked through the ruined remnant of a doorway as the canvas sheeting overheard fluttered in the strengthening breeze. Richard was glad to smell the canvas again, it smelled like safety and reminded him of campaigns in the west.

Guy of Lusignan grimaced when he saw Richard. 'You look terrible, you've ruined that surcoat. Anyway, I couldn't help overhearing. Tell me, why are we still bothering with this woman locked in this castle? We have the true cross, that is the most important thing now, surely?'

'Forget your own comfort for a moment,' Gerard replied. 'Sibylla's rescue is supposed to glory you, you cannot become regent without it.'

'It just seems like an enormous risk for not much extra reward.'

Gerard turned to Guy. The Templar was older but matched the Lusignan in size and stature. 'In the west, knights conduct matters with safety at the front of your minds. Always cautious, attacking only when you think victory is likely. Here, we do not have that luxury. Attack, always attack. We will ride south to Sela and accomplish our task. All together, and that way you shall be back in your precious safety. Then your first act as regent will be to raise an army and relieve Kerak, where you had better be brave enough to use that army. If Kerak falls, Jerusalem is threatened.'

Richard brushed some of the sand from his surcoat, but the stitching on the top part of his Templar cross had been ripped out so the cross was more of a T. 'I agree with Guy,' Richard said, 'why can't we go straight to Jerusalem, make him regent, and raise an army?'

'Go away,' Gerard snarled, 'go away now. You whimper after your family like a dog, and I won't be held responsible for what I will do if I hear your voice again tonight.'

'Come on,' Bowman said, 'you aren't going to change his mind. Let's find some of that clove wine.'

Richard stomped off into the ruins, straight past his father, who had been waiting for him. 'My boy,' William Keynes said, 'thank the Lord you survived. I have spent this whole time in prayer for you.'

'It nearly didn't work,' Richard said. 'Has it been quiet here?'

Bowman kept walking. 'I'll bring you some wine,' he said.

Richard knew he wouldn't.

'Yes,' his father said, 'and I shall be sad to leave Khirbet. It has been a soul touching experience living here so close to God for so long, and I have grown accustomed to the quiet. Nothing but the wind and occasional call of a bird of prey. I do not wish to return to Jerusalem, but I will do so gladly if it means I meet my grandchildren. I must thank Gerold too, such friendship and loyalty shouldn't be taken for granted.'

'What will you do now that the true cross is to be returned?' Richard asked.

William looked up at the flapping corner of a canvas sheet which had come loose. 'I need time to come to terms with everything you've told me. It has freed me and tortured me all at once. I will escort the cross back to Jerusalem with you, for not until it is within the Temple Mount will it cease to be my responsibility.'

'What then?'

'Whatever the new Grand Master orders,' his father replied, 'for I am a Templar until the day I pass to the next life.'

Richard remembered his father teaching him to ride and wield a lance. 'I'm here for two years, maybe we could fight side by side? You never taught me how to fight with a sword.'

'You must know by now?' William asked. 'You are a full grown man, and is that not a sword fastened around your waist?'

'I'm not very good with it,' Richard said quietly after checking that no one could hear.

William's face, for so long creased with worry and pain, creaked into a smile. 'My boy,' he even laughed, 'I remember when you used to sneak off with your sister to practise with sticks and wooden swords. You were too weak to begin properly with iron swords.'

Richard blushed. He'd been quite sure no one else had ever known about that.

'I fear my sword skills are rusted,' William said. 'I do not carry a sword and have not for some time. My assigned duties will likely be less dramatic and away from you. But it is for the best. Just knowing you live and have become such a fine young man fills my heart with hope and joy.'

Richard wanted to turn away. 'I'm glad you are hopeful, but I fear I'll lose my children. If we have to ride south, we need to accomplish Gerard's mission as quickly as possible.'

William tapped his fingers on the crumbled down ruin of a once tall wall. 'I think I can help you if you feel the burning need to return to Kerak sooner than the seneschal plans. Leave it with me.'

The next morning, as the sun rose over the devastated and lifeless Saracen camp, William Keynes wheeled his old cart out of Khirbet. It creaked as he and his old Templar companion pulled and pushed it, but it drew all the company out of the town to watch nonetheless.

Because, slotted into the square hole in the middle of the cart's platform, was a ten foot tall wooden cross. Splinters the size of spearheads hung off it and a tremendous crack ran up the centre, but it was clear what it was.

Richard frowned as he and Bowman watched. 'I thought the true cross was that kindling I found in the golden box?' Bowman asked.

Otto stood beside them. 'That was only a fragment, a cross made from splinters from this cross. This is the true cross, the actual cross on which Christ was crucified.'

'How do you know?' Richard asked.

'I spent a lot of time with your father while you were gone,' the German said. 'He was very worried. But he also told me some stories from when you were young.'

'Keep them to yourself,' Richard replied.

'He told me the cart was once gold plated,' Otto said, 'and that he and his companion stripped it off and buried it in the desert so no one would look twice at them.'

'What a waste,' Bowman groaned.

Gerard knelt down on the stony ground outside of the ruins

and prayed to the cross.

'He was happy enough with the small one,' Bowman whispered.

The Templar standard bearer prostrated himself on the floor beside Gerard, and the turcopoles chattered with excitement before throwing themselves down to the floor too.

Even some of Guy's company fell to their knees. One knight, an older man with a greying beard, wept.

Gerard got to his feet and approached the cross. He held his hand up to it for a moment, as if unsure if he should or could touch it, but then placed his hand against it.

He whispered a prayer and then turned to face the company. 'See what we fight for? With the true cross at the head of the army of Jerusalem, Saladin will flee in terror.'

'How do we know this is really the true cross?' Bowman asked Richard quietly.

'Don't you believe my father?'

The blonde man rubbed his cheek. 'A thousand years is a long time for wood to last, you know what a house door looks like after ten years.'

'It looks like the true cross,' Richard said, 'it looks old. Why shouldn't it be?'

Bowman lowered his voice still further. 'Because, young lord, there are no nail holes.'

'What? So?'

'You do know how a crucifixion works, don't you?'

'Oh,' Richard sighed. 'Just don't mention that to anyone else.'

'How do we get that back to Jerusalem?' Richard asked loudly. 'We have no driving horses here.'

Gerard bristled at being interrupted, but the question was valid and he stopped to think about it. 'We have men to pull it,' he said.

'All the way to Sela and then Jerusalem?' Richard asked. 'It sounds too far.'

Gerard put his hands on his hips. 'Do you have a suggestion or are you just trying to annoy me?'

Bowman nudged Richard. 'My shoulder hurts again.'

'Good,' Richard shrugged him off. 'My horse from Normandy is strong, stronger than any of the native horses. He has ridden alongside carts and shouldn't be afraid to pull one.'

Bowman chuckled. 'This won't be as easy as when you drove that donkey into St Malo castle.'

'It was a mule,' Richard turned to Gerard. 'I can't promise it will work, but I think I can move this cart faster than some men will drag it.'

Richard just hoped the Tancarville horse wouldn't destroy the cart, he'd seen new driving horses cause utter carnage before when being between the two shafts frightened them.

Gerard stared at Richard with unblinking eyes. 'Do you want to save the Holy Land all by yourself? Is that why you're here?'

'No,' Richard said, 'I just don't have time to waste out here in the sand.'

Gerard bowed theatrically. 'The true cross is all yours,' he said, 'but if you overturn the cart and snap it in two, you will be the reason Jerusalem falls.'

'No pressure, then,' Bowman slapped Richard on the back. 'I suppose we should fetch your horse.'

Richard hitched the Tancarville horse up and fed it some barley while he gently pressed the shafts of the cart on and off against its side. 'There,' he said, 'that's all it will feel like. And now you're getting food when you feel it.'

Gerard and the company had gone to break camp and all the canvas roofing had been packed away.

Richard didn't dare sit on the horse as it took its first steps as a carthorse, and when the wheels turned for the first time and the whole contraption creaked, the horse jumped on the spot. Richard fed it a handful of barley and it forgot about the creaking.

'We should begin,' Gerard shouted as he mounted his horse.

Richard ideally wanted a whole day to make sure the horse was happy with its new job, but he didn't have that so he mounted the horse himself. He knew he didn't have time to train the horse to respond to the usual commanders of a cart-driver, either, so he was going to have to ride it. Slowly.

Bowman rode up alongside on his new Arab horse and grinned.

'What's so funny?' Otto asked.

'Before the Young King died,' the blonde knight said, 'Richard travelled half way down France in a cart. The locals once threw a load of rotten vegetables at him. And now he's the knight of the cart again. This is hilarious.'

'It might not be so funny,' Richard said, 'that whole episode didn't end so well, did it?'

Otto frowned. 'Why, what did you do?'

'We killed a king,' Richard pressed his legs to the horse's belly and it broke into a very slow walk.

Otto shrugged. 'Hopefully you won't kill another king now, then.'

'No,' Richard said, 'I'd settle for a sultan.'

# RED LION

They came across the tower at midday. A yellow square made from yellow bricks and three-storeys tall, the tower stood at one corner of a walled courtyard made from yet more yellow bricks. The wall was the height of two men, and its proximity to the road meant that the tower blocked the company's path to Sela.

Richard sat on his new carthorse while Gerard and Guy argued in front of him. He looked around for Maynard and spotted the squire somewhere amongst Guy's company, despite the squire's black Templar surcoat. Richard decided to ask Maynard later why he'd seen so little of him during their march.

'He's hiding,' Otto watched where Richard's eyes had gone. 'He is a coward.'

'I've seen him fight and kill,' Richard said.

'Men lose their nerve,' the German said, 'he wouldn't be the first to lose it in the east.'

Richard reached down and checked the harness on the Tancarville horse. It was rubbing on his coat because it had been built for a smaller animal, but so far the horse was not suffering. 'I don't want him as a squire,' Richard said, 'I never wanted him at all.'

Otto ran his hand around the top of one of his maces. 'He is your Templar squire, so he is your problem.'

'Everything is my problem,' Richard mumbled.

Gerard shouted at Guy, and the Lusignan rode his horse away

and appeared to fall into a sulk.

The fort with its tower lay next to the stony road which wrapped around a steep mountain. On the other side of the road the mountain sloped away too steeply for a rider to traverse. Anyone who tried to follow the road would find themselves showered with missiles.

'Who garrisons it?' Richard asked.

'There is no banner flying,' Otto said, 'but I think your seneschal is finding out.'

Four turcopoles rode forwards on their black-caparisoned horses. Gerard and everyone else waited out of range of the walls and whoever stood on them. Someone did, for iron helmets moved along the battlements, but it wasn't clear whose men wore them.

The horse archers rode until they were outside the gateway, a dark-coloured wooden gate which was very much shut.

The turcopoles waited for either a greeting or an arrow, and it was an arrow that they received. A white-feathered shaft spiralled out of an arrow slit halfway up the tower, and cut through the black surcoat of one of the Christian horse archers. His hand clutched the arrow in his stomach and his companions shouted and turned their horses.

Two crossbows lowered from the wall and sent their bolts towards them.

One bolt rammed into a turcopole's arm and shattered the bone with a crack, but the other missed. The horse archers cleared the range of any further weapons and returned to Gerard.

'Crossbows,' Guy rode back. 'I told you not to bother. We could have found another way around the fort.'

'This is not the kingdom's territory,' Gerard said. 'It is unusual for Christians to garrison forts and castles out here. We know Count Raymond is holding Sela, so it stands to reason that he has quartered men here.'

'Is that good or bad?' Richard asked Otto.

'It is bad for those turcopoles,' the Hospitaller replied.

The turcopole with the stomach wound was surrounded by some of his fellows who inspected the arrow in him. He uttered no cries of pain when an older turcopole shoved his fingers into the wound and pulled the whole arrow out. Another poured a huge amount of clove wine into the wound it left behind.

Sarjeant watched and groaned ever so slightly.

Richard had seen tracks leaving the road on their journey, so he raised his voice so Gerard could hear him. 'We can ride around,' he said, 'we don't need to fight and lose more men.'

Gerard turned his white-covered horse towards the cart carrying the true cross. 'Templars always attack the enemy,' he said, 'so we will attack.'

'I thought that meant attacking the Saracens?' Richard asked. 'I didn't think it would apply to fellow Christians.'

Guy's uncovered horse sweated under him and its ribs could be seen. 'I agree with our knightly driver. I don't have any interest in sitting outside this fort until it runs out of water. We'll run out of water first anyway, and besides, those surviving Saracen horse archers are still following us, so we can't go out foraging except in force.'

Gerard shook his head. 'We can't leave this tower in our rear,' the seneschal said, 'they will know where we are going and will attack us while we besiege the castle at Sela.'

'Exactly,' the Lusignan said, 'which is the whole point of castles and forts. But they are rooted to the earth, whereas we have horses and move swiftly. We will assault Sela if you insist on dragging me there, but if we do as Richard says, the garrison here will be too far behind to bother us, for it probably only has stables big enough for four or five horses.'

The Marshal rode next to Gerard on his horse, now free from its extra blankets. The English knight sneered at Guy, but spoke to Gerard. 'You are correct, we cannot leave this thorn in our sides so that it can poke us later. They may only have a few horses, but the true cross travels slowly. Guy is a coward, that is all.'

'Coward?' Guy raged. 'I've led men into battle more times than you've shouted Dex Aie the Marshal.'

'You ambushed the queen and stabbed my uncle in the back. In his back. That sounds like the work of a coward to me.'

Guy pointed an accusing finger. 'You counselled the Young King to war, you led his army to defeat, you failed as a leader. Your views on strategy are worthless.'

'Worthless?' the Marshal's lip twitched. 'You are here because you lost your lands in the west. Because you failed as a lord. When my time with the order is over, I'm coming for you.'

'Enough,' Gerard shouted.

'We should attack,' the Marshal said. 'There are probably no more than ten men inside, their will to fight will crumble when they see we are serious.'

Guy laughed, a laugh of indignation. 'When they see we are serious? How are we going to do that? I don't see any ladders lying around, and how long has it been since we even passed a tree? Look at the ground, the rock, we aren't digging under it, are we?'

'We will take the fort,' the Marshal said through gritted teeth.

Guy shook his head. 'Oh, are you hiding a catapult?'

Bowman walked up next to Richard and his cart. He rubbed his neck. 'We do have a battering ram,' he said quietly.

'Where?' Richard asked. 'Guy is right about the lack of trees.'

Bowman tilted his head towards the cart.

'Are you insane?'

'I'm in pain,' Bowman replied, 'and want to end this whole expedition. Why not use the cross? It's just a chunk of wood.'

'Quiet,' Richard hissed. 'We all know Gerard isn't going to allow that. Besides, it'll just snap in two, and then who'll be blamed? There are enough things people can blame us for as it is.'

The blonde man shrugged, but then winced from the movement and groaned.

Guy and the Marshal still argued. 'They won't surrender just because you tell them who you are,' Guy laughed so much he almost fell off his horse.

The Marshal's eyes were wide with anger. 'They will know my name, and they will know they cannot resist us. No one knows your name, not outside the people you have robbed or kidnapped. Although that is a considerable group.'

'Don't bring that up again,' Guy said, 'we are all sick of hearing about it.'

'I was sick of being locked up.'

'Enough,' Gerard said, 'do not make me ask it three times.'

The Marshal's black surcoat heaved up and down and he

looked like he might burst. 'I've had enough,' he said to the seneschal. 'I'll show this Lusignan what I'm worth. Allow me to lead the assault. If the turcopoles shower the wall with arrows, I will scale it.'

'You?' Gerard choked on the word. 'Can you fly? Can you climb a sheer wall? You will learn humility as a Templar, learn your place. You are nothing more than another man under God, another man in the order, not better than anyone else.'

'Not better?' the Marshal couldn't believe what he heard. 'I hand you a solution to your problem and you insult me for it? You're almost as bad as the Lusignan.'

Gerard couldn't respond because he was so shocked that anyone would dare speak to him like that.

Bowman sucked air in through his lips. 'Someone's about to get killed.'

The Marshal drew his sword.

'Yes, but Guy or Gerard?' Richard asked.

The Marshal didn't strike either of them, instead he spurred his horse towards the fort.

'Damned peacock,' Bowman muttered. 'But at least once he's dead we won't have to listen to him complain anymore.'

The two crossbowmen on the wall were caught by surprise and fumbled to raise their weapons. The archer in the tower got an arrow off, but his shot was snatched and sailed behind the charging Marshal.

Turcopoles swarmed towards Gerard. One of them, the man who had pulled the arrow, pointed his still-bloody hand towards the fort. 'A Christian is in danger, we must aid him.'

'He is disobeying my orders,' Gerard said, 'you will do no such thing.'

The old turcopole shook his head. 'He fought like a lion outside Khirbet. Bravest man we know, he is surely shielded by Christ. He is our white knight and we will help him. We are allowed to aid a troubled Christian without orders.'

The turcopoles rushed forward, drawing their bows because they knew it was written in the Templar Rule and Gerard could do nothing but grumble at them.

Richard groaned. 'We can't leave him to do whatever stupidity he's planning on his own.'

'Why not?' Bowman asked.

'He'll just complain forever that we abandoned him,' Richard said, 'it's just not worth it.' He glanced over to where he'd last seen Maynard. 'Squire,' Richard shouted as loud as he could, 'bring me my warhorse.'

Maynard had been transfixed by the Marshal's advance, but he snapped out of it and led the blue roan over.

The turcopoles loosed arrows at the crossbowmen on the wall, and although none hit, the flurry of missiles kept their heads down. One held his crossbow over the wall and blindly shot it, but the bolt wasn't aimed and flew off to one side.

Richard vaulted from the Tancarville horse onto the blue roan, landing in the saddle with a thud.

'You can't seriously be going to help him?' Bowman asked.

'Come on,' Richard said, 'we both want to be done with this place as soon as possible.'

Richard kicked his horse on and the blue roan gathered himself up and exploded forwards. They charged towards the Marshal, who reached the foot of the wall, and another arrow sailed by harmlessly overhead.

The Marshal stopped his horse and then climbed up to stand on its saddle. He wobbled precariously on it for a moment and reached up to find a handhold on the wall.

He reached up, a foot slid on the wooden saddle, and his horse walked forwards. The Marshal, with no handhold, fell off the back of his horse, which startled it and caused it to run away. The knight hit the ground hard on his shoulder and threw up a cloud of fine dust.

A steady stream of arrows flowed overhead from the turcopoles, the sound of the arrows above only added to the sense of urgency.

Richard reached the fallen knight. 'I'll help you,' he held a hand down.

The Marshal picked up his sword which had fallen from its scabbard, then took Richard's hand and swung himself up onto the blue roan.

Richard climbed up onto his saddle so both men stood on the horse. It snorted but stayed still. Richard held his hands together to form a stirrup. 'Step in here,' he said, 'and maybe you can reach the battlements.'

The Marshal was too angry to speak, but his mailed foot landed in Richard's hands and he jumped upwards. The force nearly broke Richard's fingers, but the Marshal grabbed the top off the wall as he leapt. A handful of the wall came loose and showered the blue roan in stones and dust, but it meant the Marshal's other hand grabbed a newly protruding brick which didn't give way.

With a huge grunt, the knight pulled himself up, straining himself and finding a second handhold. His foot landed on Richard's iron helmet and used him to propel his feet up.

The Marshal ignored turcopole arrows as they snapped on the wall or whistled close by, and hauled himself with a great effort up onto the battlements.

Richard shook his fingers and rotated his neck around. That would hurt later. He looked up at the yellow wall and sighed. He could hear some horses approaching, but knew he had to help the Marshal as quickly as possible, so he raised his hands up and jumped. The blue roan groaned beneath him, but Richard caught the protruding brick and clung on with everything he had. His other hand scrambled around the wall, but as his toes scraped up and down, they lodged in a gap between two layers of bricks just enough to take his weight. Now committed, Richard summoned his strength and made a jump, all or nothing, to reach the top. His hand reached the battlement and with more luck than judgement, Richard climbed the wall and rolled more than stepped onto the parapet.

Where the two crossbowmen already lay dead. Their bodies sprawled on the stone, a splatter of bright red blood across the crenellations above them, the smell of iron already in the air.

Richard snatched a glance at the rest of the fort. It was indeed small, a square of walls with the tower in the corner to their left. A few men ran around the walls to reach them from their right, and at least two men down in the courtyard readied more crossbows. But the Marshal ran towards the tower. Two men with spears and wearing leather and fabric armour stood in his way.

Richard rushed after the Marshal, but the parapet was only

wide enough for one man at a time so he wasn't sure how much help he was going to be.

The Marshal swung his sword to bat a spear aside, stepped inside the long weapon's range, and cracked its owner's nose open with the pommel of his sword.

Richard realised the Marshal probably didn't need his help.

The English knight pounded the unfortunate spearman's face again and again, and blood sprayed back at him before he pushed the man off the wall and into the courtyard.

His comrade stepped backwards, drew a sword, but feared the demon that bore down on him.

The Marshal didn't stop walking, he pressed on, struck at the swordsman, who parried, then crashed into him. The Marshal grabbed the man's sword-wrist with his left hand, then arced his sword down onto the startled man's head. His first blow caused the man to cry out, the second silenced him, and the third split his skull apart as his leather helmet failed.

A crossbow bolt Richard never heard clipped his thigh as he ran, but he was wearing his mail leg armour and it did little more than rip some rings apart.

He caught up with the Marshal as he flung the second body into the courtyard. 'We need to take the tower,' the blood-covered knight said.

Richard agreed but the Marshal reached the tower's doorway first.

It was locked.

The Marshal turned and bumped into Richard. 'We'll have to go the other way,' he said.

Richard spun around, remembering that enemies were running around the wall to get to them, but saw Guy drop down onto the parapet.

'What are you doing here?' Richard asked as they met him.

'Your rude knight helped me up,' Guy said.

'But why?'

Guy snarled at the Marshal. 'I'm proving a point.'

The Marshal tried to push past Richard but there was no room. 'We don't need your help.'

'I think you do,' Guy said, 'all the horses ran off, so it's just the three of us up here for now.'

The Marshal pushed Richard roughly into the battlements to move him out of the way, the stone almost crushed Richard's nose and did crush one of his fingers.

'Out of my way,' the Marshal squared up to Guy, who wisely backed himself up against the battlements before the English knight could barge past or throw him off.

A crossbow bolt cracked into the stone wall and the head spun off and cut a hole in Guy's blue and white surcoat, but got caught harmlessly in his mail.

The Marshal charged around the wall on his way to meet the four defenders who rushed to confront him.

Guy swore and followed closely behind the English knight, the six men all meeting together at a corner of the wall. The men with spears waited at the right-angled bend, which meant all four of their spears reached the Marshal and Guy at the same time.

The Marshal never even slowed down. His sword pushed one spearpoint aside, and his left hand pushed another.

Expect that there were still two more, and one stabbed him in the left shoulder and spun the knight around. The fourth spearmen, his eyes wide at the chance that had appeared, thrust with all his might into the Marshal's face.

Guy's sword caught the spear just before it found flesh and cast it away. Another spear found Guy's arm and forced him to step back with a cry of pain.

The Marshal, delayed for only a moment, danced between the spear points which were distracted by Guy, and severed a hand holding one of them.

The spearmen howled and held up his bloody stump as the Marshal pulled the spear from his other hand and swung his sword down on the shoulder of another enemy. His blow was stopped by leather and several layers of wool, but the man still dropped to his knees.

Guy fended off the other two spearmen with desperate swings of his sword, as the crossbowmen in the yard used Richard for target practice.

Fortunately, their racing hearts put off their aim just enough that both of their bolts missed.

The Marshal whirled his new spear around in his left hand

and used it to sweep an enemy spear out of the way. He stepped into the gap he'd created and cut down into a spearman's neck.

Guy killed the fourth man, which left just the mutilated spearman alive, who held up his deformed wrist and cried.

The Lusignan sniffed once and jammed his sword into the man's mouth.

The Marshal had already jumped over the bodies and was running along the wall to where a set of stone stairs led down to the courtyard.

Richard went to follow as Guy ran behind the Marshal.

Another group of spearmen formed at the bottom of the staircase. Two of them standing in front of it, and two off to the side so they could stab up at the Marshal's legs if he tried to exit the steps.

'Wait for us,' Richard cried, 'you can't take them all on yourself.'

'These men know how to fight,' Guy said, 'just wait. They're on our left and we don't have shields.'

The Marshal paused halfway down the steps and caught his breath. His eyes checked the crossbowmen, who had pulled their strings back and slid new bolts into the groves in their weapons.

Guy flew down the steps and nearly crashed into the Marshal. 'Take your time,' he said, 'we'll attack together.'

The Marshal turned to the Lusignan and they were face to face. The English knight pushed his chest into Guy's. 'You talk like a washerwoman, as if there is any hope for men like us to die of old age in our beds.'

Guy pulled his face out of the Marshal's. 'We can try, can't we?'

The Marshal elbowed Guy out of the way and jumped off the steps and onto the bewildered pair of spearmen who waited to stab his legs from the side.

Richard jumped down the steps two at a time and rushed past Guy. 'That's our chance.'

Richard heard an almighty clatter as the Marshal landed on the spearmen and limbs tangled with spears, swords, and each other.

But Richard had two men in front of him to worry about, and they held their spears up pointing at his face. When they saw

Guy advancing behind Richard, they both stepped back to keep their distance, their faces uncertain.

Richard and Guy, side by side, reached the ground of the courtyard at the same time.

'Rush them,' Richard said.

Guy hesitated.

'Before the crossbows reload,' Richard hissed and charged. He used Durendal to fend the first spear off, but the second aimed at his stomach and he couldn't quite push it away with Sir John's dagger. The first spear whipped round and smacked his knuckles, which made him drop his sword.

Guy finally leapt into action, tried to hook the second spear away with his sword, but only succeeded in tripping over and into Richard.

Richard stumbled over and scrambled towards the stairs to get out of the way of the first spear, which narrowly missed him.

Guy's trip turned into a fall when he stepped on a trailing lace from his leg armour and his legs snarled each other up. He thudded onto the stony ground face-first.

Richard threw himself at the first spearman who went to finish Guy off, and this time Sir John's dagger reached the spear tip and turned it away from the fallen Lusignan. Richard tripped over Guy and landed on the spearman, but once they hit the ground, Sir John's dagger found its way into the man's throat.

The second spearman gripped his spear tightly as Guy rolled over and looked up at him with a gaping mouth and terror in his eyes.

The man thrust.

But the Marshal slammed into him and pushed him up against the castle wall. The Marshal's spear and sword were gone, but he still had his hands, and they gripped the spearman's shocked head and twisted so hard his neck snapped. He turned, his eyes bloodshot, his helmet gone, and his hair tangled up with bits of someone's brains.

Both crossbowmen had got as far as aiming their weapons at him, but neither pulled their trigger levers.

The Marshal breathed heavily but calmly, clenched his fists, and walked slowly towards them.

They threw their weapons down, but one crossbow shot its bolt when it hit the ground and flew at Guy, who screamed, but it glanced off the earth and missed his face by a whisker.

The Marshal advanced.

'They're giving up,' Richard said, 'leave them. We need to get into the tower.'

The Marshal stopped and thought about it while the crossbowmen fell to their knees and begged for their lives.

Richard retrieved his sword and held a hand out to Guy.

The Lusignan's face had drained of colour, and Richard pulled him to his feet. 'Thank you,' Guy said in the Marshal's direction, but he already strode towards the tower door.

'Don't you need your sword?' Richard shouted after the English knight.

'I doubt he does,' Guy mumbled and made the sign of the cross. 'Twice then I thought I was dead. Do you know what that is like?'

Richard answered only by raising his eyebrows.

The Marshal pounded on the door. 'Let me in, you cowards,' he shouted.

'That's not going to work,' Richard approached the crossbowmen. 'Who are you, who do you serve?'

The Marshal kicked the door, and when that didn't work, he stomped off around the courtyard looking for something to help him break it down.

'Let's just open the main gate,' Richard shouted over to him as the Marshal found a storeroom, 'then everyone else can come in and clear the tower.'

'I'm taking the tower,' the Marshal emerged from the storeroom with a long-handled wood axe.

'Tripoli,' one crossbowman placed his hands together as if praying.

'We serve Count Raymond,' the other said, 'we are Christians and beg for mercy.'

Richard wiped his sword clean and put it away. 'Enough blood has been spilled here,' he said.

'Especially over a woman,' Guy approached.

'We can take them back to Jerusalem,' Richard said, 'we can

make them pull the cart when my horse needs a rest.'

'That is one idea,' Guy stood above them with his hands on his hips. His shadow blocked out the sun for them and one whimpered. 'Which one of you nearly shot me?'

'I didn't ever aim at you,' the first said.

The second shot him a dirty look. 'Judas. It was you that dropped the loaded crossbow.'

Guy's lips curled up and grabbed the first man's hand. He pulled it close and in a flash of his blade, the man's fingers rolled on the yellow courtyard. He screamed.

'What are you doing?' Richard cried.

The Marshal hammered away at the doorway with his axe, the blows heavy, loud, and regular.

'They are not Saracens,' Richard approached, but Guy spun his knife around to point at Richard's eyes.

'No closer,' Guy kept his eyes on the squirming crossbowman.

'I'm not letting you do this again,' Richard said.

Guy flicked the blade back towards the crippled crossbowman and dragged it across his throat. The man grasped at it with both his good and fingerless hands as his breath began to bubble.

His companion watched in silence, accepting his fate.

Richard didn't. He grabbed Guy's knife hand in both of his and tried to twist it around behind his back.

But Guy was a strong man, and anger flowed through his veins. He spun around and punched Richard in the nose with his free hand.

Richard fell to the ground with his eyes watering as the nasal guard of his helmet served only to hurt him.

By the time he could see straight, Guy had jammed his knife into the second crossbowman's eye. Where he left it.

A crack of timber from the tower signalled the Marshal's success.

'Why did you do that?' Richard shook his head in an effort to clear it.

'Count Raymond is my enemy,' Guy said, 'and this is a fight to the death. His death.'

'You're insane,' Richard said, 'he is a Christian lord and we have a common enemy.'

Guy shrugged. 'I must succeed.'

The Marshal hacked another plank from the door, reached inside, and raised the bar which locked it. Richard was surprised that no one was there to shoot or stab at him.

'Let's just get this done,' Richard drew his sword again and went to follow the Marshal as he threw the door open and charged into the tower.

Richard entered it and looked around the square chamber. A table stood under a layer of grey dust, cobwebs between it and the single old wooden cup that stood on it. Otherwise, the chamber was empty.

A chilling scream came from up the staircase, so that's where Richard ran. He climbed up in the dark, the coolness of the staircase a welcome relief, but his body was hot and felt like he was standing next to a cooking fire.

His foot went for a step but hit something and Richard fell forwards. He brought his hands up just in time to avoid bashing his forehead on a step, but he bent his wrist the wrong way, and swore at the Marshal for leaving a body in such a difficult place.

The man moaned.

Richard, the pain in his hand for the moment excruciating, stabbed down with Sir John's dagger without thought. The blade sunk into something soft and the moan became a yelp, then a fading whimper.

Richard pulled the blade out and apologised to the man as his wrist pain turned into a throb.

More sounds of fighting came from above, so Richard picked himself up and went towards them. He didn't hear Guy behind him.

He burst out into the stark sunlight that bathed the roof of the tower. But it wasn't only sunlight that bathed the tower, it was saturated in blood and body parts. Blood dripped down the walls and oozed into puddles in the cracks between the stones.

The Marshal pushed a man away from him, the man's yellowed padded tunic was punctured in several places with stab wounds, streams of red already staining it. The Marshal's black surcoat mostly hid the blood soaking into it, but it glistened in the light as his last victim collapsed to the stone

170

floor in a lifeless heap.

Blood dripped from the Marshal's dagger. He turned to Richard and his face was mostly dripping, too. The knight walked to the edge of the tower and looked down over the company still waiting outside.

Richard went with him and watched Guy's company enter through the gates which their lord had just opened.

The turcopoles stood outside and a cheer rippled through them. They looked up at their lion and started to sing a hymn. Richard didn't recognise it, but he saw Brian tap Maynard on the shoulder and tell the squire what they sang. Bowman, Otto, and Sarjeant were not outside, presumably they were on their way to the top of the tower.

Richard decided it would be best if he left the Marshal alone, so he dodged a severed arm and left the tower, which might as well have been a torture chamber.

On his way down, Richard stepped over the body instead of tripping over it, but at the base of the tower collided with Guy.

'They sang his name,' Guy shook his head, 'he's not a hero, he's a whining weakling.'

'A weakling who killed the whole garrison apart from the two men we did, and the two who surrendered,' Richard snapped.

Guy frowned.

'He saved your life, too,' Richard said, 'and we're in a hurry, we both need to be away from here. So you owe him.'

'I think maybe we're just even,' Guy said, 'did you see that I saved his life, too?'

The Marshal descended the tower, his inhuman appearance making Guy flinch.

'We're not going to hear the end of this,' Richard said under his breath, but then turned to Guy. 'Thank the Marshal for storming these walls and saving your life.'

'I will if he thanks me for saving his,' the Lusignan looked away.

'Are you children?' Richard asked.

The Marshal wiped his face with the back of his hand but it only served to smear the blood. 'Thank you Guy, for blocking that spear.'

Guy blinked and returned the English knight's gaze.

'He's the one who wants to kill me,' Guy crossed his arms, 'so I'm happy to let our disagreement end, I have bigger things to worry about.'

'For following me up onto the wall, I am willing to forget the manner of my imprisonment,' the Marshal said.

Guy went to speak, but Richard raised a hand to him. 'Not now. He won't be this lenient again.'

'And for blocking the spear,' the Marshal added, 'I am willing to forget the brutal and unprovoked murder of my uncle.'

Guy almost burst with the urge to respond.

Richard growled at him. 'Say thank you and we can end this argument between the two of you.'

The Lusignan checked no one else was within earshot, then gritted his teeth. 'Thank you for forgiving me.'

The Marshal snorted. 'I said I would forget, I said nothing about forgiveness.'

'Heaven help me,' Richard said, 'forgive him now, before you kill each other.'

The Marshal stared into his enemy's eyes. There was pure, unbridled hatred there, and Richard knew the Marshal held a grudge as strongly as any other man in Christendom, save for King Henry himself.

But the Marshal sighed. 'I am struggling to be the better man I promised to be after the death of my lord. I will forgive you, but do not presume that we are friends.'

'Really?' Richard couldn't help himself. 'You will forgive him?'

The Marshal nodded. 'Christ preached forgiveness and we are in his land now. I will rise above my hatred.'

'That's almost courteous,' Richard said. 'Thank you.'

Guy nodded weakly.

Bowman found them and winced when he saw how bloody the Marshal was. 'God's legs,' he said, 'it looked bad enough from down there, but up close you look like a devil.'

'He fought like one,' Richard said.

'The turcopoles are calling him the red lion,' the blonde knight said, 'and Gerard has been reciting the Lord's Prayer since he appeared on the battlements. It's the first time I think I've seen him look afraid.'

The Marshal shrugged. 'I told him I'd take the fort.'

Men roamed around the newly captured fortification, and Otto poked around the storeroom while Guy's men looted what they could. It wasn't very much.

William Keynes walked in and looked from body to body around the courtyard. He spotted the blood-drenched Marshal and shook his head. 'What manner of man is this, who can inflict such terror on fellow Christians?'

'He's a peacock,' Bowman said.

'Not any longer,' the Marshal said without a hint of offence in his voice. 'Once I have served my time with the order, my heraldry will be a red lion. A red lion on top of green and yellow. Green for the tournament fields and yellow for the sand. And not once in the west shall I ever explain the reasoning to anyone, as proof of my commitment to the realm and the Angevin dynasty.'

'Fine words,' Guy mumbled.

'Enough,' Richard said. 'But keep those thoughts to yourself.' He turned to the Marshal and grinned. 'They were fine words though, you sounded almost noble for a moment there.'

'You wouldn't know,' the Marshal's serious demeanour left him and he smiled.

Otto left the storeroom and returned to the courtyard, dragging a man behind him. A man who kicked and screamed.

'Who is that?' Bowman asked. 'He sounds so pathetic I thought it was Maynard.'

'Where is the squire?' Richard asked. 'I noticed he didn't try to rush in and help when you and Otto did.'

'He says his job is to hold horses,' Bowman shrugged. 'You know what I think about him.'

Gerard entered the fort in time for Otto to drop his prisoner in front of him.

'Who are you?' Gerard asked.

'I am the castellan of this place,' the captive struggled up to his knees. 'But I am no knight, no warrior. Count Raymond will ransom me.'

'That is not my interest,' Gerard said, 'why are his men garrisoned here, far from his lands?'

The castellan's eyes darted around and noticed the fate of his men. He gulped. 'The count is waiting for his chosen husband for the king's sister to arrive from the west. She is being kept away from other suitors.'

'You are telling me this very freely,' Gerard said, 'but then I knew it already. Tell me the castle Sibylla is being kept in.'

'Sela,' the prisoner said as quickly as he could.

Raymond grimaced. 'It's almost disappointing to hear you answer me truthfully so quickly. What sort of castellan are you?'

'The sort who wishes to remain alive.'

'Your lord would have us all be slaves of the sultan,' the seneschal said, 'you follow a traitor to the one true faith.'

'My count believes we cannot push back the Muslim tide through force alone. We must seek peace to give us time to strengthen our defences and raise funds from the west.'

'That is what my order is for,' Gerard said, 'and your master is getting in our way. We will seize the princess from Sela and marry her to our own man.'

'The Templars want a puppet, do they?' the captive laughed.

'Who is he calling a puppet?' Guy stormed towards the captive.

'Sela cannot be stormed,' the prisoner said, 'its walls are higher than here and there are no trees to fell for ladders. It is perched on the top of a mountain and is garrisoned by more men than I had here. Sibylla is safe at Sela, you should go home.'

Gerard turned away from the man. 'We will prevail, but you will be spared.'

The prisoner's shoulders slumped in relief.

Guy reached him before he even knew what was about to happen. The Lusignan's knife, still bloodied from his last two executions, drove down between the castellan's shoulder blades. Air escaped with a sucking noise and the man jerked forwards with surprise. Guy kicked him to the ground, which he hit head first, and then walked away to leave him to die slowly in the centre of his last command.

Gerard watched in stunned silence.

'Why?' Richard shouted. 'Why would you do that? We could have dragged him out in front of the castle at Sela and made him tell the garrison what happened here. They would have

174

surrendered in fear.'

Guy looked at Richard, and for a moment he looked ashamed. But only for a moment, because he shrugged. 'Why didn't you say that before?' the Lusignan asked.

Richard clenched his fists. 'I didn't think I needed to. I thought it was obvious.'

Gerard's shock gave way to anger. 'You,' he pointed at Guy, 'you said you would obey me.'

'I changed my mind,' Guy stood tall. 'Let's get this job done, shall we? The guide said Sela isn't that far away.'

'It hardly matters,' Gerard said, 'thanks to you, we now have to fight a protracted siege.'

Guy rolled his eyes. 'Maybe not, we have the true cross, don't we? And when we arrive at Sela, we'll have the heads of the men we killed here dangling from the breastplates of our horses and stuck on the ends of our lances. Count Raymond's men will see the consequence of resistance and they will throw their gates open to us.'

'Will they?' Richard asked. 'Or just fight that much harder because they know what you're going to do to them. How do you know they'll surrender?'

Guy shrugged. 'I would.'

The plain beyond the tower looked much like all the others had done since they'd left the Dead Sea. It dropped away on the right of the track into a vast valley where distant mountains rose up into the blue sky. Richard rode the Tancarville horse as it pulled the true cross and slowly lost any fat that it had left.

After a while, the road snaked away from the valley and funnelled down into a rock-lined gulley. Green grass grew on the sides but there was no moisture in the sandy earth. The path descended even more and small but ancient-looking cypress trees appeared, although they weren't big enough to cast a useful shadow under the glaring sun.

Richard swore at the sun under his breath as it lowered in the sky just enough to threaten to blind him. The cypress trees, light green and not densely leafed, became more common as the road met a dry riverbed than ran across its path. The far end of the riverbed rose up in the form of a cliff, topped with more trees and bushes.

Ishmael pointed to the left when Gerard stopped and asked him which way they needed to go.

Richard didn't like the riverbed because it was stonier than the road had been, and his cart wobbled and creaked constantly behind him. Plenty of sand lay between those stones, but that just served to slow the cart down when the old wheels caught in it.

'Hoofprints,' Bowman pointed down at the sand.

Richard nodded. He'd seen them when they entered the riverbed, but they were going in the same direction as the Templar company.

'The wind hasn't blown them smooth yet,' the blonde knight squinted up ahead.

'Silence,' Gerard shouted back from the head of the company next to his bannerman. The piebald Templar banner swayed back and forth in the gentle breeze that channelled between the rocky valley sides.

'I don't think we should just ignore the hoofprints,' Bowman replied back.

'Templars do not speak while marching,' the seneschal raised his voice.

'I'm not wearing your colours, am I?' Bowman said. 'And I think you should listen to me.'

The guide nodded as the column maintained its steady progress. 'The rude knight is right, horses have been here recently. Send turcopoles.'

Gerard took a good look at the cyprus trees that lined the banks above them. They were high enough that they masked anything on the other side. 'Sela is close, isn't it?'

Ishmael nodded. 'We will be there by sunset.'

'If there are no Saracens waiting for us,' Bowman shouted.

Richard hoped there weren't any, because the horse archers from the camp to the north of Khirbet had not given up their shadowing of the company after their companions had been killed. Instead, they were always behind when Richard turned to look for them, be it on a distant hill, or waiting to enter the most recent valley. For now, with the company sheltered in the riverbed, they were out of sight.

But Richard knew they'd still be there.

'We go on,' Gerard said loudly enough that almost everyone heard.

Guy's company spoke between themselves, but with no option other than forwards or backwards available, they kept marching in the centre of the formation, a detachment of turcopoles acting as a rearguard to deter the Saracen horse archers.

'Is this even a road?' Bowman asked.

The cart caught on a large stone and the Tancarville horse had to grunt to pull its burden over it. 'Someone's been using it as one,' Richard said.

Otto rode with them. 'The rains did not fall here,' he said, 'and this wadi looks as if it has been dry for a long time.'

'So it's just a road now?' Richard asked.

The German shrugged. 'The road led here. I do not know the land this far south, but I do not like it. Too dry.'

Richard shifted himself in his saddle, the constant travelling would normally have been fine, but now his horse moved with an awkward gait due to its load and it made the inside of his thighs sore.

The riverbed ran on and on in a straight line, eventually starting a very gradual rise.

The turcopole rearguard broke away in a flurry of hooves as the Saracens came back into view, following them down the riverbed. Richard wondered if a charge against them would work now, as there was nowhere for the enemy to escape to, but Gerard didn't order one. The turcopoles instead rode in loose order to act as a screen and keep the enemy away from the true cross and Guy's company.

'Let them come,' Gerard shouted when Guy asked what they were going to do about the horse archers.

'Attack them,' the Marshal said. The blood had been wiped off from most of his face, but it stayed in his faint wrinkles and made him look older. 'Our horses are as swift as theirs and we will catch some of them. The turcopoles can shoot the rest. When this riverbed next turns, we should wait around the bend and ambush them.'

'We will conserve the strength of our horses,' the seneschal replied.

'I thought God would grant us victory?' the Marshal asked.

'We shall drive them off,' Gerard said, 'but not around the next bend. We will spring an ambush around the second next bend.'

'Why?' the Marshal groaned. 'Because you won't listen to a knight from the west?'

'Because I said so.'

Richard shook his head because he agreed with the Marshal. He'd feel much better if the Saracens stopped following their every move. The riverbed was wide enough for a dozen horses to ride abreast, but the boulders and beds of sand that littered it meant that a few separate streams of men rode in single file between the obstacles. The valley sides were barely tall enough not to let Richard see over them, but sheer enough that no horse was going to jump up and out of the channel they rode along.

Ishmael's eyes followed the sides too, Richard knew what he was thinking.

'How many horses do you think made all these prints?' Richard asked Bowman.

The blonde man let out a breath. 'Who can tell? At least a dozen, but they are all taking the same path through, almost as if it's deliberate.'

'You mean as if they didn't want us to know how many they are?'

'We're all thinking the same thing,' Bowman replied.

'This isn't the first gully or ravine we've ridden along,' Sarjeant said. 'Just because someone else has been along here doesn't mean it is an ambush. And if this is genuinely the true cross, then we cannot be defeated.'

Bowman sniffed loudly. 'I wouldn't put too much store on that, thought, old man.'

'I'm not old.'

'You drink like an old man.'

'Stop it,' Richard said, 'we survived the last ambush, and now there are not that many Saracens behind us. We can deal with another one.'

William Keynes and his white-robed companion walked alongside their cart, not wishing to add their weight to the Tancarville horse's burden. 'Your friend is right,' William said, slightly out of breath, 'the Lord will give us victory if ambushed. The true cross and Christ's teeth have great power.'

Brian, walking with William, nodded with enthusiasm.

'I'm not sure it works like that, young lord,' Bowman said quietly.

'I wish I had my father's optimism,' Richard said, 'but what do you want me to do about it? Go to Gerard and argue with him?'

Bowman sighed. 'No, he's more stubborn than the Marshal.'

The sun dropped and forced Richard to squint. It cast the earth into a warm golden glow, which on another day would have been beautiful.

'I can't see where I'm going now,' Richard said, 'I hope the horses can.'

Bowman raised his hand to shield his eyes. 'I am beginning to become tired of this,' he said.

'Tired of what?'

'Being right.'

'Why?' Richard tried to look up the gentle slope of the riverbed but the ball of light above it was too bright.

'Because,' Bowman untied his lance from his saddle.

'Oh, no,' Richard sighed.

Ishmael shouted in his language, then pointed ahead. 'Horsemen.'

Gerard didn't so much as blink in response. 'The enemy is not to be feared. The turcopoles will shower them with arrows and they will flee. Turcopoles to the front.'

The turcopoles not in the rearguard rode past their seneschal and spread out across the riverbed, drawing their bows and laying arrows on their strings.

Richard could hear hooves. Then he saw shadows descending the slope, but they did not move in the same way as the Saracen horse archers he'd seen so far.

'This is different,' Bowman shouted.

'Ghulams,' the guide cried.

'What are glue lambs?' the blonde knight asked.

Richard remembered the term from Khirbet, but his attention was more focused on the thundering of their hooves. The sand around him vibrated and he could feel their advance in his throat.

Gerard knew what ghulams were. 'Everyone with a lance, form on me,' he ordered, and the trumpeter blared some desperate sounding notes.

Guy's company rushed about changing horses and gathering weapons. Guy himself approached Gerard. 'We can go back, we can push through the horse archers and get away from whoever this is.'

'You would abandon the true cross?' Gerard asked in disbelief.

'You're not leaving me here,' Richard said, painfully aware he didn't have time to separate his horse from the cart.

'It's only wood,' Guy said.

The Marshal took a fresh lance from a Templar pack horse. 'Do you want me to call you a coward again?'

The sound of whistling arrows from the rear was joined by the rush of turcopole hooves as the rearguard engaged the Saracens in a shooting match.

'Form on me,' Gerard shouted, 'or you will all be excommunicated.'

Most of Guy's company formed on the seneschal as the turcopoles out in front loosed their first arrows at the approaching horsemen, but the range was too great.

Richard could make them out now, and saw they carried lances. Bowman and Otto went to draw their own lances from the baggage, no one was going to forbid them doing it now.

'They have armour,' Richard said.

His father clutched the cart, which along with everyone else, had stopped. 'They are owned by their lord,' he said, 'but they are the equal of western squires.'

'Not my squire,' Richard mumbled, then cast his eyes around to find Maynard.

William rushed off back to the baggage and rummaged for weapons.

Bowman rode by. 'I suppose I'll have to join this charge,' he said as he went to line up alongside the Marshal, whose horse pawed the sand and sent a cloud of it over Sarjeant as he also joined them.

'Maynard,' Richard shouted over the clamour of the approaching enemy and the archery duel behind. 'Maynard, bring my warhorse.'

He saw the squire, leading the blue roan amongst the pack horses which had been tied to the cart in one long string of animals.

William Keynes returned with a spear and watched the ghulams break into a charge. 'I think Saladin is angry,' he mumbled and reached for Richard's Templar shield which lay on the cart. 'Can I take this?'

'I'll need that,' Richard said, 'Maynard can find you one as he's clearly not going to be fighting.'

William handed his son the shield after Richard dismounted from the Tancarville horse.

Maynard brought the blue roan over, but he had to drag it and the beast pulled back on its rope against the squire, who was all haste and fear.

Maynard used both hands to tug it, but the warhorse was only enraged by being challenged and tried to bite the squire, who flung the end of the rope at its teeth to keep it away.

The blue roan flinched back and jerked itself free.

'What are you doing?' Richard ran over, he tried to stand on the end of the rope to trap the horse but missed.

The trumpeter blew some notes which sounded like an advance.

'I'm supposed to be with them,' Richard cried, sweat streamed down his back as he tried to catch his horse, which danced away from him snorting. He wasn't sure he could catch it now. 'You've ruined this horse.'

'Why is he your squire?' William asked.

'He isn't,' Richard said, 'he really isn't.'

'He scared me,' Maynard said, 'I'm sorry.'

'Don't apologise,' Richard said, 'find a shield and come back and defend this cart.'

The squire ran back to the first horse tied to the cart, which held a few spare shields, and tried to untie them, his fingers too fast for their task.

Richard held a hand out to the blue roan and the animal, even though his neck arched, approached.

Maynard united the shields but they fell off the packhorse and clattered onto the stony ground.

The blue roan jumped onto Richard's foot, but he was able to grab its rope and keep it still. Richard freed the reins as the Templars and Guy's company moved off to meet the enemy.

Maynard brought two shields back and handed one to William.

Richard mounted the blue roan but wasn't going to be given a lance in time. 'Squire, you're going to have to redeem yourself. Stand with my father. I've seen you fight, I know you can do it. Do it this one last time and you can sail back to the west.'

Maynard shook, his face white. 'I can't do the things the rest of you can do. I'm not that brave or skilled. I don't want to be here. It's too hot, the flies never stop and there is nothing to drink. I don't want to be thirsty anymore.'

Richard didn't have time to deal with him, he whirled his horse around to face the ghulams. 'Fight or die, Maynard.'

Bad comrades are worse than absent ones, Richard thought as he drew Durendal and spurred the blue roan to catch up with the charging knights. Gerard and Guy's men swept up the riverbed, now some way ahead of him, singing the psalm of David.

The turcopoles parted to let them through, but the boulders broke up the formation and the pits of sand held some horses back.

Richard urged his own on as he stared at the backs of the men ahead, most with the white and blue Lusignan surcoats, but he could see Bowman's green and Otto's black.

They lowered their lances as their horses threw up sand which got in Richard's eyes as the blue roan surged forwards with its head down.

The ghulams crashed into the knights with a roar and splintering of lances. Men on both sides were hurled from their saddles, and horses collided and fought and bit and kicked.

Richard had a fleeting thought that the Muslims were

not supposed to have armoured knights, as a ghulam burst through Guy's company and came straight at him. The warrior was covered in a shirt of small metal plates, not dissimilar to Richard's mail, but without any holes. The ghulam wore an iron nasal helm and his lance came down towards Richard's chest.

Without a lance Richard couldn't strike back, but the blue roan was fired up and when Richard asked him to canter diagonally to the left, he obliged. That put the ghulam to Richard's right, and the enemy had to shift his lance over to track him. But it meant his shield was useless, and now Richard would be able to reach him with his sword.

Undeterred, the ghulam uttered a strange war-cry and they came together.

Richard tried to catch the lance-head as it scythed towards his chest, but both horses charged so fast he was almost too late and the lance stabbed through the mail rings on his coif and grazed his neck. Roland's sword pushed the lance away and then cut sideways into the chest of the ghulam. Richard's wrist shook with the impact but the scale armour on the enemy horseman held firm.

The blue roan jumped over the sprawling body of a Lusignan squire, then veered to avoid a loose horse which bolted in front of him. Shouts and war-cries were joined by arrows as the turcopoles shot at the ghulams from behind, the arrows bursting through the melee.

Richard aimed at the centre of the riverbed where the piebald banner was surrounded by both friend and foe in bitter combat, combat which started to grind to a halt. The Marshal danced his Arab horse around it with his reins on his belt, the animal seemingly just as able to respond to his bodily commands as any western horse. His mace crushed ribs as easily as his sword cut at hands and faces.

Richard aimed the blue roan at a ghulam who struck Sarjeant's shield from behind. The former steward raised it but the blows smacked it down onto his helmet and stunned him.

Richard's sword arced down into the ghulam's neck, above his scale armour, and the man screamed out in shock and pain. The blue roan slammed into the side of the injured man's horse and clamped his jaws down on the animal's neck. The blue roan was taller and heavier than its adversary, and the small horse immediately knew it had no chance. It dropped its head in an effort to evade the blue roan's jaws, overbalanced, and threw its riders onto the floor of the riverbed.

Richard had to pull the blue roan away because it wanted to finish the horse off. A turcopole strayed too close to the fighting and a ghulam's slightly curved sword slashed through his face.

Guy fought under the piebald banner as Gerard sung the psalm of David at the top of his voice.

Richard rode to aid Ishmael instead, who galloped by with two ghulams in pursuit.

The blue roan collided with one and Richard's legs tangled up with the ghulam's. Both horses moved at such speed that when Richard's leg lodged behind his enemy's, so he simply locked his leg to the side of his horse and accelerated. The ghulam's knee was wrenched out of its joint, and Richard compounded his agony by crunching the pommel of his sword into the man's nose.

Ishmael twisted in his saddle and loosed an arrow at the second ghulam. It stuck in his body armour but didn't seem to bother him.

An arrow thudded into Richard's shield and up ahead he saw the cart, and beyond it the Saracen horse archers closing on the turcopoles they outnumbered.

Ishmael rode close to the side of the riverbed and the ghulam followed him. Richard caught up on his now frenzied horse and drew level with him. A cluster of man-sized boulders lay ahead, and Ishmael turned towards the middle of the riverbed to avoid them.

Richard pushed the ghulam towards the boulders while he struck his shield. Durendal couldn't batter through the wood, but the ghulam realised he had to jump the boulders or scream to a halt. He chose to halt, but his horse was out of his hand and chose to jump. The blue roan leapt over the boulders with a grunt, but he was tall and powerful, and cleared them with nothing more than a scrape of his iron shoes on the stones.

The ghulam's smaller horse got stuck on the boulders, hooves flailed as it tried to haul itself up with flaring nostrils, failed, and sank backwards to land on its rump.

Richard didn't see how the rider fared, for he thundered past the cart which was not under attack, and into the Saracens who pressed the turcopoles. The enemy horse archers reached the rear of the string of baggage animals and cut some free to lead away.

That was bad, Richard knew, because all the clove wine was attached to those packhorses, and without that wine, they would all be dead in a few short days. He spurred the blue roan to help the turcopoles.

One slumped in his saddle when a third arrow found him, but Richard headed into the swirling and chaotic melee without a second thought.

The Saracens ran back and forth, their young horses still running free behind their mothers, sand and dust now almost obscuring the riverbed. Ishmael's bow twanged again and again, but both sides soon ran out of arrows.

Men and horses lay on the ground amongst a forest of broken arrows, all of which the blue roan bounded over, snapping them like twigs as he went.

Richard caught a Saracen unawares and Durendal cut down to an arm bone.

There were only five turcopoles left and they bunched together behind Richard as he drove on towards the dozen horse archers. He was fed up now. He didn't want to fight anymore, he'd come to the Holy Land to find answers, to find peace, but instead these Saracens were trying to steal his wine and kill his friends.

The horse archers wavered at the advance of the blue roan and its mailed rider. Some turned to retreat straight away, but the riverbed was narrow and difficult and Richard rammed into the last five of them who couldn't get moving and got in each other's way.

The blue roan's teeth went to bite a horse's face, but grabbed its bridle instead and ripped it clean off the horse's head.

Richard ignored a sword which hit his shield, and another which struck across his mailed back, and focused on three quick blows which cut a Saracen's head and shoulder into bloody ribbons.

Against unarmoured opponents Richard could take the time to use his sword properly, and a second horse archer fell as Roland's sword stunned his wrist and then severed an artery in his neck.

The turcopoles, buoyed by Richard's attack, flooded the other Saracens and cut them down. In only a moment the surviving enemy was gone, galloping far down the riverbed. The turcopoles cheered, clearly pleased to be fighting in close combat, for they preferred that to being horse archers.

Richard turned back towards the cart and the ghulams, but so much dust swirled he wasn't sure what was happening.

'Leave them,' Richard shouted to the turcopoles, 'with me.'

The blue roan, its blood still up, cracked stones under hoof as it cantered back past the jittery baggage animals and into the dust cloud kicked up by the battle.

Richard choked and grit got into one of his eyes and made him close it. He was hot, partly with his anger at having to fight, but slowed the blue roan because in the cloud he couldn't see more than a few strides ahead, and although he could hear the fighting, he couldn't see it.

Guy rode towards him with a ghulam on either side cutting down at him. Their blades shaved wood and paint from his shield and cut notches into the sword he tried to block their attacks with.

The Marshal, blood on his arm and cheek, burst out of the dust, a cloud of it swirling behind him, and his mace shattered the shoulder of one of the ghulams.

Richard met the other, his sword swing missed but distracted the foe long enough for Guy to drag his dented and bent blade across the ghulam's bearded face.

'I can't stop saving your life,' the Marshal grinned at Guy.

'Don't make a habit of it,' the Lusignan snarled as he finished the ghulam with a thrust into his face. It reminded Richard of the blow which had killed Nicholas and suddenly he felt a blackness within himself that mixed darkly with his rage.

He stopped the blue roan next to Guy and strained his ears to work out where the fighting was fiercest.

'I can't hear anything, either,' Guy said.

The Marshal disappeared back into the dust, and the trumpet

blared out.

'Which signal is that?' Guy asked.

'I'm not sure,' Richard replied, 'it's not the attack, maybe it was the recall?'

Guy shifted his battered shield around and groaned, but he had no visible injuries.

The dust settled. 'There's the Templar banner,' Richard pointed his sword ahead.

They rode towards it at a walk, glancing around for the enemy but only finding them dead or wounded underfoot.

Richard found Gerard under the banner with most of Guy's company, although a few also lay dead and dying around the riverbed, coated in yellow sand and red blood.

Bowman and Otto were dismounted, walking from body to body and killing any of the ghulams who still lived. Sarjeant held their horses, and when Richard stopped, he could see the surviving enemy horsemen walking away towards where the sun still shone into his eyes.

'Reform! Reform,' Gerard shouted at Guy's men, who milled around chattering excitedly to each other. They told each other of victories and deeds unseen by others, their voices loud and their horses hot and panting. A few were silent, glancing around at fallen friends, and Guy's company was now half the size it had been.

Guy let out a long sigh and coughed out some dust. 'I can't believe we won.'

'Reform,' Gerard bellowed, 'they are not finished yet. That was a feigned retreat to draw us out.'

'What?' Guy groaned.

The seneschal raised his eyebrows at the Lusignan but didn't feel it necessary to elaborate.

Bowman liberated a curved bow from a ghulam along with a quiver of arrows.

'I don't know why you are bothering with that,' Otto grinned at him.

Bowman ignored him but noticed Richard. 'Ah, young lord, you made it onto your horse in the end, then.'

'I'm not in the mood,' Richard replied. The riverbed was fully visible again now, with an equal covering of friendly and enemy bodies. 'How many of them survived?'

The blonde man returned to his horse and remounted. 'No idea, but I'd wager we are equally matched.'

'Blasphemy,' Gerard said, 'we have the true cross and they are nothing but miserable unbelievers.'

'They still have sharp lances,' Bowman said.

Richard tried to swallow but his throat stuck together and he hoped he'd been able to save enough of the clove wine. He thought about going back for a drink, but remembered he was a Templar and was certainly not allowed to do that without an order. So he moved up towards Gerard and joined the Marshal, who looked uncomfortable in his saddle and had withstood many blows.

The Marshal stared back with a blank expression. 'Nothing is deep,' he said.

Richard nodded, the Marshal must be protected by some very strong charm, he thought.

Guy took his place in his company as it lined up on either side of Gerard and the piebald banner.

Ishmael returned with both of his Assassin comrades, and the guide's gaze lingered on the riverbed up ahead. 'They will come back.'

Gerard spat onto the floor. 'Good. Then we can be done with them.'

'We can't afford to lose any more knights or squires,' Guy said, 'not if we want to take Sela Castle. The path back is clear, we can go west and north back to Jerusalem.'

Gerard growled at the Lusignan. 'The Lord will guide us, did he not part the red sea for Moses?'

'Maybe,' Bowman muttered, 'but we aren't exactly Moses, are we?'

'Look,' Otto pointed his bloodied mace up towards the sunlit riverbed. 'They are coming back.'

Bowman groaned, but Richard just gripped the handle of his sword all the more tightly. The ghulams racing back towards them were keeping him angry.

The turcopoles were all out of arrows and Gerard commanded them to retrieve lances from the pack animals. As they raced back, it became clear to Richard that Guy's company and Gerard's few Templars were out of lances.

'We need lances, too,' Guy cried.

'There is no time,' Gerard shouted, 'form line.'

The trumpeter sounded his instrument once to form and again to advance. Richard pushed into line to Gerard's left, between the Marshal and Bowman, and their horses moved up the riverbed.

The blue roan snapped at Bowman's Arab and the smaller horse baulked and disappeared out from the line in fright. Then Richard's warhorse tried the same with the Marshal's, but got such a snap back he left his horse alone.

Ghulams flooded down the riverbed like a torrent of water, but then they bunched up in the centre and formed what looked curiously like a wedge.

The Marshal threw his nasal helm to the ground and ripped his face-plate helmet from the leather which tied it to the back of his saddle. He moved with a deliberate calm that impressed Richard.

'They are heading for the cross,' Gerard shouted, 'defend the true cross with your lives.'

Richard knew the turcopoles would form their own line behind, but for now the Templars and Guy's men rode out and up towards the enemy wedge without them.

The sun blinded Richard until the moment the wedge met the charging Christians.

Lances lowered and the ghulams attacked, their leader charging right between Gerard and his banner bearer, pushing both of their horses aside so forcefully that they stumbled. The piebald banner crashed to the ground as its rider and horse tumbled, and Gerard himself was thrown from his saddle. Ghulam lances skewered one of Guy's knights and sent two squires to the ground.

The Marshal deflected a lance that came for him and severed some fingers from its owner.

Richard tried to do the same, but the lance he tried to block swung around and struck the Marshal, glancing off the full face-plate helmet he'd so recently put on and temporarily unbalancing him.

Richard and those to his left had no one else to face as the ghulams funnelled their strength into their wedge. Richard halted and turned the blue roan, he saw Gerard getting up, and to his credit the seneschal had not let go of his horse when he fell.

The ghulams kept going and cut through the turcopole line, killing the four in the centre of it as they scythed their way towards the true cross and Richard's father.

'Recover the banner,' Gerard shouted and Richard remembered having sworn to lift the banner if it ever fell, and something about never riding away from it.

But his father was on that cart, Brian was probably under it, and however much Maynard annoyed him, the squire was his responsibility. So Richard spurred the blue roan and chased the ghulams.

William Keynes stood in front of the true cross, a Templar shield held before him and a spear pointed at the attackers. His companion was beside him, and to Richard's surprise the smaller figure of Brian the monk appeared with a spear held in both hands.

However brave this was, two dozen ghulams charged them, intent on capturing Christendom's most holy relic.

Richard reached the turcopoles, who turned their horses to save the true cross, but the ghulams reached it first and circled it tightly, their shields on their left and their lances stabbing over them and at the defenders. William and Brian fought back, but they had to dodge lance thrusts and did no damage in return.

Some ghulams jumped from their horses, intent on getting to the cart, while others turned and faced the turcopoles as they charged. Richard charged with them, burning rage in his veins, pushing him on and ahead of the turcopoles around him as they crashed as a wave into the almost stationary enemy.

Some turcopole lances found faces or throats, but more found shields or were turned aside by scale armour. A few of the Christian horsemen fell, but Richard thrashed out with his sword and almost chopped through one lance, then he was through and in a few quick strides he clattered into the dismount ghulams. Two dove out of the way, but the blue roan caught one on the arm and tossed him around, sending the ghulam flying through the air. Richard's sword caught one in the helmet, which knocked the helmet off.

A handful of ghulams approached the cart and used their lances to fence with William and Brian's spears. Maynard snuck out from under the cart, and he flashed his spear to cut one's ankle, and his victim dropped to the ground with a shriek.

The turcopoles fought closely with the enemy, but were not outnumbered for long, as Gerard led everyone else into the fray. Combats broke out in all directions as small groups engaged each other. Almost like a tournament, Richard thought.

In the growing confusion and rising dust, Richard pushed his horse towards the cart and cut down at the ghulam fencing with Brian.

The monk turned around and fought off the next ghulam who had been trying to climb up onto the cart.

Maynard emerged fully from under the cart and stood up. Richard reached him as two ghulams attacked the squire.

Richard pushed the blue roan closer to help and brought his sword down onto one of their helmets. Roland's sword scraped down the helmet just as the blue roan tried to rip the man's throat out, the stallion's neck curled round with savagery in its eyes. Durendal drew sparks as it scraped down the ghulam's armour, but those sparks flashed in the face of the blue roan.

Richard remembered how the horse had become afraid of fire just as the warhorse lurched away, reared up on its back legs, and spun around. This would not normally have been enough to trouble Richard, but a ghulam swung his spear at him and caught him in the middle of his chest as the horse spun a second time. The spear blade severed a few rings, but more importantly, it pushed Richard out of his saddle.

He hit the stony ground on his shoulder and his head hit a stone. Durendal fell nearby, but the blue roan snorted as it threw its back legs out in defence and then ran away down the riverbed in a panic.

Maynard fought an enemy, but back-tracked in Richard's direction.

Richard rolled in the sand and spat some out of his mouth. Sand caked half his face, scratched one of his eyes, and made his blood boil. He got up, drew Sir John's dagger, and pushed Maynard aside when he backed into Richard. The squire tripped over and fell onto one of the cart wheels with a bang and a crack of wood.

The ghulam swung his sword down in a cut to split Richard's skull, but he brought his left hand up inside the cut and it deflected harmlessly away. He plunged Sir John's dagger into the surprised enemy's face and he felt the satisfying crunch of bone.

Richard pushed the body aside as Maynard crawled under the cart. A ghulam with a sword dropped to his hands and knees to follow him.

A ghulam on horseback hurtled by, aiming his lance at Richard.

Richard dropped his dagger and with both hands grabbed the spear even as he swayed out of its path. He wrenched it from the ghulam's grip as the horseman thundered away. Richard half tripped from the force transferred into the lance, but he twisted round and thrust the weapon at the ghulam who crawled under the cart after Maynard.

The lance speared the unfortunate Muslim between his buttocks and Richard let go of it once it was well and truly buried in him. Then he ran back for his dagger and sword.

A turcopole rode past chasing an unarmed ghulam, while on the cart, Brian, William, and his Templar companion fought off four attackers who tried to get past their desperate spear blocks.

'Protect the true cross,' William shouted with the confidence that came from a veteran knight, a man who had once captured a king on a battlefield.

Richard wasn't bothered about the cross, he wanted to kill all those who were disrupting his plans for a peaceful life. He ran around the cart to get at the ghulams who battled his father.

Dust cloaked the riverbed, even more than it had before, and horses raced in and out of it as the melee lost any sense of order. One horseman that raced in cantered up to the cart on his way to attack Richard. The ghulam lowered his lance, but William thrust his spear out and the ghulam rode into it, the razor-sharp blade gashing his cheek and ripping his eyeball apart.

Richard dodged the lance as it fell from the wounded man's

grip, but a dismounted ghulam took advantage of William's action to stab him in the thigh.

Richard's father fell backwards as the leg gave way and his spear fell onto the cart. He landed on the true cross and blood from his wound stained the ancient timber.

Richard gasped with concern as Sarjeant arrived on foot and fought a dismounted ghulam who turned to face him.

Brian lunged with his spear and caught an enemy unaware in his shoulder, but in turn a spear jabbed up and into the belly of William's Templar companion. The man tried to fight on, but more ghulams arrived through the dust and it looked like the true cross was about to be captured. A cluster of approaching ghulams found Sarjeant facing away from them, so Richard ran to help him, jumped onto the back of the ghulam his steward fought, and slit his throat.

But the new ghulams climbed on the cart instead of attacking Sarjeant, and one killed the wounded Templar with a sword cut.

William brandished his retrieved spear at them, but he was sitting on the cart and wouldn't last long, even with Brian beside him.

Then more horsemen burst into view in a swirl of dust and sand. The three of them charged at Sarjeant and knocked him aside as he dove under the cart to escape them. Richard was their next target, and being right in their path, he could only think to drop to the riverbed and curl himself up into a ball.

The enemy horses cantered over him, a hoof dented his helmet and blurred his vision, while another clipped his foot and a toe burst out in pain. The same toe that had plagued him across Ireland. The pain bred rage.

Richard got up as soon as they were gone, but the horsemen turned their horses with expert precision and made to come back.

Brian went to help defend the cross, and the frenzied swings of his spear made the ghulams step back.

William pushed himself up to his feet and saw the ghulam horsemen who made to trample his son to death. William glanced at the men Brian fought and the men who Richard couldn't fight. Then William Keynes stepped away from the true cross that he had protected for years, hauled his unresponsive leg along behind him, and reached the edge of the cart. He thrust his spear out at the attacking cavalry, but he didn't just stand there, instead he jumped at them. His spear reached across to the middle ghulam, stabbed him in his lance-hand and caused him to drop it. William's body thudded into the shield of the closest ghulam and forced his horse sideways, where its hoof clipped a tall stone and sent the animal down in a tumbling whirl of men and horse legs.

Richard only had one rider left to face, so when the ghulam's frothing horse reached him, he simply rolled over the ground and out of its path. Then he sprang to his feet. The ghulam and William both lay motionless on the earth, the horse that had gone down rolled and pushed itself to its feet with a heave. Then it shook and a layer of sand left its body and filled the air.

Sarjeant crawled out from under the cart, glanced at the devastation, but looked up when Brian's screams cut through the dust that now made breathing difficult.

Brian's cry snapped Richard's attention away from his father, because the monk faced three enemies on his own.

And for a moment he held them back.

Sarjeant stood up and drew a sword he'd taken the baggage, and even Maynard appeared from under the true cross with a sword in his hand, his eyes wide and his face drained of colour.

Richard climbed up onto the cart with his dagger in his hand while Sarjeant did the same but slower. A spear caught Brian in his shoulder and he was pushed back onto the cross, which he hit with a thump. He ducked a thrust which stabbed deeply into the cross and got stuck.

Richard reached the ghulam before he could un-stick his spear. Sir John's dagger cut through his bicep and the spear stayed in the true cross. Richard's left hand grabbed the ghulam's helmet and jerked it backwards, the chin strap dug into the man's chin so he was never aware of the dagger which plunged four times into his chest.

The other two ghulams noticed Richard. One tried to finish Brian, but the monk fled around behind the cross. The other swung his curved sword at Richard, who advanced despite it. He brought his left arm up and the sword cut down the mail sleeve, grinding against the metal and tearing a hole, but doing nothing more than jar the arm beneath. Richard's dagger stabbed at the scale armour, dislodged a few thumb-sized scales but glanced off. Richard brought the dagger up and crunched it into the ghulam's jaw.

The enemy recoiled, but Richard leapt at him, grabbed his sword-wrist, and slashed with his dagger. The ghulam blocked with his own left hand, but Sir John's dagger seemed to know where his fingers were, and it severed two and a half of them. The moment of shock the ghulam suffered was fatal, because Richard jammed the dripping blade up into the man's throat.

Brian cried out for help, but Richard didn't hear him. Instead he grabbed the ghulam who attacked the monk from behind, and with every sinew of his body, hurled him backwards and down to the wooden planks of the cart. The ghulam smashed the back of his head on the wood and his sword fell from his hands.

The Muslim held his hands up and said something quickly.

'He's surrendering,' Sarjeant reached the cart.

Richard already knelt over the ghulam, but he heard neither the man's words, nor Sarjeant's thoughts on what he said.

'You are stopping me being peaceful,' Richard slammed the dagger down into the ghulam's rib cage, where it glanced off a bone and punctured a lung. He pulled it out as the man gasped.

'I want to be peaceful,' Richard stabbed again, searching for man's heart but again finding only a rib, which he shattered. 'Why won't everyone leave me to live in peace?' Richard brought his blade down again and this time it crept between ribs and found its target. The ghulam's gasps failed and his eyes stared up at Richard with fear and sadness.

Richard still only felt rage. All he had wanted was to be a pilgrim, to find the truth about his father, and raise his children quietly. Instead, his father lay on the ground with a thigh wound, and this man had made him fight. So Richard stabbed him again twice until the man went limp and a final sigh escaped his lips.

Sarjeant put a hand on Richard's shoulder and Richard spun around and nearly stabbed him too. Sarjeant caught his wrist. 'It's over,' he said.

Brian slumped down against the cross and said the Lord's Prayer.

'It's over,' Sarjeant said, he picked the dagger from Richard's hands while his lungs worked hard and blood and sand soaked into his face and hands. Dust caked his black surcoat and Richard felt lightheaded. His father, where was his father?

'I need,' Richard tried to push Sarjeant out of the way but his strength was failing him.

The Marshal rode his horse slowly to the cart, his weapons gone and his face-plate helmet missing half of the plate. He held up his right hand and tried to close it. 'It won't work,' he muttered, 'it won't work.'

'Take a breath, my lord,' Sarjeant held Richard on both shoulders to steady him.

'My father,' Richard stammered, 'where is my father?'

Sarjeant looked but when his face turned it frowned. 'Allow me to look for you,' he said.

'No,' Richard shook his head, 'I have to help him.' He shrugged off Sarjeant and slid off the cart. He almost landed on Maynard, who for some reason was back under it, and rushed over the sand to where his father lay next to the ghulam he had brought down. Richard rushed over, tears in his eyes, and he landed in a heap next to William and rolled him over.

His father slumped onto his back, his eyes open and his lungs just about moving.

'Father,' Richard tried to wipe away some sand from his father's face. 'Father.'

Sarjeant joined him and crouched down. 'My boy,' he said with a tremor in his voice.

Richard choked back tears. He looked at the thigh wound, but that still bled and his father didn't seem awake enough to be aware of it. 'You can't die here,' he said, 'not now, I only just found you. You haven't told me anything yet. You haven't seen your grandchildren.'

William's breath was shallow and rasping. His eyes stared up into the sky but didn't move.

'My boy,' Sarjeant put a hand on Richard's arm. 'Men are coming, they will see you. Be the man your father thinks you are. I know anger and sadness flows through your veins, but turn them cold, my boy, turn them cold.'

Richard couldn't be cold, he was simmering. He wanted to go to the ghulam that lay almost within reach and rip him to pieces.

The Marshal approached on foot, shuffling over with blood dripping down from the mail links on his right arm. 'Richard?' he asked softly.

Tears fell from Richard's eyes and cleared channels in the grime on his father's face. 'Don't you dare leave me again,' Richard whispered, 'don't leave me all alone again.'

Sarjeant shook Richard's arm as William Keynes took his last breath and his body stilled.

'No,' Richard whispered, 'that can't be it. Not after finding you again. What happened to having last words? I need to hear your last words.'

Richard's rapid breathing threatened to overwhelm him, but the Marshal crouched down and put a hand on his other shoulder. 'When Guy killed my uncle in front of me,' he said, 'it tore a piece of my heart away, it destroyed me. But it also made me older.'

Richard cried. He sniffed and watched the lifeless eyes of his father look up to the clear blue sky. Nothing felt real.

'You will recover from this,' the Marshal said with an unusual softness to his voice. 'You will rise above it, Richard. You are the only one of all these men who could one day ever equal me. I mean, not with a sword, obviously, but with lance and horse. Use this to make you great, not to make you small with anger and revenge.'

'Are you feeling well?' Sarjeant asked the Marshal, but the English knight wasn't. His armour was torn and his surcoat was entirely missing below the red Templar cross. A steady flow of blood coated his right hand and pooled on the floor by William's head.

Richard could hear hooves and voices behind him. He could hear the screams of the wounded, too, but only dimly. He wiped his face and said a silent goodbye to his father, then reached down and closed the man's eyes. 'You saved me in the end,' he said, 'and I thank you for that. You chose me over the cross and that must have been hard. I forgive you.'

Sarjeant started to cry. 'I'm sorry,' he said, 'that was beautiful.'

'I had more to say,' Richard said, 'and he should have been able to say goodbye.'

The Marshal pushed himself up by pushing off Richard. 'Real life is harsh,' he said, 'some things that would be better said remain unsaid. Not all of the loose threads of your life will be neatly tied up at the end of it. Everyone dies with something unfinished, but I think your father died better off than many.'

Richard felt faint.

The Marshal looked at the cloak under William. 'I think I need to die a Templar. I'm going to bring a Templar mantle back with me to the west to be buried under. It would be my great honour if you would allow it to be your father's mantle.'

'You want his cloak?' Richard asked.

The Marshal nodded. 'He gave himself for his cause, which is exactly what I aspire to do. Having the cloak will serve to remind me of my duty.'

'Whatever you want,' Richard said.

Sarjeant reached under William's surcoat to a pouch hanging from his belt. He pulled the pouch away with a snap of leather and handed it to Richard.

'What's that?'

'Your father took Christ's deciduous teeth out of the golden box when Bowman took such a liking to it. They are in this pouch. I think that you have just inherited his duty as keeper of the teeth of Christ.'

Richard frowned, he wasn't sure what that meant.

The Marshal laughed. 'Does that mean he's also now the warden of the true cross?'

Sarjeant nodded. 'I think so, which means that now, Richard, you are the guardian of the most sacred relic in the entire world.'

# CUSTODIAN

No one who died during the ambush was given a proper burial. Stones were piled up over the bodies of the Christian fallen, while the infidel bodies were left where they fell.

Richard stared at the white boulders Sarjeant and Bowman had laid over his father's body. Bowman had made Maynard lift the heaviest ones, and the squire stood stripped to his waist and drenched in sweat.

'Our father,' Richard muttered, 'that art in heaven.'

Brian sat on the cart next to Richard as the turcopoles sent a small scouting party off ahead. Only a dozen of them remained. The rest finished looting the bodies of the fallen and tying captured horses onto the string of pack animals. The blue roan was gone, Richard didn't know where.

'Our father,' Richard whispered, 'that art in heaven.'

'It isn't the time for the next prayer,' Brian swung his legs off the cart.

'I know,' Richard sighed. 'But the words mean something else now.'

'Oh,' Brian said, 'I see. At least he is closer to the Lord now.'

'Is he?' Richard asked. 'He left the true cross to the enemy in order to save me. Isn't that a dereliction of his Templar duty? Isn't that him choosing the material world over the holy at his final moment?'

Brian frowned. 'I don't think so, we didn't lose the true cross, did we?'

Richard could feel the presence of the ancient wood behind

him, now stained with both his father's and Brian's blood.

The Irish monk rubbed his shoulder and his hand came away red. 'God's will was done.'

Richard closed his eyes. He wasn't so sure about that. And his toe hurt.

The Marshal sat on the other end of their cart, Sarjeant tying a strip of cloth around his forearm, his mail shirt removed and stored in a string bag which allowed it to air.

'You will be fine if the wound stays clean,' Sarjeant told him, 'but you can't fight for a while.'

'I've still got my other hand,' the Marshal flexed his left hand, but his left shoulder was swelling up more as time went on, and Sarjeant went to bind that next.

Otto, who seemed to have a knack for finding prisoners, dragged a horse archer over to where a ghulam knelt in the sand, his head bowed and his hands bound behind his back.

The German dropped the horse archer, who had an arrow protruding from his hip, and clapped dust from his hands.

Gerard stood next to his fluttering banner and looked down at the captives. He spat onto the ground and coughed up some sand.

Ishmael joined the seneschal when he realised he was going to be needed to translate.

Richard went to sit next to the Marshal so he could hear.

The guide spoke back and forth with the horse archer. The ghulam captive tried to silence the Saracen but Gerard stepped forwards and struck him with the back of his hand, sending him reeling to the riverbed.

Ishmael frowned and turned to the seneschal. 'The horse archers who have been following us are reporting back to Saladin at Kerak. The last rider they sent told him we have the true cross. The ghulams were Saladin's response.'

'We showed him the superiority of the Templars,' Gerard mumbled.

Ishmael didn't nod. 'The siege at Kerak, they say, goes badly for the defenders. With so many nobles inside, the food will not last long, and the infidels have built a siege tower. This pig says they have seven catapults bombarding the castle. They say the town outside is long since taken.'

'Ask him about the Templar tower,' Richard raised his voice.

'It will have fallen,' the guide replied flatly.

Richard swallowed.

'I'm sure Gerold will have been prudent enough to move everyone into the castle,' Sarjeant said.

'What if he didn't?' Richard asked. 'My children are surely running out of good luck.'

'Horses are being eaten,' Ishmael relayed his next conversation. 'Or so he says. I am not sure how he would know.'

'Their words cannot be trusted,' Gerard said. 'Does he have anything useful to tell us?'

The guide shook his head. 'A few enemies survived, but few enough now to attack us, as long as we spend little time at Sela.'

'Do not presume to advise me,' Gerard said.

Guy rode over, his eyes on the prisoners.

'You are not to kill them,' Gerard told him.

Richard had half a mind to kill them himself. No one would stop him in time, and they were as guilty as anyone else for the violence that had taken place. He went to stand up, but Sarjeant clamped a hand on him that felt as big as a bear's paw and pushed him back onto the cart. 'No, my lord,' he said.

'What?' Richard complained.

'I know what you were thinking.'

As it turned out, Richard would have been too late, anyway, because Gerard swept forwards over the bloody sand and his sword severed the windpipe of the horse archer so quickly he never saw it coming. The ghulam looked up, nothing but anger blazing in his eyes, and spat at the seneschal.

Gerard's sword never paused and on his backswing he smashed the ghulam's jaw off, or almost off as it hung by a flap of muscle as the prisoner's eyes burned with hatred. The Templar's second blow knocked the man over, but it took him a while to die, face-down on the stony ground.

Richard felt nothing as he watched the executions.

Gerard handed his sword to a turcopole to clean, then looked at Richard. 'You will have to join the order as a full brother now,' he said, 'you owe us a full brother.'

'I didn't tell my father to do what he did.'

'And yet he did it anyway,' Gerard replied. 'And that is on you.

The true cross is your responsibility until it reaches Jerusalem.'

Richard sucked on his tongue instead of responding because he knew his words would not be thought out. He'd lost the blue roan and his father, and could lose a lot more before the company returned to the safety of the kingdom. He didn't really want the responsibility of the true cross on top of everything else.

Bowman drank some of the clove wine and Richard could feel Sarjeant watching him. The blonde man offered it to Richard.

'Not yet,' Gerard shouted, 'all duties must be completed first.'

'Suit yourself,' Bowman took another gulp of the undiluted wine.

Maynard looked up at the blonde man and his wine with pleading eyes.

'You heard the man,' Bowman said to the squire, 'and you're a Templar now, although I think they'll kick you out for your cowardice. Richard, I told you to get rid of him, the boy is a disaster.'

Richard knew the squire had cost him the blue roan, and probably been an indirect cause of his father's death, but the scrawny figure seemed too feeble to punish.

'You do remember he betrayed us at Grandmont,' Bowman said.

Maynard disappeared to hide somewhere in the baggage train.

'I can hardly forget,' Richard gritted his teeth and Brian patted him on the back.

'Forgiveness is a blessing,' the monk said, 'remember how you forgave me.'

'I think I'm out of forgiveness.'

'Forgive yourself, then,' Brian said, 'and you already let go of your father, do you remember? You moved on.'

'And then straight away I found him,' Richard said, 'and now he's gone again.'

'You need to get over it,' Bowman sniffed. 'We're in a hostile land, and it's the land itself that's hostile here, and you need to be fit to fight. This isn't over yet.'

Richard swallowed. 'No one is to tell my children that my father was alive, or tell Gerold. There is nothing to gain by telling them. Is that clear?'

'That's one way to move on,' Bowman said, 'I for one won't utter a word.'

Sarjeant and Brian agreed.

Richard looked at the Marshal, who stared blankly back at him.

'What do you want?' the English knight tried to lift his left shoulder but it got stuck. A cut on his cheek looked deep, and he moved as if he was thirty years older than was.

'Don't tell anyone that my father lived,' Richard repeated.

'Why would I?' the Marshal replied. 'I don't care about your father and won't be speaking to your children.'

'Fine,' Richard said. 'That's good enough.'

Gerard finally gave the order that water could be drunk, and then the much depleted company moved on towards Sela Castle. They left behind many men under white rocks, and Richard felt he'd left a piece of himself there with them.

He was running out of pieces.


A small village stood on the cliff that overlooked a vast basin between two mountains, mountains both far away and immense. They were so far away a white haze dulled their colour. In the middle of the basin they created was a tall hill with a low causeway that linked it to a derelict village. The causeway dropped halfway down to the bottom of the basin, but offered the only route up to the flat plateau on top of the hill.

'That is Sela,' Ishmael said when the company halted in the cool and shadows of dusk.

'We can't even ride down there,' Guy studied the causeway below, 'we'll lose horses off the sides of it.'

'I suppose you won't need to tie the heads of our enemies onto our horses, then?' Richard asked.

Guy frowned. 'We'll just tip them all down this hill, although it seems like a waste to me.'

'You can still walk down there with some on your lance,'

Bowman pointed out.

'You can't just hurl a dozen heads off a cliff,' Brian said, 'that's very unchristian.'

'Do you not remember what Raymond the Large did at Baginbun Head?' Richard asked.

Brian flinched and his tanned cheeks reddened. 'But I also think this is Edom from the bible. King Amaziah threw ten thousand Edomites off the castle hill.'

'Really?' Bowman snorted. 'I doubt it was ten thousand, can you imagine how long that would take? I don't think ten thousand people live in all the land we've ridden through.'

'It is what the Holy Book says,' Brian crossed his arms.

'It's not really a castle, either,' the blonde man said. 'Look, it's just a huge rock with a flat top. I can't see a tower or any walls.'

'It doesn't need walls,' Richard said, 'everywhere other than the causeway is a sheer drop, no one is climbing it.'

'It has a gatehouse,' Ishmael said. 'You cannot see it from here. A narrow gully is the entrance, cut deep into a huge cliff, and before it is a tower with a gate. Even if you take the gatehouse, the gully can be defended or blocked.'

'They must be able to get horses across,' Richard said, 'Count Raymond's men wouldn't go into that place without them.'

The guide nodded. 'Horses just go carefully.'

The breeze whipped at the piebald banner and it snapped twice as the gust refreshed Richard's face.

'We cannot starve them out,' Ishmael said, 'they have cold and dry storerooms for food, and huge cisterns to store water. All rain that falls on the plateau is stored.'

Guy dismounted and went to his baggage where a dozen severed hands had been tied to an unfortunate pack horse. Flies plagued the heads and transferred onto the nearby horses, who shook their own heads and swished their tails at them.

Guy tried to swat them away, but settled for stabbing the severed heads one by one onto a single lance until it had six heads one above the other when he held it up. 'Add the other six to another lance and follow me,' he ordered.

His men argued about the task for a moment before the youngest squire was pushed at the remaining heads with a lance.

Guy picked his way down the slope towards the causeway.

'Shouldn't we send some turcopoles with him?' Richard asked.

Gerard chuckled. 'If God wants us to be rid of him here, then so be it. But if you're so interested in his safety, then you can go with him.'

'Me?'

'Yes,' Gerard said, 'between the two of you, you are one of the most troublesome groups of western knights we've ever had. I'll forgive the Marshal because if it wasn't for him we'd still be sitting outside the last castle. Go on, go and look after our future regent.'

Richard groaned, but dismounted from the Tancarville horse that still pulled the true cross all the same. He started to walk down the slope himself when Gerard shouted. 'Have you said your Lord's Prayer this hour?'

Richard sighed.

Brian clambered up onto the cart and, with one hand on the true cross, led the hourly prayer for all the Templars and turcopoles.

'Our father,' Richard said to himself once they were finished and he could resume his journey, 'that art in heaven.'

Guy was far ahead with his macabre spear in his hands, and when Richard joined him and looked back, the company were but specs in the distance, the true cross visible above them. Guy's squire arrived with his own lance and severed heads, panting and red in the face. He collapsed onto a rock to sit and tried to catch his breath, the lance resting on his shoulder.

Something slimy dripped down Guy's spear and landed on his toe. He flicked his mail foot and the piece of head narrowly missed the squire's face. A flash of anger darted across his eyes and Richard wondered how loyal Guy's company would be to him if they had the choice to abandon his banner.

Guy ignored the fatigue of his squire and started to climb the slope up to the castle. The path wound between boulders bigger than a horse, but Richard thought a sensible animal could probably have made the journey.

When they reached the stone wall of the gatehouse, a single guard gazed down at them. 'Are you the resupply?' he asked.

Richard waved at Guy. 'Put the heads away.'

The guard realised what was on the two lances more quickly than Guy could have hidden them, but the Lusignan never tried, and instead stepped forwards and pointed the spear to the sky.

Richard groaned to himself. Without the heads, they could have probably tricked the guard into opening the gate.

'Do you want to end up like these men?' Guy shouted.

The guard didn't reply.

'Well, if you don't, fetch your commander.'

The man disappeared and left the yellow-stoned wall empty. The causeway ran up to it and although the wall was short, it blocked the entrance. On top of it stood crenellations. And behind it Richard could see the fissure in a tall cliff which signified the passage up into the main castle.

Guy propped his lance on the ground. One of the heads slipped all the way down it until it reached the knight's hand. Guy turned the head's eyes away from him and swore.

Richard sighed. 'You need to learn to speak another language other than intimidation.'

'It's worked for me so far.'

'Has it?' Richard asked as a cluster of men appeared on the wall.

The castellan of Sela Castle had a beard and weathered face that told Richard he could survive in the desert, and that this was probably not his first important mission for his master.

'Who are you?' the castellan shouted gruffly.

'I am Guy of Lusignan.'

'Is that supposed to make me open my gates?'

'No,' Guy waved the lance at him, 'but these are.'

'Whose heads are those?'

'Count Raymond's men in the last castle,' Guy grinned. 'So if you don't want the same thing to happen to you, open your gate.'

'What business do you have at my castle?'

'I only want the woman you're keeping prisoner here.'

'What woman?' the castellan replied with a straight face.

Guy threw the lance down and one of the heads ruptured on a sharp stone. 'Don't play games with me,' he said, 'I'm taking her away from here, it is merely up to you how that happens.'

'Do you know about this place?' the castellan asked.

Guy nodded. 'Someone once threw a lot of people off it. I don't care about your walls and your cisterns, either. I will not be denied.'

A chorus of chuckles surrounded the commander of the castle. He spoke to someone on the wall and then nodded and moved along it.

'I do not care about your heads,' the castellan said, 'do you think I haven't seen that before?'

The squire behind Richard exhaled. 'Can I take the heads off?' he asked.

Guy whirled round. 'If you touch them, I'll add yours.'

A crossbow bolt cut through the air and hit a stone behind the squire.

'The next one won't aim to miss,' the castellan shouted. 'Leave and do not come back.'

Richard backed away from the gatehouse until he was beyond where the bolt had hit.

'We've got more crossbow bolts than you could imagine,' the castellan shouted as Guy strolled away from the gate, 'and even more food and water. Go home.'

'Hurry up,' Richard shouted at Guy, 'before they shoot you in the back.'

'They are welcome to,' the Lusignan walked very steadily out of crossbow range, 'because if they shoot me in the back, that would be great for me in Jerusalem.'

Richard sat down on a smaller boulder and poked a finger through rips in his surcoat and into one of the many holes in his two mail shirts. He wondered how long it would take the mail-maker to repair them all.

Guy strode past and threw his lance to the rocks with a great clatter. He watched Richard. 'You should get those holes repaired.'

'You're lucky not to have some new holes yourself, acting like you're the King of Jerusalem. They might have shot you.'

'Careful,' Guy grinned, 'someone might think you care about me.'

'You don't need to worry about that,' Richard stood up, 'I

suppose we have to go all the way back now.'

Guy swore at the castellan and ordered his squire to carry his lance back for him.

Richard took pity on the young man and picked up Guy's lance to save him the trouble. He slid the remaining heads off, letting them thud onto the ground, and carried the lance back towards the true cross that stood out clearly against the dimming dark blue sky behind it.

By the time Richard climbed back up to the rest of the company, it was almost completely dark.

'I'm sure the sun sets quicker here,' Bowman took the lance from Richard and handed him a drink.

'Am I allowed that?' Richard asked.

The blonde man shrugged. 'Your righteous leader isn't looking.'

Gerard listened to Guy tell him about his exchange with the castellan.

'Kill the castellan and the rest will surrender,' Guy said.

Gerard rubbed his face. 'Yes, I'm sure they would, but we aren't going to pick him off with arrows, are we?'

Ishmael stood quietly behind Gerard. 'Perhaps I can help.'

Gerard groaned. 'Now everything makes sense,' he said to the guide, 'your companions are Assassins after all, aren't they? Does that make you an Assassin, too?'

'It matters not what I am, only that I and my companions can get to the castellan.'

'You want to murder the castellan? The *Christian* castellan?'

Ishmael's face didn't change. 'One death here grants you the castle and your prize. Any other action results in either no prize, or the prize and a great many Christian deaths. What is one compared to many?'

Gerard looked out over the causeway and into the night, which had now swallowed the hill and its castle. 'We are Templars, we do not sanction killings in cold blood.'

Bowman snorted.

Gerard raised his eyebrows at him.

The blonde knight patted his chest. 'The wine went down the wrong way, that's all,' he said.

Gerard shook his head. 'We are short on wine, from now on

you only drink when we do.'

Bowman sighed

The seneschal turned back to Guy. 'We cannot have an infidel doing the killing for us, we cannot set a Muslim blade against a Christian, to prevent such acts is why our order was formed.'

Guy shrugged.

'It doesn't have to be a Muslim who does the killing,' Richard said, 'or an Assassin at all.'

'Are you suggesting we turn Assassins for a day?' Gerard laughed at the idea. 'We are not cold-blooded murderers who skulk around in the night.'

Ishmael's eyes very slightly narrowed, but not enough for anyone who wasn't looking closely to notice.

Richard gazed at the squire, who lagged behind, and struggled to make his way up the hill with his lance. 'The guide is right, though, isn't he? We can get what we want with a single death. We do not have enough men to storm the walls, look at the Marshal, he can barely stay upright on his horse at the moment. We can't conduct a siege, for there are no trees big enough to make ladders or rams. All we can do is block the causeway and hope they are lying about their food and water supplies.'

'You want to wield an Assassin's blade?' Gerard sneered. 'Forsake your Templar vows and kill a fellow Christian?'

Richard shrugged. 'I just want to get back to Jerusalem, and then.'

'Yes, we know,' Gerard snapped, 'on to Kerak.'

Guy grabbed his squire when he finally arrived, tore the lance from his grip and kicked him back down the causeway. 'Do not amble like a lazy farmer,' Guy said as his squire tumbled down until he banged into a rock and groaned.

The Lusignan held the spear with four heads left on it and stared at Gerard. 'Now that we are here, let us be done with this business as quickly as possible. Richard has a habit of being incredibly annoying, but he is also right, a lone knife is the best option. To save you the moral turmoil you pretend to be suffering, I will wield the blade myself. I'll rescue Sibylla. I'll end this.'

Gerard chuckled. 'Your insults are weak, if you intend to goad me you shall have to do far better. But I am pleased that you at long last are willing to play your part in this.'

'Whatever you want to think,' Guy said, 'I need to be in Jerusalem. If these Assassins can get me into this castle, I'll kill the castellan and get this woman out. She had better be pretty.'

'You are empty of morals,' Gerard said, 'I already questioned the Grand Master's wisdom in backing you. Very well, you can commit a murder. But take Richard as well as those Assassins, it is his idea as much as yours.'

'I think it was Guy's idea more than mine,' Richard said, 'and I'm not sure I can help. Or want to.'

'I didn't ask your opinion,' the seneschal said, 'and if Guy falls, which is not unlikely, you will be there to finish his task.'

'What if I fall?'

'Then we shall have to rely on the Assassin's blades whether we like it or not,' Gerard said, 'but if that happens, then no one in the garrison can be allowed to survive to tell of it.'

'So, you are now happy to kill an entire garrison of Christians?' Richard asked.

'Only if you fail,' Gerard said, 'so if their deaths are required, it will be on your soul to bear the cost.'

Guy grinned. 'See Richard, intimidation works. Now you want to kill the castellan, don't you?'

Richard sighed. 'Fine then, but how are we going to get in?'

Ishmael's stern face cracked a smile to Richard. 'Leave that to me. Can you climb?'

Richard never answered the guide because he didn't know if he could climb anything bigger than a tree or a ladder. That night though, and in the blackness of the night, it hardly mattered. Ishmael and his two Assassins, dressed in black robes and with numerous daggers concealed about them, descended the cliff next to the causeway and down to the bottom of the cauldron which contained Sela Castle.

Richard and Guy went without their mail, because it was noisy, and with nothing other than weapons, water, and dates. The scramble down the rocks was slow and silent. Every time Richard put weight on his toe it ached.

They helped each other to get lower and lower, dropping

into even darker recesses of the valley between Sela and the mountains which surrounded it.

Richard had thought it would take only half the night to reach the bottom, but the crags and stones and sheer drops forced many detours, and it wasn't until the sun lit up the south side of Sela that they finally reached the bottom and stopped for a rest.

'That was exhausting,' Guy drank from his waterskin while he sat on a rock.

Richard looked up at the cool and foreboding cliffs all around. 'I can't believe we've just come down all of that,' he said. 'In the dark.'

'There is much further to go,' Ishmael said, 'we have to follow the valley around to the far side of the mountain, only then can we climb.'

'How long is that going to take?' Guy asked. 'I'm tired now and it's already sunrise.'

'I think I'm supposed to say my prayers now,' Richard said.

The guide nodded because he did too, and they performed their differing rites while Guy yawned and complained about the difficulty that lay ahead.

Richard mumbled the Lord's prayer and could only think of his father lying under a pile of rocks in a riverbed. He had died so suddenly and there had been no time for Richard to think about it.

The guide cut those thoughts short, and for the whole day they negotiated boulders and jumped chasms to get around Sela. They were so far from the summit of the mountain they could speak freely without lowering their voices. At no point could they even see the castle, so Richard at least felt they were safe from being discovered. He was less happy about the threat of injury though, for a twisted ankle would leave the victim unlikely to climb out to safety.

But that was part of the life he lived, danger was not something that could be avoided, only faced, so Richard kept going even as Guy's complaints led the Assassins to increase their pace until they were too far ahead to hear him.

Richard tried to keep up but just wasn't fast enough over the strange ground with his stinging toe, but nevertheless, as the sun started to set, he and Guy caught up with Ishmael when he stopped to wait for them.

'Is this finally it?' Guy asked.

The guide nodded and turned his gaze up to the huge natural blocks that made up the mountainside. Although sheer, the enormous blocks had gaps between, and through those gaps a path might be found.

Guy rummaged in his bag for dates but his hand came out empty. 'Richard, have you got any dates?'

Richard did, but he shook his head. 'We should climb.'

Ishmael nodded. 'If you were quicker we would make it tonight. Now I am not sure.'

'He's talking to you,' Guy swung his bag aside and made his way to the first channel between two towering stones to begin his ascent.

Once he'd gone, Ishmael pointed to the next one over. 'We go up there.'

Richard nodded and followed the Assassins up Sela's rear mountainside. He scrambled for handholds and stones gave way underneath him and rolled back to the valley floor, but up they went. Up was tiring until the heat of the day subsided, but even as it grew darker and cooler, Richard was hot and almost constantly thirsty. His fingers ached from the effort and he tried not to think about his toes.

He slipped more than once, but never fell, and when the sun rose, after more than a day with no sleep, they had still not reached the castle.

Ishmael found a ledge they could all fit on, a shelf hanging out over the wide valley which stretched away to the west, and they went to sleep. Richard made a bed out of his surcoat rolled up against the mountain for fear of rolling off. Despite the danger, he fell asleep instantly.

He dreamed of priests, monks, and wives falling from towers and walls, and woke up covered in sweat more than once. He spent a while filled with regret that he'd been unable to put his anger towards his father aside, and found sleeping in daylight difficult.

Guy snored through the day and Richard was pretty sure the Assassins made jokes about rolling the Lusignan off the shelf.

While Guy slept, Richard ate some of his dates, but he finished the last one as the sun dropped into the valley to the west and cast the sky above in a fiery orange light.

'Blood will be spilled tonight,' Ishmael said.

'Because of the sky?' Richard asked.

'No,' the guide sighed, 'because tonight we scale the final part of the mountain. Do you think we are that superstitious?'

Richard shrugged. 'My people are. Why are you helping us?'

Ishmael smiled, his dark eyebrows caught the orange glow of the evening and for once didn't look black. 'Your enemy is my enemy.'

Guy awoke and yawned. He glanced at the sunset for only a moment before moving away from the edge of the ledge.

'I am more surprised he is here,' Ishmael said.

'So am I,' Richard replied, 'he spoke of finding lands in the east but I didn't think he'd follow it through.'

'I follow everything through,' Guy snapped.

Richard almost reminded the Lusignan that he technically owed Guy a ransom from the Lagny tournament, a debt Guy had not followed through, but kept that quiet. 'How did you do it?' Richard asked. 'We landed in the Holy Land when you did, and then after a day in Jerusalem, the Grand Master wants you to be regent.'

'He recognised me as a great leader,' Guy said, 'isn't that plain to see?'

'I don't think that's it,' Richard said.

Guy stepped forwards and reached for a dagger, but Ishmael jumped up. 'Not here, are you so stupid?'

'I think he just proved the Grand Master must have had another motive,' Richard said, then wondered why he'd been so brave as to say it. Maybe it was the hunger that gnawed him, a discomfort that competed with thirst to see which yearning could annoy him more.

'Just be quiet,' Guy said, 'we've got a job to do.'

Ishmael watched Guy start his own ascent and locked eyes with Richard. 'The Grand Master plays with fire when he deals with that one,' the guide said.

Richard understood what he meant and held back from calling Guy a puppet. He also wisely waited for the Assassins to pick their own route up towards the summit before following them.

They were a long way up from the valley floor now, nearly at the top, and when Richard looked down it made him feel sick. A breeze brushed his face and ruffled his old blue tunic as the air grew thinner and the worry about falling from the climb started to be replaced by thoughts of what awaited them above.

The moon cast a silvery glow onto the bleached rocks once night took hold, and Richard's hands took hold of the last rock he needed to climb before he reached the top of Castle Sela. He pulled himself onto the roof of the mountain.

Ishmael lay flat on his belly at the edge of the plateau, his eyes peering at what constituted the castle. There was no castle wall, but the unmistakable sight of stone buildings littered the summit. Around them, great stones towered into the sky and Richard wondered why the place was called a castle at all. It looked more like the temple complex at Khirbet, the first Khirbet, although to Richard this felt like a more holy place. Sounds of life wafted over the dead space between the end of the plateau and the buildings. Richard couldn't see anyone, but he could see a plume of smoke from the centre of the complex, and thought most of the voices came from there.

The habitable area was large, dozens of buildings spread around an area that he thought was about the size of Yvetot. That thought caught him unawares. He hadn't thought about Yvetot since he'd set foot on the Holy Land.

Guy heaved himself up onto the plateau and stood up.

Ishmael sighed.

'Get down,' Richard whispered.

'Why?' Guy asked. 'There's no one out here to see us.'

Ishmael sprung silently to his feet and stopped Guy in his tracks by holding a knife to his throat.

'Wait, wait,' Guy said.

The guide hushed him and the Lusignan held his finger to his lips to signal that he understood.

'You are only here to wield the knife,' Ishmael whispered, 'until then, you follow me.'

Guy bristled for a moment, but let Ishmael lead the way towards the houses. The houses looked more like they'd been carved out of boulders than built, and Richard pressed up against the cold stone of one when they reached them.

His hands felt the rough and fresh stone as one of the Assassins peered around the building and then crept off to check the way ahead.

Richard focused on his breathing because he realised he was holding it in an effort to keep quiet.

Guy sighed with impatience, but the Assassin returned and nodded.

The moon lit the plateau, which was both a blessing and a curse, because it meant Count Raymond's men would be able to see their attackers if they happened to venture out into the night.

Entering the sprawling complex of buildings, they passed an entranceway that had been cut down into the rock long ago. The smell of water wafted up from it, cool but not pure, as if the water had absorbed some of the stone cistern which contained it.

Pure or not though, it just made Richard even thirstier.

The guide led them to a wide courtyard with buildings on two sides and ancient rock formations on the others, with a huge stone staircase carved from the rock in the middle of it.

'Did they not bother to finish building this place?' Guy asked because the staircase rose up into the sky but abruptly ended without reaching anything.

The guide shook his head. 'In this land, you cannot bury the dead, and burning them is forbidden. So the ancient people here offered their bodies to the sky.'

Richard frowned. 'So they just left them to rot?'

Ishmael shook his head again. 'Birds.'

Richard shuddered. 'If I die, just bury me under some stones.'

The guide smiled a harsh smile at Richard, and the moon reflected brightly on his white teeth. 'Wild animals roll the stones away and eat the dead,' he said.

'Our father,' Richard whispered, 'that art in heaven.' He made the sign of the cross and felt sick at the idea of a wolf eating his father's body. He didn't even know if they had wolves here, but he swallowed hard anyway. 'Which way do we go?'

The guide remained impassive. 'We do not know. This is a

large place.'

'I'm getting bored,' Guy pointed at the buildings on one side of the courtyard. 'I'm trying that one.'

Richard decided he had little choice but to try to search some of the buildings and chambers himself, for this Sibylla could be anywhere. The first building Richard tried looked like no one had stepped foot in it for a hundred years, and the second smelled so badly he knew the current inhabitants were using it as a latrine. He covered his nose, gagged, and moved on.

It was Guy who found something first. He rushed back to find Richard and Ishmael. 'I've found a building with guards.'

They followed the Lusignan through the skeletons of some carved out buildings which no longer had roofs until they reached a street corner, from where Guy pointed to a building with a canvas roof. 'See,' he whispered.

Ishmael took a long look. He nodded. 'Good chance the woman is in there. If we can take her, we do not need to hunt the castellan.'

Richard drew Sir John's dagger and felt slightly better with it in his hand. He did feel vulnerable without his mail and shield, though, so he was glad when Ishmael signalled to his two companions and they slid off into the darkness.

Richard watched the stars twinkle above for a while, the sky was clear and the stars were different to home. No owls hooted though, and fewer birds flew across the sky.

Guy drew a sharp breath when he saw the Assassins creep at the guards from either side of the building. The first drew his knife across the throat of a guard while they spoke to each other, but the second was a moment late in guessing when to strike, and his target half managed a yelp before the Assassin's blade silenced him. The Assassins lowered their victims to the floor and listened.

Richard strained his ears too, searching for anyone who'd heard the sound. He waited for a moment until Ishmael looked like he'd relaxed. 'Now we go in?'

The guide turned to Guy. 'Let us see how you wield the knife,' he said. 'It is either the woman or the castellan beyond the door. Or both.'

Guy ignored him and strode to the building as if he owned

it. The two Assassins waited by the door, ready to enter behind the Lusignan.

Richard lined up behind them, he decided the first thing he'd do would be to close the door behind them to drown out whatever went on inside.

Guy didn't think about what he was going to do, instead he turned the door handle and kicked it wide open. The old and neglected wood broke, and the door split down its front and half fell into the room.

Where five men stood with open mouths, rooted to where they sat, staring at their shattered door. They sat on two benches on either side of a table made from another old door. On it was food and drink, and while Richard grew envious over it, Guy lunged.

The Lusignan reached the table as the men reacted, standing and drawing daggers and swords. But Guy was too quick for the first man, especially as he'd been facing away from him, and his blade dug in between his shoulder and his neck.

Richard went to close the door, but realised there was no point as the two Assassins rushed either side of Guy and dispatched their chosen targets.

One of the men flashed a knife and it sliced an Assassin's arm. Richard went to help, raising Sir John's dagger as the enemy, a strong man, pushed the Assassin's blade aside and stabbed him in the chest.

Richard stabbed his upper arm because that's all he could reach, and the man recoiled back as Guy tangled with the last surviving man.

Richard's foe reached around and caught the arm wielding Sir John's dagger, stopping Richard from retaliating.

From nowhere Ishmael was somehow behind the man, and his dagger stabbed him in the shoulder, arm, neck, and neck again. Count Raymond's man released Richard's wrist and sank to the ground.

Guy finished the last man, who took his bench over as he fell, the wood clattering against the stone wall so loudly it echoed around the carved stone building.

'Everyone in Sela will have heard that,' Richard said.

Guy's eyes went from enemy to enemy, checking they were

all dead or dying. The surviving Assassin ensured their final victim would never rise again, then went to check on his companion. The Assassin's wound was in his lungs, blood pooled in the folds of his robes and Ishmael shook his head. He said some words to the man, who nodded more strongly than Richard expected, and then the guide drove his wet blade into his companion's neck. For a brief moment he looked sad.

When everyone stopped to listen for signs that they'd been heard, a dull and subdued sob floated out from deeper in the shadows of the room.

Guy wiped his blade clean on his tunic and put it away as he went to investigate. He pushed a curtain aside which led to a dark room and the sobbing grew louder.

'No, no,' a woman's voice cried, 'I'm important, you can ransom me back to my brother.'

'We aren't Muslims, and we're not here to hurt you,' Guy held out a hand, 'we're here to rescue you. Well, as long as you're the right princess.'

Guy's voice was kinder than Richard had ever heard it, and the Lusignan entered the dark room and came out leading a woman. She was a head shorter than Guy, thin and wearing a green dress stained yellow with dirt and sand. Her brown hair was down only just past her shoulders.

Guy pulled her into the light cast from the broken doorway and her pale face took in the room. Her face hardened and she spat at one of her fallen guards and Richard raised his eyebrows.

Ishmael nodded. 'We should leave.'

'Obviously,' Guy replied.

'Thank you,' Sibylla gazed up into the Lusignan's eyes, which softened when they looked back.

'Kidnapping is a terrible thing,' Guy said and placed his other hand on top of the woman's.

Richard suppressed a snort and shook his head.

'What is your name, my gallant hero?' Sibylla asked.

'I am Guy of Lusignan, and I have spent days climbing the harsh rocks outside to reach you. I have braved the sun and risked death by scaling this fortress so that I can free you from these evil men.'

'That's enough of this rubbish,' Richard said, 'we need to be going.'

Sibylla stared up at her rescuer and Richard wondered how long Guy's spell would last.

Everyone's attention was snapped back into focus a moment later when Ishmael stepped out of the building and was greeted by an arrow which flew by him and snapped in half on the wall next to Richard.

'I told you,' Richard bent down and picked up a sword from the floor.

'If we stay here, we die,' Ishmael nodded to Guy. 'We rush out now, whoever is waiting for us.'

'I will protect my princess,' the Lusignan said, and Richard thought he might actually mean it.

They burst out of the broken doorway and into the street. The moonlight reflected on the pale stone of buildings, but it also glinted on the menacing iron of spears and crossbows.

The guide ran straight ahead, aiming for the street they'd arrived from, and a crossbow bolt whistled across them from one side.

Three men stood in Ishmael's way, but he never hesitated and Richard sprinted to catch up with him as he charged. One of the three enemies drew back a bow and aimed at Sibylla as Ishmael crashed into the man next to the archer.

The bow twanged and an arrow cut through the air. Guy swung his princess out of its path with a great heave, but it meant the missile hit him in his left shoulder.

Richard threw his looted sword at the archer to stop him drawing again, and by the time the man stood back up, Richard was on him, plunging down Sir John's dagger.

Shouts of alarm burst out all around Sela, and somewhere someone rang a bell.

Ishmael and his Assassin ran along the street.

Sibylla clutched Guy. 'Are you hurt?'

'Of course I'm hurt,' Guy said, 'there's an arrow in me. But it missed my heart.'

'It's a small target,' Richard mumbled and picked up the bow and two arrows from the dying archer. Footsteps and shouts approached from behind so Richard ran after the guide.

'Come on,' Guy commanded the princess, and dragged her along with his good hand.

Richard rounded a corner and a man bumped into him. They bounced off each other and Richard dropped the bow and arrows. The man stood back and squinted in the moonlight. 'Turn around,' Richard said, 'walk away.'

The man frowned. He had bushy eyebrows that met in the middle and confused eyes.

'You don't need to die,' Richard said, 'run.'

The one-eyebrowed man took a step back.

Where Guy collided with him.

Richard sighed.

The Lusignan let go of his princess and wrapped his hand around the stunned man's head. Then he pounded it into the nearest wall which it hit with a squelch and a crack. Guy let go and the body crumpled. 'Do I have to do everything myself?' he looked at Richard.

'Just go,' Richard replied.

Sibylla looked down at the man with a now slightly misshapen head, and Richard wondered if she would cry or faint.

Instead, the sister of the King of Jerusalem kicked the head once herself.

Guy grabbed her as she went for another kick and pulled her down the street.

Richard looked down at the bow, decided he probably was wasting his time with it, and ran after the rest of his party.

Ishmael already waited at the edge of the plateau when Richard reached the open ground before it. He sweated despite the cold of the night, and he could hear the men chasing them.

Guy lowered Sibylla down to the other Assassin and they began to descend from the plateau.

A bolt spiralled past Richard as he caught up with them, and he had a moment of regret about the arrows he'd dropped. Richard lowered himself down, his eyes having one last look at Sela and catching a fleeting glimpse of five or six men rushing after them.

The party scrambled down the rocks as quickly as everyone dared, but the fall was more dangerous than their pursuers, and climbing down took longer than going up. Richard still checked every foothold before he went down and swore at how long it was taking. The moon was on the other side of the castle now, so they worked in shadow, feeling for rocks to grip and praying that toeholds wouldn't give way. Richard's heart pounded in his chest and he prayed that he wouldn't die from a fall. That was not the way he wanted to go.

Our father, he thought, that art in heaven.

Stones fell from above to signal that Count Raymond's men had not abandoned the chase. Guy winced and gasped as his wounded shoulder caused him discomfort, but no words of complaint escaped him as they had done on the way up.

They reached the ledge where they had slept and Richard allowed himself a moment to close his eyes and catch his breath. His fingers and toes hurt from the strain on their descent, and when he looked up, he wished he'd kept the bow or at least had a spear, for then their position would have been easily defendable.

Guy held Sibylla in his arms, large arms which enveloped her. She didn't cry, but she looked down at her leg. A leg she wasn't bearing weight on. 'I landed badly on it,' she said quietly, as if embarrassed.

'Can you still climb?' Guy asked.

Richard didn't hear a reply, but he heard Sibylla sniff.

Guy stepped back and nodded to himself. 'I've had enough climbing,' he said, 'enough fleeing. I'm going to be the regent of this whole kingdom, and this woman is going to be my wife. I will not scurry around mountains like a rat, nor make her hobble the whole way.'

Sibylla tilted her head at Guy. 'Wife?'

'He wants to be a king,' Richard looked up at the rocks above where Count Raymond's men drew ever nearer.

'I don't want to be a king,' the Lusignan said, 'I just want to save the kingdom.'

'No, you don't,' Richard said, 'you don't care about the kingdom, you just want some land here because you lost all yours in France.'

'Don't speak to him like that,' the princess balled her fists.

Richard's mouth dropped open. 'You're defending him?'

'We do not have time for this,' Ishmael also watched for movement above.

'This man rescued me,' Sibylla said, 'like in the romances. No one shall speak ill of him.'

'Well, what now?' Richard asked.

Guy grinned. 'We're going back up.'

'We can't go back up, there are men chasing us.'

Guy led the princess back to the wall and pushed her against it. 'Stay there,' he said. 'We'll press ourselves against the mountainside in silence, and when they drop onto the ledge, we only have to push them off.'

Richard went to argue but the voices above were too loud, so he pressed himself against the rocks and drew his dagger. He glanced down at the blade, its once gleaming length now stained with black lines and spots where blood and damp had eaten into it. The lines looked like the veins in a leaf, and he wondered if the dagger was alive. It certainly knew its purpose.

A man's legs lowered right in front of Richard's eyes and kicked around to find a rock to step on. The feet flailed around and almost kicked Richard in the nose.

'I can't find a way down,' the man cried.

They didn't know the ledge was there, Richard thought. He put the dagger away and grabbed the ankles of the dangling man. Then he pulled. The man screamed as his fingers were ripped from the stone and his body thudded onto the ledge. Richard pounced, redrawing his dagger, but the fall had cracked the man's skull and he lay on his back with dead eyes staring up at the stars.

Richard backed towards the cliff as a man dropped down and landed on the ledge on his feet. He went to cry out but Guy pushed him on his chest with two hands and he reeled backwards, out into thin air, and plummeted to his death.

'What's going on down there?' one of the count's men asked from above.

'They must have fallen,' another voice answered.

'This is a fool's errand,' the first man said, 'we should turn around and go back.'

'The castellan will throw us out of the fort.'

'That's better than falling to our deaths for some woman.'

'Amen,' the second man replied, 'she was a sour-faced one, anyway.'

Sibylla grunted indignantly.

'What was that?' the first man asked.

'Someone's down there.'

Richard closed his eyes and sighed.

'You know what,' the first voice said, 'I'm going up. I'm not dying for this.'

A shower of grit fell down as the voices faded away.

'Now can we go down?' Ishmael whispered.

Guy shook his head. 'I am a man of my word, and I said we are going back up. So we're going back up.'

'How does that help us?' Richard asked. 'We are free to go back the way we came now.'

Guy climbed up off the ledge and held a hand down to Sibylla.

'This is madness,' Ishmael looked at Richard.

Richard shrugged as the princess took the Lusignan's hand and, despite his wounded shoulder, lifted her up.

'You westerners are odd,' the guide said, 'you are too lazy for the hard work of the journey so you choose death instead.'

'I'm not choosing death,' Guy said even as he climbed further up, 'I'm choosing glory.'

'I think he believes himself,' Richard said to the guide, shrugged again, and started to climb back up towards Sela.

He overtook Guy and Sibylla quickly and soon caught up with the count's men. They complained as they climbed slowly, so noisily that they came into view as he pulled himself up onto a boulder. It would be best if those two didn't make it back to the top, he thought.

So he ascended hand above hand, pushed up from his toes, and closed in on Count Raymond's men. One had a crossbow slung on his back, and Richard had to slow down to continue his climb in silence.

Until he was almost close enough to touch the crossbowman's foot, when the stone his hand was on came loose and tumbled down the mountainside with a clatter.

The crossbowman looked back, looked down, and saw Richard below him.

Richard whipped out his dagger, reached up and drove it into the man's foot. He cried out as Richard scrambled to get a good enough hold on the cliff to avoid falling. He clung onto a stone and breathed so hard it sucked in some grit and he nearly choked.

The crossbowman howled and tried to place his foot on a rock, but couldn't.

'Come on,' his companion shouted down.

'I can't use my foot.'

'Just get on with it.'

Richard, now steady, climbed up.

'He's coming to get me,' the wounded man cried, fear threaded through his voice.

'Then climb up, you fool.'

'But it hurts.'

Richard felt no pity for the man because of his answer. He could imagine how the Marshal would chide any man so unwilling to help himself. Sir John's dagger felt no pity either, as it sliced into the guard's other ankle until it hit stone.

The man screamed as he fell from the stones. He bumped off the mountain and down onto Richard, who half tried to batter him aside and half tried to grab his crossbow. His hand, even with the dagger in it, closed around the stock of the crossbow and for a moment the wounded man hung from it. Then the leather strap snapped and he fell. He screamed as he dropped past the others and Richard heard his body splatter onto the ledge.

Richard squinted into the night to spot the last enemy, but he couldn't see him above and so resumed his ascent. He could hear the others beneath him but Ishmael hadn't caught up yet, so when Richard reached the plateau he slammed the crossbow onto it and dragged himself up and onto his belly. Lying on his front, and with his eyes forward, Richard peered into the dark as his rapid breath blew sand away from his face.

The guard Richard was chasing hadn't got much further, he wheezed and gasped air, facing away from Richard and too out of breath to notice him.

Richard pushed himself up to his feet as quietly as he could and swung the crossbow. One of the arms scythed through the man's ear and pierced his brain. The weapon's arm broke and the guard went limp and dropped to the ground.

Richard marvelled at the crossbow for a moment and that he'd finally managed to kill an enemy with one. But it was useless now, so he dropped it by the man as Ishmael clambered up onto the plateau with his companion close behind him.

There were no other guards visible, and it was quiet when Guy pulled Sibylla up and she brushed herself down.

'Why isn't there anyone here?' Richard asked.

Ishmael mumbled something in his native language, and Guy made the sign of the cross.

'We've killed four,' Richard said, 'and I'm sure I saw more than four chase us here.'

'The others surely went for help,' the guide said, 'we should not stay here.'

Richard sighed. 'I know, although coming back up here feels like returning to the lion's den.'

'You know the story of Daniel?' Sibylla asked.

'Obviously,' Richard's eyes darted from Guy to the princess, 'but now that we're up here, we need to get to the gate, seeing as that's our only way out of Sela.'

'Right then,' Guy said, 'which way is it?'

Ishmael walked across the clearing and back towards the houses where they'd found Sibylla.

'That way, I suppose,' Richard noticed the guards had left their shields at the plateau's edge before their descent. He picked one up and followed the guide.

Guy didn't because he was supporting the princess, and they made slower progress away from the treacherous cliff.

Once they were amongst the carved out buildings Richard could hear voices and shouts from deeper within the settlement. 'They will all rush over to the plateau soon,' he said to Ishmael as they peered around a street corner.

The guide nodded. 'But they will not be stupid enough to abandon the gatehouse. Clearing that is a task for us. Me and my companion, not you.'

Richard stood aside as Ishmael and his Assassin skulked off into the shadows across the street and made their way to the deep gorge which led to the gatehouse.

Richard waited for Guy and Sibylla, who walked even more

slowly now. A group of guards ran down the street and Richard dragged Guy and the princess aside to hide in an alleyway. Once the guards had gone, they scrambled out quickly and found the gorge.

'Wait here,' Ishmael said from the entrance to it, 'and hold the entrance to this gorge. It is wide enough only for two warriors, so the two of you can delay the count's men if they come this way.'

Richard nodded and lifted his stolen shield up. 'Of course, but we won't last for too long.'

'We do not need too long,' Ishmael grinned and he and his Assassin disappeared into the impenetrable darkness of the gorge.

Sybilla shivered and the tall rocky sides of the gorge that loomed overhead were both comforting and oppressive.

Guy looked up at the black rocks above. 'I hate this place,' he said.

'Me, too,' the princess replied. 'I shall be glad to be rid of it.'

'We aren't out yet,' Richard said, 'and if they bring a crossbow, my shield isn't going to be enough to save us.'

'You always think of the worst,' Guy said, 'always complaining.'

A flicker of light shone on the wall of a distant street back inside the castle.

'Well,' Richard said, 'it looks like my worries are coming true. If I die here, I'm going to come back and haunt you.'

The flicker of light grew and then a group of men burst out of the street and approached the gorge.

'Step back,' Richard said, 'it's better if they don't know we're here, then we can catch them by surprise in the dark.'

The Lusignan signalled his agreement by taking three steps into the gorge until they were cloaked in the blackness of it.

Richard braced himself and raised his shield up. In the enclosed space he drew Sir John's dagger instead of Durendal, and then he waited.

Guy shifted his feet around and cleared his throat.

'We should have rolled the body off the cliff,' Richard mumbled.

'What?'

'The guard,' Richard said, 'they've just found his body and realised we've come back up.'

'Then this is your fault,' the Lusignan said with too much volume in his voice.

'Don't make this my fault,' Richard said, 'just don't run away now.'

'I'm not going to run away.'

'He will stand,' Sibylla said, 'he is a brave and noble warrior.'

'See,' Guy said, 'she already knows me better than you do.'

The castellan was in the midst of his guards, which Richard thought was probably every fighting man left in Sela, for they poured into view as they narrowed into pairs to file through the gorge.

Where they received a nasty surprise.

Richard saw the white eyes of the lead man widen as they spotted him in the gloom. Sir John's dagger struck between them and the guards all bumped into each other as Richard's victim stalled.

'What are you doing?' one cried.

Guy's sword arced down as he tried to use Richard's shields for cover, and he killed a second man.

The castellan's men realised they were in a fight and the next two men lowered their weapons. But their eyes hadn't adjusted to the near total darkness of the gorge, and Richard brushed aside a lowering spear and drove his dagger into its owner's chest. On the third stab the man fell.

Guy's opponent carried an unloaded crossbow, but he managed to bring the weapon up to block Guy's attack.

The Lusignan kicked him in the groin instead and followed up with a more successful strike. The next few moments were a blur for Richard as he battled to hold his ground, but then the guards stepped back.

'Crossbows,' the castellan shouted. 'The gorge is straight and they have nowhere to hide.'

'That's a shame,' Guy said, 'I thought we were doing quite well.'

'We should probably back up a bit,' Richard said.

'Can't we just hide behind your shield?' the Lusignan asked.

'We can't all do that, not all three of us.'

227

The first bolt spiralled over their heads, its flight echoed off the tall sides of the gorge and sounded like a stone thrown down a well.

Richard planted the shield on the ground and knelt down behind it. Guy went behind him and pushed the princess into place behind Richard.

Another bolt glanced off one side of the gorge, bounced past the shield and shattered on the opposite wall. A splinter hit Richard on the arm and he swallowed. He would rather be on a horse. In his mail.

Richard thought he heard voices from behind them, but the sound was drowned out by the next bolt, which skidded off the ground and crashed into the bottom of his shield. The bolt cracked the shield back and it thumped into Richard's leg. That was going to bruise.

The next bolt penetrated the shield, splitting the grain of the wood, and came to a stop a finger's width from Richard's eyes. He reached around to pull it out and again heard a noise from the direction of the gatehouse.

Guy also turned to listen to it. 'We can't hold on two fronts, we should surrender now before they close in.'

'It's not over yet,' Richard said.

'I know you're only thinking of my safety,' the princess said, 'but this man is correct, your honour requires you to fight a little longer.'

Another bolt narrowly sailed over Richard, but he was more concerned with who was coming from the gatehouse. 'Turn and face them,' he said to Guy, 'that's more than two men coming, so it can't be Ishmael.'

'Who is Ishmael?'

'Our guide,' Richard replied in exasperation. 'How do you not know his name?'

'Oh,' the Lusignan said, 'but we're trapped, we can't fight our way out of this.'

'They're going to kill us if we yield,' Richard said, 'after we've killed so many of their friends, so just stop complaining and face them.'

'Speak to Guy with the respect he deserves,' Sibylla went to stomp her foot, but it was still sprained and she yelped with pain.

Richard couldn't help smiling at that, and that smile only widened when he heard one of the war-cries coming from the gatehouse.

He smiled because it was in a language he didn't understand, and it was Otto, in his black surcoat, who nearly cut Guy in half with his sword. The Lusignan fell over backwards trying to get away from him, and Otto's sword reached his nose before the German paused and laughed. 'God smiles on you today,' he grinned.

Guy rubbed a small cut on his nose. 'Get off me.'

Richard nodded at his friend. 'They have crossbows,' he said as a bolt hit a rock and snapped into three pieces.

'I can see,' Otto replied.

Sarjeant appeared from the gloom, and Richard could sense the presence of other men behind him. 'My boy,' the big man smiled and let out a breath. Even in the dark Richard could see how cracked his lips were.

'Forwards,' Gerard's voice boomed through the gorge, 'forwards until no one is left to stand against us.'

'You heard the man,' Otto leapt away from Guy, raised his black shield before him, and strode towards the source of the crossbow bolts.

Gerard and his bannerman led the turcopoles and Guy's men through the gorge, they pushed past Richard and the seneschal merely grunted at Richard as he went.

Bowman advanced behind them, dragging Maynard by the arm. 'Come, squire,' the blonde knight said, 'this is your first chance to start redeeming yourself. Go and fight.'

'I want to,' Maynard moaned, 'let me go.'

'Fine,' Bowman did, 'but if you come back with a clean sword, I'll use it on you.'

Maynard scurried off up the gorge and towards the sounds of battle that broke out when Otto and Gerard exploded out from the gorge and into Sela.

Guy stood up and touched his nose again. 'I'm going to avenge your captivity,' he said to the princess. He ran off up the gorge with his sword drawn.

Richard sighed because Sibylla clasped her hands together

and watched her saviour go.

Sarjeant had stayed. 'Do you know where the castle's stores are?' he asked.

'There are many buildings,' Richard said, 'and there are cisterns full of water.'

'Water,' Sarjeant said, 'I must drink, can you show me?'

'Why are you so thirsty?' Richard asked.

'We only have the clove wine,' Sarjeant said, 'and I feared if I touched it I would be lost. So I have made do with prayer.'

'I told him that was stupid,' Bowman said, 'praying never seems to do anything at the best of times.'

'You did not complain that much,' Sarjeant said, 'you took my ration.'

Bowman shrugged.

'Of course,' Richard said, 'we'll find you the water. They must have ample supplies of all kinds of drink here.'

'Praise the Lord,' Sarjeant said.

A few loud screams signalled the end of the brief battle, and it wasn't long before Guy reentered the gorge with a severed head in each hand. He dropped the ghoulish trophies at the feet of the princess.

Sibylla giggled. 'You are a great hero. My Perseus, my Theseus.'

'Really?' Richard said to himself.

'Who is this woman?' Bowman asked. 'Surely she isn't the princess we've come to rescue? What woman swoons at two freshly removed heads?'

'A Lusignan woman,' Guy replied proudly.

'She's your sister?' Bowman said with surprise.

Guy frowned. 'I could kill you for that,' he said, 'this is Princess Sibylla of Jerusalem. But she will be a Lusignan before long.'

Bowman couldn't stop himself laughing. 'It's all just working out so well for you, isn't it? They will find you out, mark my words.'

Guy sniffed and went to Sibylla, who embraced him as if they were already married.

Otto returned from the battle to tell Richard it was over.

'Did the squire fight?' Bowman asked.

'I never saw him,' Otto replied.

'We'll have to do something about him,' Richard said, 'he's getting worse.'

'Leave him here,' Bowman said, 'before he does something we regret.'

'I'm not sure he can do much worse than he already has,' Richard said, 'but we should give him one last chance. My father once said that if you spend enough time with someone, however stupid they are, they will do something to surprise you.' It occurred to Richard that Maynard had surprised his father by getting him killed, but pushed that thought away and mumbled the Lord's Prayer instead.

'Well,' Bowman glanced at Guy, who still hugged the princess, 'we've seen everything now, so I suppose anything is possible. But one more misstep from that squire, and I will kill him.'

# THE OASIS

Richard only had the chance to sleep briefly in what remained of the night. He opened his eyes at dawn but they stuck together and urged him to go back to sleep. His body ached and his throat was parched.

Sarjeant and Maynard helped the turcopoles break down Gerard's tent and Richard could hear the sound of folding canvas on the other side of their small camp.

'Why does he get a big round tent?' Bowman asked. He rolled his bedding up and went to tie it to a packhorse.

'Because he's the seneschal,' Richard said, 'and in the Templar Rule it says he gets a round tent.'

Bowman snorted. 'I'm not helping with it.'

'No one asked you to,' Richard sat up in his bed and yawned. Dew dotted his blanket and his ever-growing beard. They were all bearded now, except for Brian who couldn't grow one, and the squire, who Richard assumed couldn't either.

Brian offered Richard a drink of water, which he needed. 'We can head back to Jerusalem now, can't we?' the monk asked.

Richard handed the empty cup back. 'I don't know. As Bowman keeps telling me, we have to go where we're told. I thought I'd like the freedom from responsibility, but it turns out I don't.'

The monk bit his lip. 'I enjoy suffering for Christ as much as the next man, but I would rather like to be back at the holy city now.'

'I'd like to be at Kerak,' Richard said, 'so I expect one of us is

232

about to be very disappointed.'

When Gerard addressed the company a short time later, it was Brian who was to be disappointed. 'The turcopoles are loading packhorses for you,' the seneschal said. 'We shall return to Jerusalem to install Guy as regent and muster the army. You and your small company shall take the true cross directly to Kerak.'

Richard's heart skipped a beat, but he frowned. 'That road was dangerous, and you propose we travel back along it with only a handful of men?'

Gerard nodded. 'We must travel fast, for the fate of Kerak is at stake. We cannot wait for your rickety cart, but at the same time, the true cross must reach Kerak. The guide will find you quiet roads to travel on. Move at night, hide in the day.'

Ishmael stood close by with his face as still as the mountains all around.

'I suggest you repair your cart,' Gerard said, 'it looks and sounds old.'

'It is old,' Richard replied.

'Thanks to the stores from Sela, your packhorses have enough food and water to last until Kerak,' the seneschal said, 'just ensure that you get there. When our new army arrives on the hills outside the castle, they should be able to look over it and see the cross. Take it to the highest point you can so that it stands out against the sky. The army shall see it and be inspired to victory. The cross can only reach that mountain if you ride back north, and Saladin's men will not be looking in that direction.'

'Won't it be too small to see?' Richard asked. 'The mountains around Kerak were huge, the cross will be just a speck on the horizon.'

'Do not doubt the Lord's plan,' Gerard replied, 'and do not question me. You have your orders. Obey them.'

Richard nodded.

'Kerak is the key to the Holy Land, if it falls the door to Jerusalem swings open and Saladin will have a clear path. Your father had the true cross under his protection and this duty is now yours.'

Richard swallowed. He already had enough duties and he

didn't really want this one. He also hadn't enjoyed driving the cross from the ambush site to Sela, and had no wish to keep on doing it any longer than was necessary.

Gerard watched him. 'Your face is a record of your struggles, and I have seen your hands. You are a hard man, Richard. I think you may be hard enough to pull this off.'

'It seems like a risk to me,' Richard said, 'but I do want to return to Kerak, so we will do as you ask.'

'I'm not asking.'

Richard half bit his tongue.

'Leave your templar surcoats and caparisons here,' Gerard said, 'they would mark you out, and you will wish to pass for merchants if anyone sees you.'

'Very well,' Richard replied. That seemed sensible, especially as he remembered that captured Templars were executed on the spot.

Gerard nodded and went to prepare himself to leave. He had the cylinder containing the Assassin's message on his shoulders, the strap repaired and the message still unread by himself.

Two men lifted the Marshal into his saddle with a grunt, and the knight himself moaned as he settled into it. He stood up in his stirrups so his assistants could pull his surcoat free from underneath him, and he stifled a painful yelp as he did.

'He's not lifting his left arm, either,' Bowman stood next to Richard as the Templar trumpet blew a note which signalled the start of the march.

The Marshal rode over, his face a picture of calm and never betraying his obvious pain. 'I wanted to say thank you,' the English knight said.

'What for?' Richard asked up at him as he rolled up his damp bedding.

'For freeing me from captivity at Castle Lusignan.'

Richard widened his eyes and struggled to find any words.

Bowman didn't. 'God's teeth,' he said, 'that took you long enough, didn't it?'

'Do not push me,' the Marshal said, 'I have risked my life for all of you more than once, and I am trying to consider others in my thoughts. I have done much for you.'

'We appreciate it. Thank you for that,' Richard said. 'What you did at the Red Tower was a deed worthy of a romance. The tale of how you conquered it alone will be told around hearths across the world.'

'I have no need for that,' the Marshal smiled faintly, 'I have chased worldly vanity for too long. I would ask you that you tell no one of my deeds.'

'Really?' Bowman asked.

The Marshal nodded.

'So a peacock can change its feathers,' the blonde knight said.

'Don't mock me,' the Marshal said.

'Why not?' Bowman asked. 'You can't fight me at the moment, can you?'

'I will heal quickly enough,' the Marshal said, 'and I will join the army, which will go to Kerak. I will be there to save your family.'

'Thank you,' Richard said, 'and I hope you heal well.'

'I always do, for I have not yet done what I was put on this world to do.'

'That rich heiress?' Bowman grinned.

The Marshal shook his head. 'That's not what I meant, but that too. If a man as unholy as Guy can capture the sister of a king, then I surely will marry high.'

Richard nodded.

'And not to mention what he did,' the Marshal looked at Bowman.

'What did I do?'

'I know how much time you spent with the Irish princess at Richard's castle,' the English knight replied, 'and you are more lowly born than Guy.'

'I'm not more lowly born than you.'

'My father,' the Marshal began, but sighed. 'It matters not.'

'I do not doubt you,' Richard said. 'But this might be goodbye. If we do not reach Kerak, please look after my family.'

The Marshal frowned for a fleeting moment. 'You have my word.'

'Thank you,' Richard slipped his black surcoat over his head and immediately felt too warm. Then he remembered he was to leave it behind and took it off. 'If the worst happens, you can have my silver too, just leave a suitable offering with the Templars.'

'Don't give it to him,' Bowman said, 'he'll just spend it on horses.'

'What do you think I want to spend it on?' Richard grinned.

'You owe me a blue roan,' the Marshal said.

'Maynard owes you a blue roan.'

The Marshal shrugged. 'There is enough silver for a hundred blue roans. I shall use it to secure your children's futures through marriages.'

'You have my thanks,' Richard bowed to the knight.

'Do not thank me, just survive so I don't have to bother.'

'And there's the old peacock,' Bowman rolled his eyes. 'You've ruined the moment.'

'Gerard is gone,' Richard said, 'you should go before he punishes you.'

The Marshal nodded. 'Goodbye Richard.' He turned his horse and rode off after the Templar banner.

Guy sat with his company, all arrayed to march, and watched him go.

'What's he waiting for?' Bowman asked.

Richard tied his bedding to his horse. 'I don't know, or want to know.'

Guy said something to his men and they kicked their horses and cantered towards Richard's small company.

'What are you doing?' Richard cried, but the knights and squires in their blue and white surcoats ignored him and rushed at their freshly loaded packhorses. They cut their ropes and dragged the surprised animals away.

Richard drew his sword and chased them, but he was on foot and they flew out of range. 'Come back,' he shouted, 'those are ours.'

'That's got my bedding,' Bowman cried in disbelief.

Guy walked his horse forward next to his bannerman. 'The credit for the relief of Kerak will go to me, and me alone. I will not share my victory with some old piece of wood. When it is said that Kerak was saved, it will be only my name they cheer.'

'That doesn't mean you have to steal our supplies,' Richard stood and caught his breath. 'This will kill us.'

'I'm not killing anyone,' Guy shrugged. 'My men will not harm you.'

'Taking our water and wine is killing us,' Richard said, 'in the heat we won't last three days without it.'

'That should slow you down, then,' Guy grinned.

'We'll die.'

'The Lord will judge me.'

Richard laughed. 'You don't believe that.'

'No, which is why I'm doing it,' Guy said, 'although the kingdom clearly needs me, so I'm sure the Lord will judge me favourably anyway.'

'If we survive this,' Richard cut his sword through the air for effect, 'we will tell everyone how you have behaved.'

'What about how you behaved when you failed to repay your ransom?' Guy asked. 'Which you still owe me. And what about the yellow horse, he is still mine.'

'We recaptured my horse fairly,' Richard replied, 'which by tournament law means I don't owe you.'

The Lusignan shrugged. 'I don't care enough to argue about it. But I do not want the cross getting in the way of my first victory. This is not personal.'

'You are not suited to ruling anything, and the nobles of the kingdom will not stand your barbarity,' Richard said. 'Condemning us to death? You cannot treat your allies and friends like this.'

'But you aren't my friends,' Guy said, 'it is because of you that I lost my lands in France in the first place.'

'Haven't we fought together?' Richard asked. 'Haven't we stood next to each other on top of Rocamadour's walls? You made a decision to save a holy place, to do good.'

'Yes, and look what it got me.'

'It isn't about what it gets you,' Richard said.

'Aye,' Bowman shouted over, 'we do it all the time and never get anything for it.'

Guy shook his head. 'I tried acting the way you and the priests want me to, but that failed me. It got me exiled to this godforsaken wasteland, which is a clear sign of the futility of your ideals. So now I'm going to trust myself and do things my way.'

'Your way?' Richard cried. 'Murdering Christians?'

'I already explained,' Guy half turned his horse away, 'I'm not killing you. This is politics, nothing more. I think I'm getting good at it.'

Richard let out a deep breath as the Lusignan turned his horse in the direction Gerard had gone and rode after him. His company followed, leading the stolen packhorses.

Bowman slid his new bow from his horse and strung it.

'This is murder,' Richard shouted after Guy.

The blonde knight reached for an arrow.

'Don't bother,' Richard turned and walked towards the cart, 'you'll only miss.'

Bowman held the arrow for a moment, looked between Guy and the bow, and his shoulders slumped. The one he'd hurt outside Qal'at caused him to flinch. 'Right then, what now?'

'Well,' Richard reached the cart and looked up at the big wooden cross, 'we've been left alone in the desert with nothing to eat or drink, so I have no idea what now.'

Brian sat on the edge of the cart's platform, watching the dust from their former comrades rise up into the morning air. 'I'd suggest praying, but I think we are beyond that now.'

'You think so?' Bowman re-tied his bow to his saddle.

Maynard sat on the earth where he'd been knocked over by Guy's men. He put his head in his hands and cried.

'Oh, for pity's sake,' Bowman tightened his horse's girth more forcefully than he normally did.

'Ishmael,' Richard searched for the guide and found him standing next to his horse. 'We can refill water from this village's well, but what then? Can we find water on the way to Kerak while avoiding the main road?'

The guide's face was darker than usual. 'We cannot retrace our way back along the road we took, for it is devoid of water and full of danger. But if we go east, into the sands, then we can move from oasis to oasis and fill our skins.'

'What's an oasis?' Bowman asked.

'A blessing in the sands,' Ishmael said, 'they are islands of green in the yellow. Life surrounded by nothingness. Moving between them is how the bedouin travel.'

'Who are they?' Richard asked.

'You have seen their caravans,' the guide replied, 'they are the people who were here first in this land. They trade with the Christians, and favour them more than Saladin, so we should be able to move between the oases in safety. I know the oases, we can use the smaller ones which will help us avoid Saladin's caravans and soldiers.'

Bowman scratched his neck. 'I don't understand this place, Muslims on our side?'

The guide raised his eyebrows. 'Do you see a cross around my neck?'

'I know,' the blonde man frowned, 'I'm just surprised.'

Sarjeant looked up from the cart and Otto grinned.

'Don't say a word,' Bowman growled at them.

Sarjeant grinned, but only briefly. 'I wish you had all listened to me in Normandy and not come here. Every time here, expeditions end in sunburn and thirst.'

'We are here,' Richard put his sword away, 'and we need to shore up this cart after Maynard cracked the wheel. We'll find some nails and wood in this old village somewhere. Then we will take the cross to the nearest oasis. Which way are they?'

'Towards the sand,' Ishmael said. 'East. I must warn you, westerners do not fare well in it. They often turn mad looking at the endless dunes of sand.'

'We'll see about that,' Richard replied, 'our skin might be peeling off from the sun, and we might be too hot, but we have got this far.'

The guide nodded slowly but didn't reply.


A day later, and as the Tancarville horse's hooves sank into the dry sand with every step, Richard turned to Ishmael, who rode alongside the cart. 'You were right, I do not like the sands.'

Ishmael grunted. 'This is the camel sea. Horses are not king here.'

Richard jumped off the cart and everyone had to help him push it up a dune. The wooden wheels, patched up slightly with scavenged wood, disappeared into the sand on every turn, but slowly their combined efforts moved the cart on and on.

Brian walked with his hood over his head, but he sweated and didn't speak. Maynard trudged on behind, not helping to push the cart, and was subsequently ignored by everyone else who strained and sweated under the sun to maintain their meagre progress.

Their first night was a cold one, and they huddled together under the cart for warmth. Richard gave his food to the Tancarville horse, but Ishmael promised the first oasis would be reached the following day.

'Can't we just dump the cart and find some wood further on? Make a new cross?' Bowman asked when they woke the next morning. 'Or travel at night.'

Ishmael nodded. 'We should travel at night, but you westerners usually refuse. So we suffer under the sun instead.'

'You could have mentioned that,' Richard said, 'but now we don't have time to wait the heat out today.'

'I think the seneschal even told us to move at night,' Bowman said, 'but my head hurts and I don't remember properly.'

Ishmael shrugged. 'I apologise for my assumption.'

'We should leave the cart,' Otto nodded. 'It will slow us down.'

'My father protected this cross for how long? Ten years? I can't just leave it in the sand,' Richard said, 'it is all I have left from him.'

'That's not true, is it?' Bowman said. 'You've still got his golden spurs.'

Richard nodded. 'We keep the cross.'

No one complained further, and as the sun dropped below the horizon and cast the clear sky in an orange glow, they spotted trees between two looming dunes.

The ground hardened and the horses made quicker progress. The sand gave way to bushes, then trees, and suddenly they were looking at an island of lush greenery that seemed so far out of place that Richard doubted his eyes.

He didn't doubt his touch though, not when he thrust his head into the water and the freshness of it made him gasp.

Bowman jumped in without even removing his mail, causing a great splash which spooked the horses. He stood up in the pool, shaded by palm trees, and then dropped down into the cool water. 'That is the best feeling I've ever had,' he shouted.

Brian knelt by the water and drank, as did all the horses who were just as thirsty as the men.

They gorged on water and filled every container they had, then rested in the shade and soaked their feet in the pool.

'Do not do that,' Ishmael said, 'it pollutes the water for drinking.'

'We don't care,' Sarjeant said, 'it's too good.'

The guide shook his head and looked away. He suggested they remained at this oasis the next day and carried on only as that day cooled, and Richard couldn't argue with him. Mostly because he didn't want to, just the shade he thought was worth killing for.

Darkness settled around them and the horses took to eating the bushes and pulling leaves from the smaller trees. The oasis was long and thin, nestled in a valley of dunes.

Brian fell asleep on the cart next to Maynard, while Richard watched Bowman light a small fire.

'This is good,' Richard sat down with his back against a palm tree. 'This is all we need. Water, shade, food.'

The blonde knight got his flame and stood back as the kindling took.

Ishmael dropped a pile of dead wood next to the fire. 'This is the lifestyle of the bedouin, moving from oasis to oasis.'

'You said. Do they fight each other?' Richard asked.

The guide nodded. 'They use the long spear and bow as well as you do, but they do not impose their will on others.'

Richard frowned. 'Don't blame me for us being here.'

'Your kind is never happy with what it has,' Ishmael said, 'so you are always unfulfilled.'

'I could be content here,' Richard mumbled.

Bowman sighed.

'Are you about to tell me I'd get bored in a week?' Richard asked.

'I was,' the blonde man said, 'but something more important is happening.'

'What?'

'Someone is coming.'

241

Richard followed the direction of Bowman's gaze. Something moved up at the far end of the oasis. 'Of course they are,' he groaned.

Ishmael watched as black shapes grew nearer and larger. 'It is the bedouin. They will leave us alone if you allow me to do the talking.'

'You'll have to,' Richard said, 'seeing as we don't speak their language.'

A line of camels lurched along the oasis, under the trees and towards Richard. Their riders wore loose-fitting black robes with white headdresses wrapped around their heads. Their camels wore tassels and decorations of beads, and made loud groaning noises as they stopped and their riders considered Richard's party.

Richard glanced at the pile of very European-looking saddles and wondered how they had believed they might pass for locals.

'Tie the horses together,' Richard said to Brian and Maynard, 'and get away from the water. I don't want them to think that we have dirtied it or taken too much.'

Ishmael sniffed. 'You are learning,' he said, 'I will speak to them. Keep your men together and ensure they do nothing to cause trouble.'

Richard looked at Bowman, who held up his hands and closed his mouth.

Otto waved the others over, and everyone gathered around Richard and the cart.

The bedouin stayed on their camels and waited.

'What are they doing?' Brian asked.

'They are deciding what to make of us,' Richard replied.

'Why aren't they drinking?' the monk asked as the camels swung their heads towards the water and growled.

'The aren't sure if they can trust us,' Bowman said.

Ishmael reached them and started to talk. After a while, the lead rider dismounted his camel and stood closer to the guide and continued their conversation. His eyes were never far away from Richard and his party.

Sarjeant stood next to Richard rubbing the pommel of his sword. 'Their eyes are burning holes through me. I do not like this.'

Two more bedouin dismounted and clustered around Ishmael.

'This doesn't look like a friendly greeting to me,' Bowman said, 'I should get my bow.'

Sarjeant scoffed and Bowman went to push him.

'Don't,' Richard said, 'they're supposed to be on our side, just wait and be quiet.'

'How sure are we that they're on our side?' the blonde man asked.

'Ishmael must be sure, seeing as he's gone over there by himself,' Richard said.

Two more bedouins joined the three around Ishmael, who still spoke to their leader, although with a louder voice.

'Just look relaxed,' Richard said, 'hands off weapons, try not to look concerned.'

'I am concerned,' Sarjeant said.

'We are fewer than them,' Bowman shrugged, 'they have no need to be bothered by our presence.'

'Unless they think we're despoiling their oasis,' Richard said, 'which I think they see as theirs. We are not supposed to be here.'

Sarjeant nodded. 'Those men know we are not Muslims.'

'They will if you keep talking and their ears are keener than ours,' Richard hissed.

Ishmael slid a foot backward through the sand, deftly and imperceptibly retreating a step.

'That's not good,' Bowman said.

'Don't do anything,' Richard said, 'we don't know what's happening.'

Maynard waited behind the others. 'We should attack first,' he said with a trembling voice.

Bowman burst out into laughter. 'You mean you want us to attack them first for you?'

The guide and the bedouin spun to look at the source of the laughter.

'What did I tell you,' Richard sighed.

The blonde knight stopped. 'It was only a laugh, it's not like I drew a sword.'

'It will either defuse the tension, or make things worse.'

Sarjeant watched a bedouin go back to his camel. 'I think it made things worse.'

'Can I get my bow yet?' Bowman asked.

Richard shook his head. 'They way you've been with the bow lately, you're more of a danger to us than the enemy.'

Brian shuffled over to a palm tree to hide behind. 'We don't actually know they are our enemy,' he said.

'Then why are you hiding?' Richard asked.

'Because I'm a man of peace.'

Bowman snorted.

Another bedouin returned to his camel and rummaged in his baggage.

Richard watched and licked his lips. 'Ishmael said to do nothing,' he whispered. Despite himself his hand drifted to Durendal, and he noticed some of the bedouin glanced over to him. 'They could just be getting food or even gifts,' he said, 'draw no weapons.'

'Young lord,' Bowman said, 'I've got a bad feeling about this.'

'We've all got a bad feeling about this,' Richard said. 'But I don't want to be the one who starts a fight. We can't afford to lose anyone else.'

Ishmael stepped back another step, this time with less finesse.

Maynard shook, Richard could hear him, but then the squire turned and ran away. He cried in fright, tripped on a stone and fell face-first into the sand.

Bowman sighed. 'I think he just started it.'

The bedouin by their camels slipped bows from cases and strung them. Bowman went to fetch his bow, skidding across the sand, and Ishmael whipped out two daggers and faced the three men surrounding him.

'For the love of,' Richard stepped forward and drew Durendal.

Sarjeant and Otto were beside him, but Ishmael's last remaining Assassin was faster and ran to aid his companion.

Bowman cursed as in his haste he dropped his bowstring.

Richard ran, Sarjeant just behind him, as Ishmael leapt at a bedouin.

The other Assassin dodged one incoming arrow, but the

next caught him in the hip and it spun him around. He kept running, ignoring the shaft, and slashed at the other bedouin circling the guide.

An arrow from Bowman flew between two camels and Richard heard him swear.

Ishmael cut a robe but not the man he fought, who caught him with the pommel of his curved sword and sent him sprawling to the ground.

Otto took an arrow to the thigh and fell, but Richard kept going, not knowing if he was in time to make a difference.

The other Assassin clashed with a bedouin who lunged to finish Ishmael off, and they crashed to the ground together.

Richard swung his sword at a bedouin, who swerved out of the way and surprised Richard with the speed of his counter. Sarjeant blocked it for him and rushed on to push the smaller enemy to the ground. Except the bedouin who had knocked Ishmael down stepped into Sarjeant and stunned him with a blow to the side of the head.

As his former steward staggered sideways, Richard cut at the man but missed.

Bowman yelled a war-cry nearby as he approached, but Richard found himself alone facing four bedouin. 'I could do with some help,' he said as two of his opponents grinned at him.

Bowman charged, right past Richard, and collided with one and they fought on the ground when they both tripped.

The other Assassin screamed as a knife stabbed him, but Richard couldn't look away from the three men who now advanced at him with naked blades.

'Bowman,' Richard said.

'I'm a bit busy,' the blonde man rolled over his enemy as they fought over a single knife, sand flying up all around them.

Brian covered ground quickly to reach Richard, a spear in both his hands and a wild cry on his lips. The monk planted himself at Richard's side and flashed his spear toward the enemy.

'Thanks for coming,' Richard said, 'but I don't think we'll kill four of them on our own.'

'But we have the true cross,' the monk cried.

245

'I don't think we do.'

'What?'

Richard backed up a step. 'There are no nail holes.'

Brian frowned. 'What do you mean?'

'The cross has no nail holes.'

'Oh,' Brian's shoulders slumped.

Richard took a deep breath. 'So, shall we get this over and done with? Are you ready?'

Brian gripped his spear and swished it at a bedouin's face. 'I'm ready.'

Richard heard the rush of footsteps behind him, then felt a blast of air go by as Maynard the squire attacked all four bedouins. He swung his sword in a great arc, which sent the enemy backwards, and threw himself at their leader.

'Now,' Richard shouted.

The bedouin leader, the tallest amongst them, brought his sword down and caught Maynard on the upper arm.

Brian charged with Richard, and the bedouin hesitated at the fresh chaos that swirled about them.

Maynard's sword drew blood from the leader's hand as Richard clashed with another enemy. Their swords locked and Richard could smell dates on the man's breath. They wrestled with their swords until they twisted and Durendal fell to the sand. The bedouin stabbed at Richard, the blade jammed into his mail shirts and the man looked up in surprise when Richard ignored it and drew Sir John's dagger. The dagger found no armour to thwart it on the bedouin.

Brian shouted with everything his lungs had, giving himself courage, and the wild swings of his spear were enough to make his foe back away from him.

Maynard howled and cut and stabbed, but he faced two men, and one of them sliced a deep gash in his shoulder. The young man dropped to a knee as Richard charged in to help him.

The leader turned to face Richard, who scooped up a handful of sand as he ran and threw it up at the bedouin's face. The leader dodged it, but Richard stayed low and dove at the man's legs, sweeping them out from underneath him. The leader thudded onto the sandy ground and Richard reached up and plunged his dagger into the man's thigh. He cried out as

Richard twisted the blade and then scrambled up so he could stab the man in his groin. Then Sir John's dagger then found the man's stomach and the bedouin screamed so loudly Richard pushed himself away from him, then looked to the squire.

Maynard was still on one knee and batted away a sword swing from the bedouin who circled around to get behind him.

There was another scream from where Bowman struggled with his enemy, but Richard hurled himself at Maynard's attacker. The squire tried to help but sank to the ground as the bedouin backed away from Richard who had fury in his eyes. Except he slipped on Maynard's dropped blade and staggered.

The bedouin took his chance and cut Richard across the stomach while he fell. He felt the metal rings of his two shirts crunch and felt the air being ejected from his lungs. He hit the ground gasping for breath that didn't come. His head spun but he raised his hand to catch the wrist of the bedouin who tried to finish him.

Richard kept his grasp firm and pulled the man down into the sand with him. Both men lost their weapons but the bedouin soon got on top of Richard, his hands flailing in the direction of Richard's sand-filled eyes.

Someone nearby died, but men of all kinds sound the same when they die, and Richard had no idea who it was.

A spear point burst out from the bedouin's shoulder, and behind it Brian the monk sang the psalm of David.

'To you the glory,' Brian tugged at the spear and the bedouin cried out as he was thrown onto his side like a skewered boar. The monk stood on the man's back and wrenched his spear free.

Bowman walked over, his mail dripping with blood, and thrust a knife into the throat of the man Brian had skewered.

Men still screamed, and their anguish echoed back and forth over the oasis. Richard didn't know who they were or who had already died, but the world darkened and then went black.

He opened his eyes and was immediately aware of how much

his head hurt. He could feel the coolness of shade on his skin, and when his eyes focused, he sat up and looked around. Everyone lay or sat under a palm tree near the water. Sarjeant tied a jagged strip of linen around Otto's thigh, but bright blood stained it even as he wrapped it again and again. Richard knew mail armour was good against arrows, but not always, and he said a prayer to give thanks that no missiles had hit him.

The camels had scattered and one sniffed the Tancarville horse, who sniffed it back.

Maynard lay next to Richard, the cut in his shoulder bandaged, but his face deathly white and his breath so shallow as to almost be gone. A stomach wound oozed blood, and his eyes stared blankly up to the gently shifting palm fronds that provided the shade.

The Assassin's body lay where it had fallen amongst the bedouin, but Ishmael sat up against the palm tree with Bowman holding a cup of water to his lips.

Richard groaned when he tried to stand up and had to sit back down.

'Good,' Bowman glanced over, 'I wondered how long it would take you to wake up, especially when you don't seem to have taken any real blows.'

'Speak for yourself,' Richard felt the mail around his stomach and winced. That was going to hurt riding. Every single step. 'How is Maynard?' Richard didn't want to look down at the young man.

Bowman shrugged. 'Things come full circle, don't they? He is finished.'

'He saved us.'

'He sold us out,' Bowman said, 'he tried to get me hung, do you remember that?'

'I remember,' Richard rubbed the back of his head. 'But my father was right, eventually he surprised us.'

'Took long enough,' Bowman crouched down over the squire and sniffed.

Richard dragged himself closer to the squire. 'Can you hear me? Thank you, Maynard, your attack saved us.'

The squire nodded weakly.

'You might not wield a sword again,' Richard said, 'but that cut missed your lungs, and your stomach wound doesn't seem too deep.'

Maynard's unblinking eyes stayed on the swaying palm fronds above him.

'Don't honey your words to him,' Bowman said, 'he knows how injured he is, and knows that this is what he deserved.'

'There's no need for that,' Richard said.

Brian carried over a bag from a camel and dropped it by Richard. 'I will say what needs to be said for the squire. He knows he is about to journey to the next life. He has the look. The same as Sir Rob at Lagny.'

Richard shuddered. Another young life was fading away too soon. 'I can do one last thing for you, Maynard.' He picked up Durendal, which he assumed Bowman had recovered for him, and knelt over the squire. 'Bowman, fetch my father's spurs.'

The blonde man swallowed and went to Richard's horse, which he had to peel away from the camel it had befriended. He'd heard horses didn't like camels, but could see no evidence of that. The camel followed.

Maynard's eyes glowed ever so slightly and he managed something which might have been called a smile. He coughed.

Bowman returned with the shining but dented pair of spurs. 'I'll put them on,' he said.

'Really?' Richard asked.

'You're right, young lord,' the blonde man knelt down, 'his charge did save us. Or you, at least.'

Richard held his sword up while Bowman tied on the first spur.

'You see,' Richard said to the squire, 'you're about to become a knight. Once this last spur is fastened, you will be Sir Maynard.'

The squire's lips curled up at the ends.

Richard looked down at his ankles and watched Bowman slide the spur onto a heel. 'See,' Richard glanced back at the squire's face, but he didn't finish. Maynard's face was still. He drew no breath. The oasis was silent apart from the animals which munched on the foliage. Richard thought at least this was a better place to die than the cold and dark chamber in Lagny Abbey.

Brian shook his head ruefully. 'Make haste, angels of the Lord, who are taking his soul and offering it in the sight of the Most High.'

Richard sat down with a thump. 'That wasn't fair. He died before the second spur.'

Bowman looked up and dropped the spur in silence. He sat down too and shook his head.

Richard wasn't sure that the blonde man's eyes were entirely dry. 'I can't take this,' Richard said, 'will everyone die here?'

Otto grunted as Sarjeant pulled his thigh bandage as tight as he could. 'We will all die,' he said.

Bowman turned away, and Richard heard him sniff. 'Why are you upset? You hated him.'

'I don't know,' the blonde knight said, 'I don't know why I'm bothered.'

'I hate this place,' Richard said.

'I told you not to come here,' Sarjeant said, 'but no one listened to an old man, did you?'

'It's too late now,' Richard said, 'we are here and need to get to Kerak. But we aren't going to make it there, are we? What else is going to go wrong?'

The friendly camel which had followed the Tancarville horse stretched its head down and rubbed the side of it on the repaired cart wheel. It creaked, cracked, and then a part of it snapped off. The camel regarded the wheel with disdain and moved on.

'Oh, come on,' Bowman shook his head, 'I take it back, Maynard can rot in hell. He's dead and he's still trying to get us all killed. If he hadn't cracked the wheel before, the camel wouldn't have broken it now.'

'We can't even fix it,' Richard said, 'we don't have any nails.'

'The cart be damned,' Bowman said, 'and damned the damned cross too. It isn't real anyway.'

'Fine,' Richard sighed, 'we'll leave the cart now we can't take it. I'll shave off some of the wood so we can make one of those smaller crosses. It'll have to do.'

Ishmael stretched his neck around. 'We have camels now, without the cart we can make good speed through the sandy sea.'

Richard looked at the bodies sprawled over the oasis. 'And

we have their robes. With them over our mail and saddles we might finally pass for natives. This doesn't have to happen again.'

'That would be for the best,' Ishmael nodded.

'Otto,' Richard said, 'are you able to ride?'

The German shook his head. 'No, but tie me to my horse and I shall steer it. I'm not riding one of those camels.'

Bowman frowned. 'I hate camels.'

The guide stood up. 'Learn to ride them,' he said, 'for we must travel with haste.'

'Why?' Richard asked.

'Because the bedouin told me about the siege,' Ishmael said, 'Saladin's catapults have destroyed the gate into the castle of Kerak and have reduced one of its towers to rubble. They think the assault will happen in a few days. The army of Jerusalem may not arrive in time.'

# THE REGENT

The white hills to the southeast of Kerak were topped with a generous scattering of green trees. The hills, bright in the dawn light, plunged down to valley floors below, the valleys which stretched around three sides of Kerak Castle.

Richard left his horse under a grove of trees on an eastern hill and looked out towards the castle where his family, he hoped, was trapped. He could see the town to the right of the castle, and in the distance beyond both of them was the hill over which they had ridden into Kerak the first time.

That felt like a long time ago.

Smoke still rose from the town, but this time the roofs of the buildings were caved in and some walls had fallen down with them. The population of the town had changed, too, for now it was home to some of Saladin's men. The town was far away but Richard could make out the shapes of people moving to and fro between buildings. He could see some catapults as well, wooden structures with piles of stone ammunition beside them, and men winding back their shooting arms. A stone was placed in a catapult bucket and soon after, the contraption loosed its projectile over the rest of the town and at the castle, which it crashed into and broke some yellow bricks away from one of the towers.

The defenders of the castle did not impassively watch as their fortifications crumbled around them, instead they used their own smaller catapults to launch their stones back at the Saracens. When he thought to look for them, Richard could notice plenty of their smaller stones scattered around the town. The Christians had effectively destroyed their own town defending themselves.

Beyond the town, and dotted across the hills behind it, were a series of large Saracen camps. Riders on horses and camels moved from one to another, and the smoke from the camps fed a cloud which hung over them.

Richard ran his fingers down the rosewood tree next to him as he studied the scene before him. The almost velvety smell of the trees flooded him, their scent as overwhelming as the task before them.

'There's no army here waiting for us, then,' Bowman joined him to scrutinise Kerak.

'I suppose Guy will have to share his glory with us,' Richard muttered. 'If we prevail.'

'If we survive,' Bowman put a hand on his shoulder. 'And I don't know if the German will, his thigh is looking bad.'

'We've all got through wounds like that before,' Richard said.

'Aye,' the blonde man sniffed the air, looked at the trees, then left whatever he was thinking unsaid.

'The sun's rising behind us,' Richard said.

Bowman nodded. 'So it is.'

'Which means no one would have seen our cross until sunset anyway.'

'If we still had it.'

Richard gazed over the ring of valleys the castle stood defiantly in the centre of. 'It really is a cauldron, isn't it? Something is going to happen here, I can feel it.'

'It's happening right now,' the blonde knight said, 'the Saracens are breaking into Kerak.'

Ishmael finished securing their stolen bedouin camels and joined Richard under the rosewood tree. The guide watched for a moment. 'There is too much activity. The bedouin were right, the enemy is pushing for an assault.'

'The defenders won't enjoy that,' Richard mumbled.

Bowman rubbed his inner thighs. 'Well, young lord, I didn't enjoy riding the camel, but you still all made me do it.'

'It got easier,' Richard shrugged, 'and we wouldn't be here yet if we'd stuck to the horses.'

'What do we do now?' Bowman asked. 'Now that we are here with no cross, and no army to inspire.'

Richard tapped the linen bag which hung from his shoulder. It had a chunk of the abandoned cross in it, although he wasn't sure why he had bothered. His eyes searched for the Templar compound he had left his family in. He couldn't see it, for the town was just about big enough to obscure the building.

The guide nodded to himself. 'My brothers will end Saladin's life here. Word will have reached whomever we have placed by his side.'

'How long will it take?' Richard asked.

'The command may have reached the Assassins, but they strike when they are ready.'

'But the siege is still happening,' Richard said, 'it should have been done by now. I have seen enough of your kind not to accuse them of cowardice, but could they have failed?'

Ishmael remained tightlipped.

'Could they have failed?' Bowman asked. 'You do all seem to die very easily, I have to say.'

'No Assassin fears death. Only failure, and Saladin is worried about us already, he will be well prepared.'

'We can't wait any longer,' Richard said, 'look at the walls, they aren't as steadfast as they seemed when we were first here. There will be a breach in the defences soon.'

'Patience,' the guide said.

'I can't stand here and watch the Saracens slaughter my family,' Richard said, 'not when I don't know if the Assassins have already tried.'

'You see,' Bowman said to the guide, 'he's not very good at waiting. Although in this case I agree with him. How do we know your people aren't already dead?'

'We do not.'

'Can we do it?' Richard asked.

Ishmael blinked a few times.

'Well, can we?' Richard asked again. 'It only takes one good strike to kill a man, and with a dagger I'm as good as anyone.'

'I do not disagree with that,' Ishmael said, 'but do you genuinely wish to kill Saladin yourself?'

'I don't want to,' Richard said, 'but at the rate the wall is falling, tomorrow my family will be killed unless I do.'

'You are no Assassin.'

'Actually,' Bowman said, 'he has quite literally done this before, and to a king no less.'

The guide frowned.

Richard felt embarrassed and the memory of how he and Nicholas had killed an Irish king scratched at him. 'That was different.'

'This is different,' Ishmael said, 'this is different to all other tasks because Saladin is expecting an attempt.'

'Why?'

'Because we have tried before.'

'Oh, great,' Bowman groaned, 'so he truly will be ready.'

Ishmael sighed. 'You are not skilled enough to reach him.'

'I don't need to reach him,' Bowman grinned, 'one arrow will do, won't it?'

'Really?' Richard asked.

The blonde man's grin faded.

'It needs to be a knife,' Ishmael said, 'even without this man's lack of aim.'

'Can you do it?' Richard asked.

The question hung in the scented air, although the guide neither blinked nor showed a trace of emotion. 'Perhaps,' he said after a moment, 'but it is hard when the Assassin is not already in employment in the target's household.'

'I know if we do this, then we won't come back,' Richard said.

'Don't throw your life away so easily,' Bowman said.

'I'm tiring of it, anyway,' Richard half grinned, but his friend didn't grin back.

'I will attempt it,' Ishmael said, 'as my order has commanded it. But we will both die, whether we succeed or fail.'

'We still have to try.'

'While I will attempt it if you insist, think first,' Ishmael said. 'You are rash, do not act too quickly out of haste or fear. I am prepared to die for my order, but it is not my task. The men we have in Saladin's guard or household will strike when appropriate, it is better to wait for them. Their chances are far better.'

'What if that's after Kerak falls?' Richard asked. 'I'd rather fail beforehand and spook Saladin into breaking the siege and going home. Before he kills my children.'

'If the worst should happen,' the guide said, 'then God has willed it and you should accept His will.'

Bowman snorted. 'He's not one for accepting anyone's will, God's or otherwise.'

Richard shook his head. 'I'm not accepting it. I'm going to kill Saladin and I'm going now. I can't sit around here waiting for someone else who may or may not do it in time.'

'Think it through, young lord, and listen to the guide. Don't get yourself killed unless you absolutely have to. Who will care for your children if you die?'

'The Marshal will.'

The blonde knight laughed. 'You honestly think so?'

Richard nodded. 'The sun and heat have changed him, they have forged him into a new man. He promised to look after them, and I think he will keep his word.'

Bowman crossed his arms, the folds of his bedouin robes ruffling as he did so. 'It's your life.'

'It is,' Richard replied, 'but look at the castle, it's being slowly degraded.'

Bowman let out a long breath. 'Fine, young lord, I think we're all dying here, anyway. I'm sure we'll all go with you.'

'No,' Ishmael said, 'it is bad enough for just one who does not speak the language. If there are more of you, our chances lessen. Two of us are needed to get through the guards, but only two.'

'That sounds sensible,' Richard said, 'Bowman, when we go, can you find some wood to make a new cross? Then display it when the army arrives?'

The blonde man looked around at the rosewood trees. 'Shouldn't be too hard, we've got an axe.'

'No,' Richard said, 'it has to be more convincing.'

'The last one wasn't very convincing.'

'Then hammer some nails into the new one,' Richard said, 'find something impressive.'

'I have no idea what you're talking about,' the blonde knight said, 'but I'll do my best.'

'We just need a cross here when Guy finally arrives.'

'If he arrives,' Bowman said.

'I think he will,' Richard said, 'he needs to, or he will lose any authority he has. And even if he failed to become regent, the king will send an army to relieve Kerak. You know how important everyone says it is.'

'I doubt the fool will manage to become regent,' Bowman scoffed.

'I actually think he'll manage it. Not for long, mind.'

Bowman shrugged. 'Who cares? Sarjeant and I will see what we can find for a new cross for you.'

'It's not for me. Although you can bury me under it.'

'If they leave anything to bury,' Bowman said with a stony face.

Richard locked eyes with his friend for a moment. 'It doesn't matter. But thank you for everything.'

Bowman nodded. 'If it looks too difficult, just turn around.'

Richard nodded back, then turned to the guide. 'Let's go.'


The two camels lurched along the track which led to the largest Saracen camp. It sprawled out from the town and part way up the hills which surrounded it. Richard wrapped his robe around him and pulled his beard out of it. It was long enough now for him to pass for a Saracen, or at least he hoped it was.

Ishmael rode next to him, the track well worn now and littered with horse and camel dung which no one was picking up. A caravan of camels waited at the outside of the camp for permission to enter, their cargo of bundled arrows wrapped in hides but weighing down the animals.

The guide rode along the caravan, ignoring them, and Richard knew he had to keep his mouth shut. He didn't need to ask Ishmael to know the mood in the camp, though. Men moved around or sat in groups speaking to each other in hushed tones, there was no singing or dancing, and Richard knew they could sense the moment of danger for them drew near. They expected an assault just as much as Richard did.

A company of ghulams left the camp in pairs, and Richard

had to fight an urge to stare at them. In their armour, they looked more like Christian knights than he felt comfortable to admit.

Ishmael stopped at a barricade in the road and spoke to one of many sentries. Their chatter was rapid and Richard could make no sense of it, but Ishmael grinned and the sentry laughed and waved them in.

'What did you tell him?' Richard whispered once they were clear.

'Nothing,' the guide watched the nearby tents and fires, 'I told him his mother was happy to see me last night.'

'And that worked?'

Ishmael shrugged. 'We look like bedouin, sound like bedouin, and smell like bedouin. But the sentry thinks the assault will begin tomorrow or the day after.'

Richard frowned. Darkness was falling and the glow of fires washed over the hills as the Saracens prepared for the night. 'Then tonight is the night,' he whispered. 'Tonight is the night Saladin dies.'

Inside the camp, Ishmael tossed a coin to a boy to look after their camels, then they dismounted. Richard didn't like the smell of the beasts, although he had grown used to it.

He followed the guide as he walked through the camp until they reached a stone well. Ishmael let the bucket down.

'What are we doing?' Richard asked.

'What we would be expected to be doing after a long journey,' the guide replied. He studied the camp around them. 'We should look to buy some food.'

Richard's stomach rumbled almost in response, and he nodded.

Ishmael led him to a campfire where he bartered for some cakes. They walked away and ate them. The cake had a peppery and citrusy flavour.

'Cardamom cake,' Ishmael said, 'it is only made by my people, but these soldiers are mercenaries from the east.'

Richard liked the small cakes, and slipped one into his bag to give to Bowman if he made it out of the camp alive.

The guide walked through the campfires, taking a winding route towards a great pavilion that stood covered in gold in the centre of the camp. As they drew near, Richard's apprehension rose. There were more armed men and he could see fences around the pavilion. He started to worry.

A man walked towards them. He was a short man with dark eyebrows and tanned face, which marked him out from everyone else in no way whatsoever.

Ishmael's hand slid inside the folds of his robe. Richard didn't do the same, although Sir John's dagger was inside if he needed it.

The short man stopped and held up two empty hands. He said something in Arabic and then turned to Richard. 'Your face is like a fire in the night. All can see what it is.'

Richard was taken aback. He was even sure knew the voice.

'What are you doing here?' the man asked, then shook his head. 'Nevermind, just go away before you're caught.'

Richard stood his ground. 'We have a task.'

'Do you remember me?'

Richard nodded. 'From the Mount of Olives, you are Count Raymond's man.'

'Ah,' Ishmael said, 'Miles the Syrian, you have delivered messages to my people. I have seen you before.'

'Then you know I am a man of my word and that we are on the same side. Leave. Whatever it is you wish to do, turn around and go back. You walk like a westerner.'

Richard frowned. How did a westerner walk?

'There is only one reason you would risk coming here,' Miles said, 'and you can't succeed. You need a reason to get within the fences, and a reason to get inside his pavilion. Then there are rooms within that tent filled with guards you need to get through. You can't fight through, not without an army. So don't even try.'

Ishmael looked to Richard. He clenched his fists. 'There has to be a way in?'

Miles nodded. 'If you are a known servant or an army commander. Are you either of those?'

Richard gritted his teeth. He felt his motivation slip away, leaving a hole which was replaced by a sense of loss. 'But the siege has to be broken.'

'Leave that to me,' Miles said, 'I have delivered a message

from Count Raymond and I'm awaiting Saladin's reply. If it is favourable, then Kerak will be saved.'

Richard scowled. 'You were in Saladin's tent? You should have killed him when you had the chance.'

'Kill him?' Miles shook his head. 'Another would take his place and the Saracen tide would continue to batter our shore. Saladin is reasonable and cautious, and that is something we can use to slow him down, to buy ourselves time. Saladin's replacement might be more aggressive, and despite what everyone says in public, our kingdom is weak and vulnerable.'

'The siege needs to end,' Richard said, 'before Saladin breaches the wall.'

'On that we agree. But I will not kill Saladin, especially when I approached as a messenger. That is a sacred and protected duty, and besides, I have no wish to be cut down in Saladin's tent.'

'I have no such worry,' Richard said, 'let me accompany you to receive his reply, and I shall do it then.'

Miles checked no one was too close to listen. Then he shook his head. 'I would not do that even if I could. You would never be allowed in, you are not known. Raymond will negotiate an end to the siege. Saladin is a wise man, and courteous, too. Do you know of the wedding which took place here?'

Richard nodded.

'Saladin agreed not to bombard the tower in which the ceremony took place, and he has still not aimed his catapults at it. He does not wish to harm the great ladies of the kingdom. This is a man we can make a deal with.'

'The army of Jerusalem should arrive soon,' Richard said, 'I don't think you'll have time for your deal to be struck. Either Saladin will breach the walls, or the Christian army will arrive and fight him off.'

'The king is too unwell to lead it,' Miles said, 'which is why Count Raymond seeks another way.'

Richard didn't want to mention Guy. 'I think the army will be here regardless.'

'Then you have no business in the camp. Leave now,' Miles said, 'before we are overheard. We should not be seen together as it is.'

Ishmael put a hand on Richard's arm. 'Saladin is more cautious than ever. There is nothing to be gained by the guards killing us before we even enter the pavilion.'

'I have to try.'

Miles's face flashed red. 'Saladin fears the Assassins. He has surrounded his tent with lime ash so their footsteps are recorded, and he has guards surrounding his tent as well as within. There are lanterns hanging all around the tent, ropes with bells no one can climb through, and other contraptions I have not seen. Do not waste your lives, especially as your attempt would endanger mine.'

Richard glanced at the guide, but his dark eyes bored into him and he said nothing to contradict Miles.

'So we go back without even trying?' Richard asked him.

'I have no problem with dying, but I do not seek a pointless death,' Ishmael replied, 'and it is apparent that we cannot reach our target.'

Richard scuffed the ground with a foot, but checked himself before he got too carried away, although also because his toe stung.

'Turn around,' Miles said. 'If the army approaches, then this will be a battlefield. If you are captured, you will be tortured to death. Leave now.'

'There is nothing we can do here,' Ishmael said.

Richard turned back to the castle, which he could see over the town that separated him from it. A catapult stone hurtled through the air and crashed into the top of a tower. A shower of bricks fell from it and smashed into the ground below in a cloud of dust. 'Fine,' he hissed, 'but I'm not happy about it.'

They left Miles, retrieved their camels, and rode back in the dark around the cauldron and to their tree-topped hill.

A night breeze rustled the leaves above them as they tethered their camels. No fire lit the camp, but in the gloom Richard could hear the snorts of horses and the swishing of tails that fought against a horde of buzzing insects.

Richard found his companions sitting under a tree. Bowman stood up to greet him, a wide smile etched on his face.

'Are you that pleased to see us?' Richard asked.

'The fact you are still breathing means you failed,' Bowman

261

said, 'but it means I get to show you what we found.'

'What?' Richard's eyes narrowed. 'Did you find wood for a new cross?'

The blonde man shook his head. 'We didn't find any nicely cut timber lying around, no.'

'Then what are you so happy about?'

The blonde knight's eyes shone. 'Come and see this,' he said and beckoned Richard to follow him into the woods.

Richard tripped on a root as the undergrowth closed in. 'What is it?' he asked with annoyance. 'Before I lose my teeth falling over.'

'It's over here,' Bowman crouched down at a bush and dragged something out from under it. It was long, and then the arms of a cross appeared.

Richard couldn't believe his eyes. 'What is that?'

The blonde man stood up and put his hands on his hips. 'It's just what you wanted, young lord, it's a cross.'

'A cross. I can see it's a cross. Where did you find it?'

'I've told you before,' Bowman grinned, 'don't go asking questions you don't want to hear the answers to.'

'Is it made out of gold?' Richard could see it glint faintly as beams of moonlight darted here and there through the canopy above.

'Well,' Bowman said, 'I don't think it's all gold, I think they have just covered it in a layer of gold.'

'Where did you get it from?'

'Are you sure you want to know?'

'No,' Richard replied, 'but tell me anyway.'

'You see,' the blonde man began, 'we went looking for a village, seeing as the villages here should be loyal to the lord of Kerak, so we followed the first road we found.'

'You stole the cross from a loyal Christian village?'

'Who do you think I am?' Bowman asked.

Richard raised his eyebrows.

'I'm hurt,' Bowman said, 'but I'll have you know that we did not take it from Christians.'

'Then how did you find it? You didn't get it from the Muslims.'

'Actually we did,' Bowman's grin caught the moonlight. 'On

the road, we came across two men with the cross strapped to a pack-camel. Sarjeant snatched the reins while I chased the men off.'

'So you did steal it.'

'From the enemy,' Bowman complained. 'They stole it first. I'm sure we can give it back once the Saracen army leaves.'

'Gerard will know this isn't the true cross,' Richard said.

'The last cross wasn't the true cross, either,' the blonde man replied with a shrug. 'So why do you care if this one is?'

Richard looked down at the cross, which was almost as large as the last one. 'I suppose a cross is a cross.'

'We can drag it out to the edge of the woods in the morning,' Bowman said, 'and stand it against a tree. When the army arrives, they'll look at the castle and see the cross standing above it.'

'It won't look so big from there,' Richard said. 'And how will they know it's supposed to be the true cross?'

'Because Gerard will be there telling them it is,' Bowman said, 'he told us to take it here, so he'll be expecting to see it.'

'Guy won't be,' Richard managed a smile, 'and God help him if I see him again.'

Bowman's face darkened. 'He's as bad as Maynard, they both tried to kill us.'

Richard made the sign of the cross. 'Maynard atoned. I don't think Guy knows the meaning of the word.'

Bowman nodded grimly. 'Aye, the squire did.'

'Thank you,' Richard said, 'this cross might just do the job. The army can decide if it is an omen, a curse, or the true cross, but we've done everything we can.'

'They will be happy to see it,' the blonde man said, 'they will rush towards it and lift the siege.'

Sarjeant found them. 'You like our cross?' he beamed.

Richard chuckled. 'I'm more surprised at your involvement to be honest. This seems more like a Bowman-scheme than something you'd do.'

'I shall do whatever gets me out of the Holy Land the quickest. I never want to smell or taste cloves again.'

Richard smiled at his old friend. 'If I ever own land again, I'll ban cloves from it.'

Sarjeant, his face more worn than before, smiled back.

Brian shook Richard awake. He lay on his back with the sun glinting through the branches which swayed softly above him. The smell of the rosewood hit Richard next, but only then did Brian shake him hard enough that he truly woke up.

'What?'

The monk's eyes were bright and he pointed towards Kerak. 'They're here.'

'Who is?' Richard rubbed his eyes. He'd slept fitfully, dreaming of chasing his children through a dark forest in which he could only ever catch fleeting glimpses of them.

'The army,' Brian said, 'the army of Jerusalem.'

Richard's dream evaporated. He sat up, pushing Brian out of his face. 'The cross, fetch the cross.'

Bowman and Sarjeant dragged it from within the wood, leaving a trail of sand behind them.

Otto groaned from next to Richard, the German's face covered in sweat and his face red. Richard would find someone to tend to him once the enemy had gone, but there was little he could do for him now.

He followed the cross and helped Sarjeant and Bowman lift it up and lean it against the last tree in the wood. The sun was behind them, so the gold remained in the shade.

Two catapults loosed stones at the same time, the thumping noise of their arms echoed around the valleys, and their stones reduced Kerak still further. The Saracen camps were hives of activity, groups of horsemen wheeled around and bodies of infantry congregated.

Brian came to watch, wiping sweat from his brow. 'Look, there,' he pointed beyond Kerak to the northern road on the most distant hill. The road on which Richard saw banners. He felt the tension within himself release, tension he hadn't realised he'd been holding. The vanguard of the army of Jerusalem galloped along the road, specks in the distance, but Richard could identify one group as turcopoles by the speed and manner in which they rode.

'The Templars are in the vanguard,' Brian said, his voice high with enthusiasm.

'Come on,' Richard urged them on, 'ride all the way, ride all the way to Saladin's pavilion.'

Bowman looked back at their golden cross. 'The sun isn't on it.'

Sarjeant sighed. 'Then this didn't work. They shall not see the cross in the shade. It is just another tree over this distance.'

'If they attack,' Bowman said, 'then it worked.'

The Templars rushed along the road, and Saracen horsemen rushed to meet them. The enemy got close, then turned and spread out, loosing arrows as they went, although those were too small to be seen from so far away. The Templars chased them but didn't catch them, and after a short pursuit, they stopped and retreated.

'What are they doing?' Richard moaned. 'Fight them.'

'They are just the vanguard,' Sarjeant said, 'the army will need to arrive and prepare a full attack.'

'We don't have that time,' Richard said, 'not if they take all day.'

The army of Jerusalem took all day. A village of tents sprang up on the road, and smaller Christian camps orbited it. Horsemen and infantry moved all over every hillside, but they never formed at the edge of the camp to advance. All day they made their camp, and all day Saladin's catapults continued their bombardment of the castle the army had come to save.

Richard watched the sun drop below the horizon behind the Christian camp on their distant hill. 'Well, that didn't work,' he said mournfully. He sat on the ground and pulled the hood of his robe over his head.

Bowman leant against a tree behind him. 'Guy is a coward,' he said, 'so I'd wager Guy is leading this army.'

Richard thought the blonde man was probably right. 'Maybe he's spotted the cross. He stole our packhorses because he didn't want the cross to steal his glory, so maybe he's outraged and waiting for the Saracens to come and take it down.'

Bowman grunted. 'No one in the enemy camp is looking this way, they'll all be looking at the new army. I think we're safe.'

Richard sniffed and drummed his fingers on his leg. 'Maybe they aren't paying that much attention to the castle, either.'

Bowman sat up. 'I know that tone, young lord, it sounds like you've got an idea. Please keep it to yourself.'

Richard watched the fires on the wall of the castle and the fires in the town. 'This idea is a great one,' he said.

'It can't be any worse than the last one,' Bowman said, 'but I still don't want to hear it.'

Richard turned to the blonde man and grimly nodded. 'While everyone watches to see what Guy will do, we're going to break my family out. We're going into Kerak.'

# KERAK

Getting past the Saracen sentries was just as easy the second time around, because Ishmael found the same one as before and traded insults as their camels took them by.

Richard and Bowman were dressed in their bedouin robes, their mail and swords left behind in the bushes where the golden cross had been hidden again. Armed with only concealed daggers, they left their camels with Ishmael and made their way into the town on foot.

They passed campfires where men slept or nervously found things to occupy themselves with. Great lines of grazing horses and camels crisscrossed the landscape, and their odour floated on the breeze and was strong enough to warm the cooling night air.

Richard could see the army of Jerusalem on their hill, fires ablaze, but it was into the ruins of Kerak's town that he and Bowman walked. They stepped over and around chunks of masonry that reminded Richard of the chunk that probably still lay outside the door to Yvetot's church. Rats scurried between their feet, rats that were fatter than they should have been, and somewhere in the ruins, a group of Saracens burst into laughter.

The two of them walked between buildings and rounded a corner to come face to face with one of Saladin's catapults. The engine of war was unattended, its crew elsewhere, so Richard hurried past it.

Bowman followed, but then paused and ran back to it. He

examined a few parts of it, then half slid out the iron pin which held the arm onto the weapon's frame. He returned to Richard and winked.

They edged closer and closer to the castle, and snuck between two groups of guards when they reached the edge of the occupied area. Bowman peered around corners and led the way slowly as they reached the foot of the castle unseen, cloaked by the night.

The stone wall towered up above, but the wall was broken and piles of rubble lay all around. Richard crept away from the gateway, however, and over to where the mountain under the castle fell away to the valley floor. Hugging the yellow walls, and with dust rubbing off onto their robes, they skirted the base of the castle until they were away from the town and the sloped skirt of the castle was beneath them. There was barely enough room to walk between the wall and the almost sheer slope.

'Don't look down,' Bowman grinned, then looked up.

Richard did look down, but focused on where his feet were going. He had to step over some caltrops, twisted pieces of iron scattered by the defenders to pierce the foot of any attacker who stood on them.

'Maybe we should look down a bit,' Bowman said when he spotted them. 'It's been a while since you've complained about a foot injury, and I'm enjoying the peace of that.'

Richard ignored him and the pain from his toe which he had deliberately not mentioned, and instead looked up at the tall walls he needed to scale.

'What is your plan?' Bowman asked him. 'We don't have a ladder, and we aren't climbing this without one.'

'I was going to ask,' Richard said.

'Ask?'

'Hello?' Richard shouted up at the walls.

Nothing happened.

'Is anyone there?'

Nothing but the wind made any sound, except for a dog which barked in the town.

'There has to be someone there,' Richard bellowed.

And he was right, because his cry was answered by a

crossbow bolt. It shot down at them, missed, and clattered off the stone skirt under the castle.

'We're Christian,' Richard shouted, 'don't shoot.'

Two heads appeared above, their iron helmets reflecting the moonlight.

'We're from the relieving army,' Richard said, 'help us up.'

Bowman pressed himself against the wall in anticipation of another missile, but what came down the wall instead was a knotted rope.

Richard smiled at his friend. 'See?'

Bowman rolled his eyes. 'Yes, but you're going up first.'

The climb caused Richard's muscles to burn, and his hands stung when he reached the top and was hauled over by two defenders. Their faces were hollowed with worry and their hands were dirty. Their surcoats were red but covered in yellow dust and black oil from their armour.

Richard stood on the wall and brushed himself down.

'You are dressed like an infidel,' a guard with a narrow nose said.

'How else were we going to get this close?' Richard replied. He gazed into Kerak, a long castle on its long ridge, and inside it stood stone and wooden buildings which had been pelted by catapult stones, many of which remained where they had rolled to a halt.

A baby cried from inside, and Richard remembered why he was there. 'Where are the families being housed?'

The guard shrugged. 'Everyone is wherever they please.'

Richard considered the castle's towers and the buildings nearer the gateway. 'We'll start at the stables, as that's the only place they could be keeping our horses.'

'Horses?' the narrow-nosed guard spluttered into a laugh. 'We've eaten all of those.'

'Eaten?' Richard cried.

Bowman caught Richard's arm as it plunged into his robe to retrieve his dagger. 'You don't need to kill him,' the blonde man said, 'it's not his fault.'

'If someone's killed my horse, I'll find everyone in this castle who has eaten even a single mouthful, and kill them.'

'Then you'll have to kill Lord Raynald and all the highborn

ladies,' the guard replied.

'So be it,' Richard tried to shrug Bowman off, but his friend was bigger and stronger.

'What happened to no more killing, young lord?'

'That was before someone ate my horse,' Richard shouted, 'I'll kill them all.'

The guard backed away into his companion. 'They're just horses,' he said, 'it's not as if they're of any use during the siege.'

Bowman almost lifted Richard off his feet as he tore him away from the guards. 'Come on, the stables will be near the gatehouse so it won't take us long to find. Let's find your family and see if we can calm you down.'

'You're not going to calm me down,' Richard let Bowman push him towards a tower. 'Let go of me.'

'Very well,' the blonde man pushed Richard into the tower's doorway. The tower once had a fighting platform at its top, but that had been knocked off and moonlight therefore lit the staircase as they descended.

'If my family isn't safe,' Richard's words echoed down the spiralling stairs, 'I'll gut everyone.'

Bowman ran two steps at a time behind him. 'You sound like Guy now, calm down. Don't let it overcome you.'

'Just as you didn't let your rage overcome you when you saw Geoffrey Martel on the field at Corbie?'

'Alright,' Bowman said as they reached ground level, 'then do better than I did.'

'I'm not calming down,' Richard strode across the bailey, the battered gatehouse on his right and various damaged buildings to his left. He passed a family lying dead where they had sheltered, a crow with an ashy-grey coat pecked at one of their heads.

Richard's blood cooled when he saw another family huddled behind a broken wall, the mother's belly large and the father's face scarred with some kind of rash. Their child was so thin he marvelled that it was still alive.

Bowman caught up with Richard as he was questioned by a guard who was missing a hand. The stump was bandaged, but he still pointed his sword at what he thought were two bedouins.

'Get out of my way,' Richard told him, 'we're Christians.'

'You're dressed like heathens,' the one-handed man said.

'Are we?' Richard ignored the sword point and pushed it aside. 'I hadn't noticed.'

Richard entered the longest building in the bailey, which he correctly guessed would be the stables. It was a long barn with no partitions or stalls, the floor coated in a thick layer of straw, and a high roof. Normally, horses would have been tied along the two long sides next to each other, but now there was just one, and it was loose.

A band of men jumped away from the wild sword swings of a man, a man who was old but moved like he was far younger.

'Gerold?' Richard frowned in the dark stable. Two holes in the roof let the moonlight in and shone a blueish light on the confrontation.

A dog in the stable barked but Richard couldn't see it.

Bowman bumped into the back of Richard and pushed him onto the raised bed of straw. 'What's going on?'

The men spread out and two tried to grab the horse. It spun around, mane flying through the air, and its hind legs kicked one in the ribs with an almighty crack.

'Gerold?' Richard shouted.

'My lord?' Gerold shouted back.

Richard realised what was happening. He drew Sir John's dagger and ran over the spongy straw.

Gerold fended off a man who was quicker than him, and he backed up towards the wall. The invisible dog barked viciously, and a man with a long stick poked at the darkness where the dog presumably was.

Another attacker cut at the horse with his sword, but the animal jerked its head out of the way and retaliated with a hoof.

As Richard ran, he was sure a smaller figure wielded a sword next to Gerold.

'The Red Child,' Bowman shouted as he ran behind Richard, 'while it's nice to see him doing something useful, it's probably best if he doesn't kill anyone.'

Richard un-gritted his teeth and realised the blonde man was right. He slammed to a halt and took the biggest breath he

271

could. 'Stop, in the name of the Knights Templar,' he shouted at the top of his voice.

The combatants froze.

The dog stopped barking and the horse walked into a beam of silver light which almost made his coat shimmer.

'Solie?' Richard asked.

Solis whinnied his high pitched whiny and trotted straight past the man who had been trying to eat him, knocking him to the straw with a bump. The stallion shoved his face into Richard's and pushed him back a step.

Richard couldn't speak, a tear of joy ran down his face and he rubbed the yellow horse's nose.

'That horse is a Templar horse,' Bowman coughed when he reached the battle site, 'he is not to be eaten.'

'Orders have been given,' the man facing Gerold said, 'all horses can be eaten.'

'Not this one,' Richard had to push Solis's head out of the way as the horse tried to lick him.

'He's food, and we're tired of eating rats.'

'This horse,' Richard had to push Solis aside, 'is a crusader. He is a Templar horse, and Templars do not eat their horses. Haven't you heard the story of the second crusade, where everyone else ate their horses, then were defenceless when the Turks attacked?'

The man scratched his neck.

'And who saved the crusaders who'd eaten their horses?'

'The Templars.'

'And how did they do that?'

'Because they had given their own rations to their horses,' the man looked down at the straw.

'Exactly,' Richard said, 'so you will go without food, and this horse will remain strong.'

'But we aren't Templars.'

'I am,' Richard approached the man, Solis following over his shoulder.

'You don't look like one, you're dressed like an infidel.'

'Do you see this horse?' Richard asked. 'Can you see the cross on his flank? He's taken the cross, he is a Templar horse, and if you are still in this barn by the time I catch my breath, I will kill

272

all of you.'

Bowman grinned. 'He is not joking, and we have come a long way to save this horse, so I suggest you walk away while you still can.'

The men picked up their comrade who had several broken ribs and helped him out of the barn.

Solis pinned his ears back and went to run at them, but Richard shouted at him and he came back to lick Richard again.

Judas emerged from the shadows with his tail wagging and sat down next to Bowman.

Gerold sheathed his sword. 'We've been in here for days keeping men like that away. I never thought I'd see you again.'

'You'll never believe who we found,' Bowman beamed.

Richard elbowed him. 'More of a what,' he said, 'we found the true cross.'

'Incredible,' Gerold said, 'there's a rumour going around that it was stolen from Jerusalem. Who stole it?'

'No one stole it,' Richard said, 'it was in the keeping of an old man full of remorse.'

Gerold frowned and looked at Bowman.

'Don't look at me,' the blonde man crouched down and rubbed the black dog's belly.

The Red Child put his sword away and approached, his red hair and dark eyes showing no sign of fear from the confrontation he had been part of. He stopped so close to Richard that he felt an urge to back away from the child, but the child halted and looked up. His sword, the full sized sword taken from Sir Thomas's hall in Normandy, and that had been dragged along the ground ever since, finally broke through the bottom of its scabbard. The waxed linen thread that held the leather together gave way and the sharp blade poked through, and promptly stabbed Richard's unarmoured right foot. He hopped away and looked down as red stained his brown leather shoe.

'I'm sorry,' the Red Child stepped back.

'It's not your fault,' Richard shook the foot but it didn't help.

'No,' Bowman said, 'it's yours for letting him keep that sword. He's far too young for it.'

'No, I'm not,' the Red Child's eyes flared.

'He isn't,' Gerold said, 'he killed a man on our retreat into the castle.'

'Of course he did,' Bowman muttered.

'How did you gain entry into the castle?' Gerold asked.

'We asked nicely,' Richard replied.

Gerold shook his head ruefully. 'You certainly have your father's intelligence. But why? Why would you come into this place when things are so desperate?'

'To get you out,' Richard said, 'to get my children out.'

Gerold rubbed his chin. 'Then I am afraid that your bravery has been in vain.'

'Why?'

'Your daughter is ill.'

'Lora?' Richard's heart beat loudly in his ears and he thought of the rash he'd seen on the man outside the stables. 'What is wrong with her?'

'A sweating sickness. Many have had it here, many have died, and she cannot be moved.'

'Take me to her,' Richard said.

Bowman stood up from Judas. 'I'll stay here with the horse. And you, young Henry the man-slayer, you stay here on guard with me.'

The Red Child stood tall and nodded up to the blonde man.

Richard left the stables, although he had to tie up Solis to stop him following, and with each step he made his foot bleed more from the Red Child's sword wound. He went with Gerold to a house with too many families all huddled together in it. He could smell their waste and their fear, and could see a small stream of what he hoped was water flowing downhill and out of the front door.

'Lora?' Richard asked into the dark room.

A figure stood up from the middle of the mass of humanity hiding within. 'Richard?' it asked.

Richard's eyes acclimated to the lack of light and he could see it was Alice who shuffled towards him. Her hair was matted and the silver circlet was gone. Dark circles marred her typically clear eyes.

Richard saw a boy next to her and recognised him as his son.

'Alexander,' he crouched down.

Alexander reeled back and threw his hands up. 'A Saracen, help me,' he cried.

'No,' Richard said, 'I'm your father.'

Alice caught the boy as he fled. 'Alex, it really is your father, be polite. Go to him.'

'But he left us again.'

Richard was torn between his heart breaking at the look on his son's face, and the frustration of having to explain himself yet again. He squatted down and forced a smile. 'Are you looking after your sister?'

Alexander shook his head. 'I'm too young to do that. Aunt Alice is doing that.'

'Aunt?' Richard looked up at the Lusignan woman.

She shrugged. 'They have no mother and are aware of the dangers in the world, why not allow them a small comfort?'

Richard gave his son a hug even though the child tried to wriggle out of it. 'I suppose they need someone when I'm not around.'

'Which seems to be all the time,' Alice said.

'You sound like,' Richard stopped himself as something caught in his throat. He let his son go and he returned to Alice while Richard wiped his eyes.

A man in the house coughed several times loudly and Richard wondered how safe it was to be in there. 'Why are you living here with common folk?' he asked. 'My children are nobly born.'

'In the beginning we stayed within the inner walls,' Alice said, 'but when the food started to run out, the high born ejected all those they didn't favour.'

Richard bit his tongue. 'Cowards. If Lora suffers more, then I will hold Lord Raynald personally responsible.'

'As if you are powerful enough to make such statements,' Alice sneered, 'you are a Templar knight are you not? You are a dog following your master's commands. You cannot make threats against the great men of the kingdom. Settle for looking after your children, if you are even allowed to do that.'

Richard's anger returned, but he choked it down. 'I am here, aren't I? What more can I do?'

'You could have taken us with you.'

'You know I couldn't, women and children cannot travel with the order on their business.'

'Your daughter needs care, care which only holy houses can offer,' Alice stood so close to Richard he could see two lice making their way through her tangled hair.

'I am working to lift the siege,' he said, 'but I came here to get you all out.'

'She cannot move,' Alice said.

'So Gerold told me, but your brother is here with an army, so it seems we will have to rely on him to drive the enemy away.'

'Guy is here with the army?' Alice frowned. 'I thought he rode with you?'

'He did,' Richard nodded, 'until he didn't. He returned to Jerusalem to become regent and raise an army to relieve Kerak.'

'So that is his army on the hill?'

'I think so,' Richard looked at his daughter who was asleep.

Alice sighed. 'My brother, I have come to see, is nothing but a craven fool. He will not attack unless victory is assured, he would rather watch us starve to death.'

'That's why I'm here, to rescue you before Kerak falls.'

'How many times do you need to be told that Lora is too weak to move?'

Richard thought he could see his daughter shivering under her blankets. 'I can see that she can't move, but I can take Alexander out at least.'

'I won't go,' Alexander cried and hugged Alice's leg.

Children, Richard thought to himself, they were so much more difficult than horses.

'You can't get your horse out either,' Alice said, 'the gatehouse is being bombarded so you can't rightly ride out of it. Or winch him over the walls, I can see what that head of yours is thinking.'

'I doubt I can get him in a sling again,' Richard said.

'He's only drinking clove wine now,' Alice said, 'and we've just run out of that, so he's refused water all day.'

'Maybe horses aren't easy either,' Richard mumbled.

'What?'

'Nothing.'

'I'm sorry you can't get your horse out,' Alice reached out and held Richard's hand, 'I know you value him at least as highly as your children.'

Richard just pursed his lips.

The Lusignan woman smiled. 'No other man I've ever met sees their horses as anything other than tools.'

'There is no reason why you can't feel affection for your tools,' Richard said.

'You are most odd.'

Gerold had remained outside, but holding up his cloak over his mouth, he entered the house. 'You could take Alexander out of Kerak. I will stay here and protect your daughter and horse.'

Alexander narrowed his young eyes at Gerold.

'I can't separate him from his sister. And if we can't all ride away, it's more dangerous outside the castle than in it.'

'You should leave while you can,' Alice said, 'I will keep her safe, at least if the sickness does not claim her.'

Richard closed his eyes. 'This has all gone horribly wrong. I wanted to get you all out and now I'm going to just leave you all again. I know what my father felt.'

Gerold put a hand on Richard's shoulder and squeezed. 'Despite what the priests tell us, I do not believe that the sins of the father pass to the son.'

'And yet I seem to relive them,' Richard groaned, 'I have forgiven my father's sins.'

'He would be proud of you,' Gerold said.

'He was,' Richard said to himself.

Gerold wrinkled his face.

Richard almost told him, but the old man's eyes were soft and Richard didn't want to break his heart. 'Thank you, both of you. If we survive this, there will be better times for us.'

A woman in the building's corner screamed, and an older woman next to her checked her. 'The baby is coming,' she announced.

'No, not now,' a man complained.

'Tragedy surrounds us,' Alice squeezed Richard's hands, 'but knowing you are here will give us hope. Go and make my brother help us.'

The pregnant woman screamed and grabbed the man next to her.

'What is wrong with her?' Alexander asked.

'She is having a baby,' Alice replied, 'and then she will die.'

Alexander frowned. 'Will Lora die?'

Richard started to lie but caught himself. 'The truth is,' he said to his son, 'I do not know. Pray to the Lord and give her all the food and water you can. Be there for her, can you do that?'

The boy nodded. 'Are you leaving us again?'

Richard pressed his lips together to steady himself. He nodded.

Alexander peered up at Richard with his round eyes and his family nose. He sniffed. 'We are used to it,' he said, 'we will be well.'

Richard swallowed.

'You should make haste,' Gerold told him, 'the faster Guy attacks, the better for all of us.'

'What makes you think I can do anything to influence Guy?'

Gerold shrugged. 'I am sure you will think of something.'

Richard thought about it. 'I will. I will either get to Guy or get to Saladin.'

'Saladin?' Gerold almost choked.

'I'll get to him,' Richard said, 'and I'll lift the siege.'

Alice punched Richard gently in the chest. 'Don't you dare, you'll never get out alive.'

'No,' Richard looked into her eyes, 'but you might.'

Alice blinked away whatever she felt.

Richard stepped away from her, said goodbye to Alexander, and left the claustrophobic room as the pregnant woman wailed into the night.

He rushed back into the stable.

Bowman looked up from the dog. 'Where is everyone?' he asked.

'Lora can't travel and Solis can't leave because we can't go out through the front gate. And no one else wants to go.'

'So what was the point of this?'

'Now I know my family is alive,' Richard glanced at the Red Child but felt little for him.

'We can take this one,' Bowman nodded at him.

'No,' the Red Child said, 'I will stay to protect the horse.'

'Really?' Richard squinted at him through the moonlight.

The Red Child stepped forward and nodded. 'It is my duty and I will see it through.'

'You are just a child,' Richard said, 'I can get you out of Kerak, why wouldn't you want that?'

'I will prove myself to you,' the Red Child crossed his arms.

Bowman laughed. 'He surely means it, he sounds a bit like you.'

'He's not mine,' Richard snapped, then regretted it when the Red Child's face saddened. 'I'm sorry, you know I didn't mean it.'

'I'll show you,' the Red Child stuck his chin out, 'your horse will be alive when you return, or I'll be dead beside him.'

Bowman shrugged. 'Well, he's made his choice. What are we doing now, young lord?'

'We're going back to Ishmael, and then the three of us will fight our way to Saladin.'

'Right,' the blonde man raised his eyebrows. 'We've already tried that once, and you were persuaded not to follow it through, or have you already forgotten that?'

'No,' Richard said, 'but we're out of options, unless you think we can convince Guy to attack the Saracen camp.'

Bowman sighed. 'No, I don't think anyone can convince him of anything.'

'Which means we'll have to find a way to get to Saladin,' Richard said, 'he's only a man, and he is surrounded by men, and all men make mistakes.'

Bowman didn't bother to argue, and instead told Judas to stay. The dog whined at him as he left, and Bowman was uncharacteristically quiet as they made their way across the bailey and to the point on the wall where they had climbed into Kerak.

The rope was coiled up on the parapet, and the two guards were still at their posts.

'Let that back down,' Richard asked them.

'No,' the guard said, 'you can't leave, that's deserting.'

'We came in with a message,' Richard said, 'and now we're taking an answer back.'

'No one told us that,' the guard replied, 'you need a written order with our lord's seal on it to leave the castle.'

'I don't,' Richard said, 'we are not part of your garrison, are we?'

The two guards exchanged a glance.

'If we leave,' Richard added, 'your food will last a little longer.'

'That is a fair point,' the second guard picked up the rope and hurled it back down outside the wall. 'You had better be going then.'

'Mind you, it's safer inside than out,' the first guard said as Richard clambered onto the battlements, which hurt his bleeding foot, and started to lower himself down.

'We're going anyway,' Richard said.

'Your problem,' the first guard said.

'Their funeral,' the second added, and they laughed.

'Probably,' Bowman clapped one on his shoulder and followed Richard down the rope.

Richard let himself down the rope, his injured foot causing pain each time it gripped a knot, until he was close enough to the ground to jump. He let go of the rope and landed on the stony ground, straight onto a caltrop. His left foot burst out in pain as the iron tip ripped through his flesh and appeared through the top of the foot.

Bowman placed himself down more carefully. 'What did I tell you?'

'I forgot about them,' Richard picked his foot up and jerked the caltrop out. He threw it with venom down the mountain and swore.

'You'll struggle to sneak up on Saladin now,' the blonde man managed a wry grin.

'It's not funny,' Richard's foot felt as if a red-hot coal burned away inside it.

Bowman glanced along the wall towards the enemy camp. 'I don't think they've heard you, but you better be quiet from now on. We don't want anyone looking too closely at us.'

Richard took a tentative step and winced. 'I'll do my best, but I can't run.'

'Good thing we don't want to run,' Bowman picked his way back between the two Saracen guards and they reached the buildings around the catapult. Except that now the crew had returned and were winding the arm back.

Bowman signalled at Richard to wait, so he sat down and rubbed his feet.

'We can't creep past them,' Bowman whispered, 'we shouldn't be here and they will know it.'

Richard was too busy wishing his feet didn't hurt to think too much about it.

Bowman swore under his breath as the catapult clicked into place and the crew started a prayer. It sounded like a song, drifting through the night, but at the end of it, the crew's captain triggered the weapon. The arm holding the stone snapped forwards with a great rush of air, but the pin holding it in flew out of place and the arm flipped over itself and landed on one of the crew members. The stone ammunition flew up into the air and towards Kerak, but the unfortunate crew member cried out as his leg was crushed by the now detached wooden catapult arm.

Bowman slowly turned his head back to Richard with a huge grin across it.

'Can we go?' Richard hissed.

Bowman nodded. 'Look normal.'

They got up and walked past the catapult as the crew clustered around the fallen comrade and levered the catapult arm off him. Richard made the sign of the cross once they were safely beyond the catapult, then followed Bowman back towards their camels.

Richard hobbled slowly, but in the dark and in the bedouin robes, no one gave them a second glance.

Ishmael asked Richard what had happened by raising his eyebrows at him, and Richard responded with a shrug. Then he looked up towards their tree-topped hill to see if the cross was visible.

'I can't see it, either,' Bowman said.

'No,' Richard said, 'but look.'

The blonde man had already seen, and after a sharp intake of breath he whirled round. 'Torches.'

'Someone is riding up the hill,' Richard said.

The guide snapped his head around, saw the five

or six flaming torches making their way along the road, then untied his camel.

'Someone is going for the cross,' Richard said.

'It could just be a foraging party,' Bowman looked at his camel with disgust.

'At night?' Richard asked.

'Fair point,' Bowman mounted his camel cautiously while Richard did the same. Both his feet hurt in the stirrups but he couldn't worry about them now. He needed to get up to the hill and make sure Brian, Sarjeant, and Otto were safe.

'It's too far,' Bowman whispered as their camels moved into a walk.

'We can't just abandon them,' Richard said.

'They'll hide,' Bowman said, 'I'm sure they'll hide.'

'I hope so,' Richard said, 'because we won't get there in time.'

# CAKE

An owl hooted as Richard raced up the mountain on his camel. Bowman and Ishmael were behind him, their camels all going as fast as they could through the night. Richard cursed the owl. Why did there have to be owls here, too?

Hoofprints occasionally dotted the track, but Richard didn't need to follow them to know where the men with the torches had gone. They rode fast, as fast as horses would have, and as the lights from the siege grew dimmer behind them, suddenly Richard could see torchlight flickering through tree trunks up ahead. He thought about dismounting and approaching carefully on foot, but his feet hurt, and he knew time was against his friends who had stayed amongst the trees.

Richard burst out to where the cross had been, but it no longer stood against its tree. Otto was still propped up against his tunk, except he was motionless and the bodies of three Saracens lay around him.

In the clearing, Brian struggled between the grip of two men, men larger and stronger than him, who dragged him towards their comrades on horses who waited on the road.

Bowman and Ishmael skidded to a halt beside Richard as they all baulked at the scene they'd interrupted.

Four Saracen horsemen, two with torches and two with their swords already drawn, raised them and yelled a loud war-cry.

Another two Saracens who already stood on the ground drew back their bows and let arrows fly. One hit Ishmael in the shoulder and another caught in Richard's robe.

Ishmael's camel was hit by the next two arrows before the guide could dismount, and the animal roared and bumped into Bowman's as both panicked. The guide was thrown to the ground where he landed awkwardly, and Bowman slid off his camel as it turned and bolted back the way they'd come.

Richard got off his own camel as it was likely to be the next target for the arrows, but when he hit the ground, Ishmael still lay on it and Bowman rubbed his head after he'd landed awkwardly.

The four Saracen horsemen charged at Richard, who backed away from their oncoming horses. He drew his dagger and waved it at them, but it felt horribly inadequate.

Bowman got up to his knees and looked up. An arrow narrowly missed his neck and he fumbled to find his knife.

The horsemen thundered on, and Richard knew he had nothing to fend them off with. He held Sir John's dagger above his head. 'Surrender,' he shouted at Bowman.

'There's only a few of them,' the blonde man cried. An arrow grazed his thigh despite his robes and he winced. Bowman looked up, considered the eight men against them, their own lack of protection, and threw his knife down. 'Fine, there might be too many of them.'

Richard closed his eyes as the horsemen slammed to a halt in front of him, showering them both in a fine mist of white dust. When he coughed and wiped the dust clear, something hit him square in the face, and his vision was lost.

Richard opened his eyes a moment later to find a Saracen pointing a sword at him while another tied his hands together with a rope.

Bowman almost punched a Saracen but thought better of it and gave in. Their captors shouted at them, but their words were foreign and Richard looked for Brian.

The monk's hands were bound in front of him and a Saracen already led him from his horse.

'Are you hurt?' Richard shouted to him, and received a blow to the face for his trouble.

Brian shook his head, but his eyes went to Otto, who still hadn't moved.

The German's head faced the leaves above him and his eyes

were open. Richard gritted his teeth and the Saracen behind him pushed him and he stumbled, his head aching and his feet hurting with every step.

The cross was gone, and Richard noticed drag marks leading back into the trees. Sarjeant must have dragged it away, because his former steward was nowhere to be seen. That was good, Richard thought, at least someone might have got away from this mess. Three maces lay around Otto, one snapped at the shaft, and Richard felt sorry for the man. It was only because of Richard that he was here.

But he didn't get any time to mourn the Hospitaller, because Bowman was punched in the face and dragged next to Richard. A Saracen with pale face and blue eyes peered at them and asked them a question, but Richard could only shrug back. The Saracen shook his head.

Richard glanced into the trees to where their weapons and mail had been hidden, and luckily it looked like the area remained undisturbed. At least the cross hadn't been found.

The Saracens briefly checked the surrounding trees, but it was dark and the cross had been hidden deeper than they had so far ventured. Richard waited to hear the sounds of Sarjeant ambushing them as they conducted a superficial search, but no sounds came. Instead, two Saracens went to Ishmael and dragged him over to the pale-faced man. Richard thought he might be their leader as he seemed to give them orders. The man's face recoiled with disgust when he pulled out two of the guide's daggers. The knives were small but sharp, and the pale-faced man immediately pulled Ishmael's unconscious head up and slit his throat. Blood drained out onto the white, stony ground, illuminated by torchlight, and the man stored the Assassin's knives in a bag. He barked more orders while Richard watched the life leave the guide. He'd liked him.

Bowman coughed out some dust but he didn't feel like getting hit again, so otherwise maintained his silence.

The two of them were tied up in a line with Brian, and led behind a horse back down the mountain. It was a slow walk with a torch-bearing Saracen right behind them, and each step made Richard's feet seem so painful that he prayed they would fall off. It was also a long walk down towards the camp, and despite the terror their destination filled him with, Richard craved an end to the walking. He had to endure stares from the Muslim inhabitants of the camp that engulfed the town, Richard didn't suppose too many other prisoners had been taken since the town itself had fallen. Luckily the darkness tempered his humiliation, which was also overshadowed by the burning pain coming from both of his feet.

Relief came when they reached the Templar compound where he had once deposited his children.

'That's ironic,' Bowman muttered as they were all led in.

The tower that crowned the compound had partly fallen, but the main walls were intact, and inside they were taken to a chamber with no window and what looked like a carpet for a door.

Each end of the rope that bound their hands was tied to a ring on the wall, and because of that, they were left to stand or sit in the middle of the room with no chance to move.

A guard stood in with them, but he didn't look concerned and contented himself with taking a drink from one of several waterskins which lay on a table. A kind-looking Saracen entered and dropped a bag next to the waterskins. He said something to the guard, who grunted, put his drink down, and turned to face the captives.

'It's not like we're going anywhere, is it?' Bowman mumbled to himself.

The kind-looking man watched them.

Brian groaned. 'At least you are well, they killed the Hospitaller.'

'I saw,' Richard said, 'at least he took some with him.'

Bowman shrugged. 'He was gone anyway with that wound.'

'We should have been allowed to bury him,' the monk said.

'The Saracens didn't even bury their own,' Richard watched the kind-looking man watch him back. 'Which seems strange.'

'They were in a rush to capture the cross,' Brian said, 'they did not stumble on us.'

'I don't think we should talk about that,' Richard said.

'Why not?' Bowman coughed up some grit.

'Because I think he can understand us,' Richard stared into the Saracen's eyes, but they were unmoving.

'Him?' the blonde knight looked up. 'He looks as simple as the rest.'

Richard waited to see a flicker of anything, but the kind-looking man remained impassive. He thought about everything Ishmael had told him, searched for something, then had an idea. 'Christ is the true prophet, your Muhammad is nothing but a false prophet.'

The kind-looking man's eyes flared, only for half a moment, but they flared.

'There,' Richard nodded, 'he understands us.'

The Saracen sighed. 'Where is the cross?'

'What cross?' Bowman asked.

The kind-looking man didn't look so kind as he swept across the room and cracked Bowman in the face with the back of his hand. 'That is for calling me simple.'

Bowman had to lower his head to his hands to rub his face.

'We saw the cross, too,' Richard said, 'we went to find it. It isn't ours.'

'You are the leader,' the Saracen stood above Richard.

'I wouldn't really call him a leader,' Bowman said, and was again hit in the face.

'Stop talking,' Richard told him.

'He sounds like the leader,' the Saracen said. He walked over to the table and took out one of Ishmael's knives. 'Do you know what this is?'

'A knife?' Richard replied.

'The man rode with you, so I think you know.'

'He was our guide.'

The kind-looking man thought for a moment. 'Do you know whose people carry these knives?'

Richard shook his head.

The Saracen opened Richard's bag, which was also on the table. He took out the cake Ishmael had bought for them in the camp. 'Do you know what this is?'

'Food,' Richard said, 'our guide gave it to me. I don't know if he bought it or made it.'

The kind-looking man watched Richard for a while. Richard wondered if the man was avoiding naming the Assassins.

'How did you employ the guide?'

'We are fresh from the west,' Richard said, 'we asked a man at the port for a guide, and he sent us the man who you killed.'

The Saracen spat onto the floor. 'He was a dog. What was his name?'

'We never asked him,' Richard replied.

The Saracen snorted. 'Of course not, why would you? Why are you wearing bedouin robes?'

Richard had to think before answering. 'When we saw the cross on the mountain, we knew we could only reach it in disguise.'

The kind-looking man raised his eyebrows. 'It is no matter, in daylight we shall search for the cross. It will be found.'

'Are you going to take us to see Saladin?' Richard asked.

The man's face broke into a frenzied laugh. 'You are mad. Maybe you are truly fresh from the sea. Do you think Saladin wants to see you?'

Richard had heard a lot about the man. He also wanted to kill him. 'I'd quite like to see him.'

'So would I,' the kind-looking man said, 'but I have only ever set eyes on him from afar. The likes of you are not fit to worship the ground he stands on.'

'What if I had something important to tell him?'

The Saracen laughed. 'You do not. I do not even need to pull off your fingernails to know that.'

Brian's hands flinched.

'Do not mind your hands, monk,' the kind-looking man said, 'it is your head you should be afraid for. In the morning, as the sun rises, you will be given a choice. You will be asked to convert to the true faith.'

'Why would we do that?' Bowman asked, his voice stifled by the blood oozing from his nose.

'Convert and be sold into slavery, that is the best you can now hope for, infidel.'

'You are not selling it,' Bowman replied.

'No, I am selling you.'

'I will not convert,' Brian said almost firmly.

'Then you will die.'

'Oh,' Richard said, 'that's the choice, is it?'

The Saracen nodded and folded his arms.

'Why didn't you say so?' the blonde man said. He coughed. 'Then why don't you tell me of your religion?'

'You can't convert,' Brian shouted, 'you cannot forsake Christ.'

'I can,' Bowman said, 'what's he ever done for me?'

'What's he?' the monk lost his words and looked to Richard for help. Brian shook his head and stared up at the Saracen. 'I shall stay true to my faith.'

'Then at dawn you will die.'

Brian pressed his lips together. 'That is fine by me, I've seen enough death, my own is of no matter.'

'Slow down,' Richard said, 'we've got until dawn to think about it.'

'What is there to think about?' Brian asked. 'You can't just convert either, you're a Temp...'

'Brian,' Richard shouted, and the monk stopped. 'I know what I am,' he searched for the words, 'I'm a temporary pilgrim to the Holy Land, but you don't need to go shouting about it.'

The monk frowned, then understood.

The Saracen groaned. 'It matters not, you can continue to argue without me having to hear you. Your voices scorch my soul. If we do not find the cross and you convert, then I will pull out your teeth until you reveal the truth. Otherwise, you have until dawn to decide your fate.' The kind-looking man threw Ishmael's knife onto the table and left his guard alone with the prisoners.

Richard sat down and let out a breath. 'Brian, what were you thinking?'

'About what?'

'You nearly said I was a Templar, and you, you joined too. Do you not remember what happens to captured Templars?'

The monk shrugged. 'It's happening to me tomorrow anyway, why prolong it?'

'I've never been too close to Christ,' Bowman said, 'perhaps this Muhammad can offer me something more?'

Brian blinked at the blonde man.

'I don't know,' Richard said, 'I can't help my family if I'm dead.'

'You can't be serious?' the monk cried. 'You will both burn in hell.'

'How bad can that be?' the blonde man sat down and sighed. 'Do you never listen to priests?'

Bowman chuckled. 'Have you ever seen me listen to a priest?'

'I have only ever seen you in one holy building which wasn't being pillaged or destroyed.'

Bowman nodded. 'There's your answer, then. I'm for staying alive.'

'It's not dawn yet,' Richard said, 'maybe we can escape?'

'Not with that guard watching us,' Bowman looked at the Saracen who sat by the table trying not to fall asleep. 'Even if he does look like a camel.'

'I wonder where Sarjeant is,' Richard said, 'I hope he is unhurt.'

'Well they didn't capture him,' Bowman said, 'and I didn't see his body. From the sounds of it, they never saw him.'

'The sensible thing for him to do would be to get into Kerak and rejoin my family,' Richard said.

Bowman groaned. 'This might be a surprise to you, young lord, but not everything is about you. Sarjeant is allowed to fend for himself, it isn't normal to just break into a besieged castle. Besides, he doesn't know your family is even alive in it, does he?'

Richard lowered his head into his bound hands. 'You're right. Hopefully he's making his way to the Christian army as we speak.'

'If he doesn't end up here with us,' Brian muttered.

Richard pulled at the rope around his wrists, but it just made them tighter.

'He might be a terrible bore,' Bowman said, 'but I hope the old man makes it.'

'He's not that old,' Richard said. Then he wondered if he was going to get any older himself, or if the morning would bring the end. He almost didn't mind the idea. In the silence, he heard the occasional thwack of a catapult, and then a distant crash when its projectile hit the castle, but he couldn't sleep.

It was two cats fighting outside their room that jolted Richard fully awake from the stupor he'd unwittingly fallen into. Their screeching cut through him and he sat up and saw the faintest glow of sunlight coming through the curtain that was their doorway.

A catapult shot and the resulting crash was a loud one. There was a low rumble and then a cheer.

Bowman awoke with a start, his eyes looking around. 'What was that?'

Richard gulped. 'I think they've breached the wall.'

The cheers grew louder and the blonde man rubbed his eyes. 'That's the only thing they'd be cheering so hard for.'

Richard sighed. He could feel his wounded feet pulsing, and patches of dried blood soiled the floor where they'd spent the night. 'Great,' he said, 'so I'm stuck in here to overhear the final assault, just so I can hear my family being murdered. I might as well choose death alongside Brian.'

'It doesn't have to end like that,' Bowman said, 'just convert.'

Brian opened an eye. 'No, don't.'

Richard thought about it again. 'I'm not living as a slave, will you? Think about it, serving someone else, being bound to them, not having your own thoughts or actions.'

Bowman raised his eyebrows, congealed blood underneath them. 'I serve you.'

'That's different,' Richard said, 'or at least I hope it is.'

The blonde knight sniffed, a slight upward curl on his lips. 'It is, young lord, but I'd leave you if you got too big for yourself, and don't forget it.'

'I promise I won't get too big for myself for the rest of my life,' Richard grinned back. He looked down at the ropes. 'But I'm not converting. I'm not betraying what I believe in. What my father died for.'

'He didn't die for his God, he died for you,' the blonde man said.

A drumbeat struck out in the air and a trumpet blasted a succession of short notes.

'So repay him by staying alive,' Bowman added.

'He wouldn't want that,' Richard replied.

'Fine,' Bowman sniffed and tried to touch his nose but couldn't quite reach. 'I will just have to die alongside you, then. I hope that makes you feel quite guilty.'

The sound of footsteps rushed by the compound, and their

guard woke up.

'He's not the quickest,' Bowman watched him.

'I think they are gathering to assault a breach,' Richard said.

'That's quite obvious,' the blonde man said as a horse flew by outside with its rider shouting something, his voice excitable.

'It's going to happen,' Brian sighed.

'This would be the perfect time to break out, wouldn't it?' Bowman grinned.

'Do you have a plan?' Richard asked.

Brian looked up as if doing so would help him hear what was happening outside. 'It is as if God has sent the opportunity when we decided to remain faithful.'

'I think the breach happened first,' Bowman said, 'you were just asleep. Like a typical monk.'

'Monks get up early. But what is your plan, then, that will take advantage of God's grace?'

Bowman chuckled. 'Plan? I don't have a plan.'

'You sounded like you had a plan.'

'Well,' Richard said, 'we're all sitting here tied to the floor and that guard is sitting over there, and I don't think there's much we can do about it. We've tried pulling the rings out of the walls.'

Bowman shook his head. 'As simple as it is, this prison isn't one we can get out of. There is nothing sharp we can cut the rope with. Chewing through it would take a week.'

Brian's face paled. 'So we actually do have to die?'

'I'm not going quietly,' Bowman turned to the guard. 'You, fetch me breakfast.'

The guard stared back.

'He can't understand you.'

'I know, I'm trying to annoy him,' Bowman said, 'if he came close enough we could kill him.'

The guard sat back on his chair and didn't get up.

'Come on,' Bowman shouted at him, 'you must want to punch me in the face?'

The guard turned his attention to the table and the wineskins on it.

Outside there was another rush of feet.

'They will start soon,' Richard said.

Bowman sighed. 'It doesn't look like we're going to conjure up a clever scheme here.'

The curtain was pushed out of the way by a robed hand and a bedouin entered the room. The guard half looked up, but didn't seem too interested.

'Oh, no,' Brian moaned, 'they haven't forgotten us. I thought they might forget us. They're going to kill us in front of the castle, aren't they? To herald their attack.'

Richard nodded. 'That's quite a good idea, let's hope neither of them understand you.'

The bedouin spoke to the guard.

The guard didn't look up but handed him one of his array of waterskins.

Richard thought for a moment that the man was a rather broad bedouin. The man sniffed the waterskin.

'Cloves?' the bedouin shouted and the guard looked up at him in shock.

'Cloves?' Richard repeated as the bedouin threw the waterskin at the guard, then lunged at him and knocked him off his chair. The two men slammed onto the hard floor and bumped against a table leg, which rattled everything on top of it. The bedouin was the bigger man, and he hit the guard's head against the table leg once, then twice. The guard went limp and the bedouin drew a dagger and made sure of his permanent silence. The thrown waterskin leaked red liquid all over the white stone floor, pooling in depressions and filling the room with the scent of cloves.

'What's happening?' Brian asked.

The bedouin stood up and looked over the table.

'Fighting over wine?' Bowman asked.

'He said cloves,' Richard said, 'but not in Arabic. Don't you see?'

The bedouin sniffed one waterskin, tossed it aside, then tested another. He turned around and gazed down at the captives.

'Sarjeant?' Richard asked. 'You came back for us?'

Sarjeant lifted the skin to his lips and drank.

'Cut these,' Bowman shook the ropes that bound his wrists, 'what are you waiting for?'

Sarjeant swallowed. 'I haven't drunk a drop of anything for over a day, and he offered me clove wine? I'm drinking this water before I help anyone.'

Bowman shook his hands more frantically. 'Don't get me wrong, I've never been happy to see you before, and I am now, but God's legs, what are you waiting for?'

'Did you not hear me?' Sarjeant drained the skin and searched for another. 'I am thirsty, so very thirsty.'

'Come on,' Richard said, 'let us out, they will be back for us soon.'

'I don't know,' Sarjeant said, 'everyone is running around outside, they are all very excited.' He finished another skin, threw it onto the guard's lifeless body, and nodded.

'Curse you and your drinking problem,' Bowman snarled. 'Cut our ropes.'

'You have a strange way of saying thank you,' Sarjeant said.

Richard held his hands up. 'I didn't know you spoke Arabic.'

'You didn't ask, did you?' Sarjeant crouched down and held his bloodied knife out.

'Sorry,' Richard shrugged. 'I know you spent time here, but didn't think about it.'

Sarjeant cut the ropes around Richard's wrists and for a while they hurt even more. He tried to shake the pain away.

Sarjeant freed the others as Richard went to the table and retrieved his dagger and bag. He added Ishmael's knives to it.

Bowman took his own knife and Brian said a prayer.

'We aren't free yet,' Richard said, 'we're still in their camp.'

'We do still look like the bedouin,' Sarjeant cleaned his knife and put it away.

Richard nodded. 'Luckily. Everyone, it's time to leave.' He pushed through the curtain and into the courtyard. There were fresh horse droppings by a tie-rail, but there were neither horses nor men present. In the direction of the castle, a cloud of dust rose from the town, and everywhere there was shouting and the beating of drums.

Sarjeant pointed south. 'There are horse lines that way, we can easily steal some horses and get away from here.'

Richard looked east, towards Saladin's pavilion.

'No you don't, young lord,' Bowman said, 'not now we've just saved our skins, don't even think it.'

'We should kill Saladin.'

Bowman looked up to the sky and groaned, the black sky which had a blue tinge to the east as dawn approached.

'This is our one chance,' Richard said, 'to stop the assault before they enter Kerak. You know what happens to anyone inside once they break through the walls.'

Bowman frowned because he did.

Richard didn't wait for any more complaints and left the Templar compound. Outside on the street, a horse narrowly missed running him over, but he ignored both it and a company of archers who moved behind the horse at speed.

Richard made for Saladin's great pavilion, turned a corner and was almost knocked off his feet by an advancing cavalry detachment.

In a square in the distance, bundles of arrows were unloaded from camels and being dished out to horse archers.

Richard decided to go a quieter way, down the next street, but when he entered it, a familiar face stared back at him. Twenty paces away was the kind-looking man, but upon seeing Richard his face changed to fury.

'Back,' Richard retreated, 'back.'

'What?' Brian stumbled into him.

'Oh,' Bowman realised and grabbed the monk to haul him out of the street.

'Run,' Richard said as loudly as he dared, and they all sprinted back along the street and back past the Templar compound.

A chorus of trumpets sounded from the direction of Saladin's tent, but that was behind them now as they flew towards the edge of town.

Richard turned down an alleyway, ran a few steps and realised it was a dead end.

Bowman pulled up beside him and wheezed. 'We started in an alleyway that wasn't an alleyway, I suppose it's only fitting we end in one.'

Richard frantically searched for a way out, but the alleyway backed up onto a dark wall, so dark he hadn't noticed it.

Sarjeant kicked at a door along the alley. 'Help me,' he said, 'if you aren't too busy fawning over each other.'

Richard looked down at his feet. 'I'm not kicking anything.'

Bowman glanced at the door, then aimed one solid kick where the lock was. The doorframe splintered with a crack and the door swung open with a painfully loud creak.

Sarjeant was inside before Richard could say anything, and he followed into a long chamber the length of the alleyway.

In which sat three men, all dressed in Christian clothing.

'Miles?' Richard gaped at the man who dropped his pottery cup when he saw the intruders. It smashed on the ground but Miles was too stunned to care.

'What are you doing here?' Miles asked as everyone flooded into the room.

'Shut the door,' Richard spun around and closed it behind Brian. 'Is there something we can push up against it?'

Mile frowned. 'Why?'

'Because a furious-looking Saracen is chasing us.'

'Use the table,' Miles stood up and grabbed the long table that was the centrepiece of the room. Together they jammed it against the broken door, ignoring the plates that fell from it as they went.

'Lean on it,' Richard said, 'in case they try to push it open. And be quiet.'

Bowman put his weight on the table. 'I'll hold it.'

'Shush,' Richard added his own weight and then waited.

'If they catch me helping you,' Miles hissed.

'Whose side are you on?' Richard whispered. 'Maybe Gerard is right about Count Raymond?'

Miles didn't answer because he heard footsteps from the alleyway that wasn't an alleyway.

Brian's eyes were wide and his lips tight as shouts came from their pursuers. A man tried to push the door open, but it didn't give way. He tried again and something hit the door with a thud.

There was another shout, and then the footsteps faded away.

Richard sank down to the floor as the tension in his stomach tightened into a ball. 'If they hadn't breached the wall, we'd never have got away with running through the town.'

'God gives with one hand and takes with the other,' Brian said.

'Shut up,' Bowman snapped.

Richard looked up at Miles, who sweated and breathed heavily. 'Why are you still here in the enemy camp?'

'As I told you before, I am on the count's business.'

'I thought you were waiting for a reply, that must have come by now?'

Miles only shrugged.

Bowman stretched his arms out and rubbed his wrists. 'I think perhaps he's been working a bit too closely with the enemy.'

'Saladin is not in a rush to respond, he was probably waiting to see how his siege went.'

'Quite well, it seems,' Richard moaned.

'Precisely,' Miles said, 'so you can see why I am still waiting for my reply.'

'That doesn't matter now,' Richard said, 'and we don't have time for this. We need to get to the pavilion.'

Miles closed his eyes and sighed. 'We have been through this before, have we not?'

Richard's eyes gleamed. 'We have, but I've got an idea. Will Saladin watch the assault?'

'Most likely,' Miles replied, 'if it were to succeed, then he would want to be there to gain personal glory from it. But have you already forgotten what I told you about the risk of replacing him?'

'What if I promise not to kill him?'

'Here we go,' Bowman walked around the room looking for food.

'Of course you won't kill him,' Miles said, 'you will never have the chance to.'

'I'm not looking for your permission,' Richard crossed his arms, 'and you can't hold us here.'

'I have two men,' Miles stood tall, but still he was shorter than Richard.

Bowman laughed as he found a loaf of bread and ripped it in two. 'Even the old steward can take those two men by himself. You'll all be dead before I finish this bread.'

Sarjeant puffed himself up and both of Miles's men took steps back.

'We are leaving,' Richard said, 'thank you for your concern, but I suggest you do the same.'

'You are all idiots and will get me killed along with you,' Miles said.

'Do you want Kerak to fall?' Richard walked towards the door which fronted onto the main street.

Miles shook his head.

'And do you think the Saracen assault will succeed now that they have a breach?'

Miles folded his arms and said nothing.

'Well then,' Richard said, 'let me try. There is no harm in trying, is there?'

'Very well,' Miles said, 'if Kerak falls, then Jerusalem is almost undefended. The kingdom itself hinges on Kerak staying in Christian hands.'

'Then get out of my way.'

Miles stood aside, and Richard gingerly opened the door. It let in the sounds of trumpets and more horsemen riding by, but the search party had moved on.

Richard left the chamber, followed by his companions, and they took the quietest route possible towards the great pavilion in the neighbouring encampment.

From around the corner of a building, Richard caught sight of it and the open space around its fencing. Three companies of foot soldiers formed in neat squares in front of it, facing the entrance, as a man strode out surrounded by well armoured bodyguards.

'It's him,' Richard gasped. He could only see the back of the man, slim and shorter than he'd expected, but wearing mail armour on his arms and with a billowing green cloak around his shoulders. He wore a conical helmet that seemed to be heavily inscribed with something in gold, but walked swiftly and with purpose. The companies of foot soldiers chanted something at him as he passed between them and into the town.

'Good,' Richard said, 'he's going to watch the assault.'

Bowman peered over Richard's shoulder. 'I never thought we'd see him, but how do you suppose we kill him now? There's a few hundred men between him and us.'

'Remember what I told Miles?' Richard grinned. 'We aren't going to try to kill him.'

'What are we doing, then?' Bowman asked. 'He's walking away from us.'

The foot soldiers marched off behind their leader, leaving the open space looking very empty.

'We're not here for Saladin,' Richard said, 'we're here for his tent.'

The screens of the great pavilion acted like the surrounding wall of a castle, and as Richard examined one, he knew he couldn't just knock them down because their posts were braced with thick wooden buttresses.

Bowman tried anyway. His first kick did nothing, and his second rattled the joins between the screens, but then Richard told him to be silent.

'Someone will hear that,' Sarjeant looked left and right along the screens.

'They're all with Saladin,' Bowman jumped up to grab the top of the screen and tried to pull it down. It didn't move.

'Enough,' Richard said, 'he's right, someone will hear that, and you can't pull them down.'

Bowman gave up and swore. 'This was your idea, I'm just trying to help.'

'Maybe we could charge the front door?' Richard rubbed his chin.

The blonde man groaned. 'And just hope that if there are any guards, they happen not to be wearing their armour, and are also fewer than us?'

'Then we need to get through these screens,' Richard said.

Sarjeant ran his hands up and down them. 'They are strong, Saladin has spared no expense.'

Richard scuffed his foot under the screen.

'That will not work,' Sarjeant said, 'it is on hard ground and even if it were on grass, we have no tools.'

'If only we had a siege ladder,' Richard said.

Bowman grinned and stood up to the wall, then held his hands together in a cup in front of him. 'I'll be the ladder.'

Richard looked at his hands. 'That's going to hurt my feet.'

'Walking is hurting your feet,' the blonde knight said, 'ignore it.'

'Easier said than done.'

'What would the Marshal tell you?'

Richard tapped his foot in annoyance but flinched from it. 'He'd tell me to ignore it.'

'Well then.'

Richard clenched his teeth and stepped into Bowman's hands. The blonde man heaved him upwards and Richard hurled himself up onto the screen. He scrambled over the top of it, then fell headfirst down the other side. He landed with a bump as Bowman's head appeared above the screen. Sarjeant helped him up and the blonde knight joined Richard on the other side, although he lowered himself down much more gently.

'You need to stop doing that,' Bowman laughed at him.

'At least there are no caltrops here,' Richard stood up.

The canvas pavilion was only a few paces away, but before it lay a smooth bed of ash and a tangle of lanterns and bells.

'How are we getting through all of that?' Richard asked.

Bowman put his hands on his hips and studied the obstacles. 'The ash is easy enough,' he said, 'we'll just smooth it back down on our way out.'

'What about the bells?' Richard said. 'The lanterns at least we can ignore, but those bells are on a tangle of ropes. It might as well be a hedge.'

Bowman sucked in a breath. 'How badly do you want to get in here?' he asked.

'You know how badly,' Richard replied. 'But I don't want a company of guards to come swarming over us. It will take us an age to climb our way through those ropes without making any noise.'

Bowman sniffed. 'I can't promise that it'll be silent,' he said, 'we just need those damned trumpets to blare again. That will be our moment.'

Richard looked up into the air and waited. Then he waited a

little longer. The trumpets didn't sound.

The blonde man had his knife in his hands and he waited too. 'They wouldn't stop playing the cursed things earlier,' he said.

'Any moment now,' Richard said and looked at Bowman. 'Any moment they'll play again.'

'What's happening?' Sarjeant asked from the other side of the screen.

'We're waiting for the trumpets,' Richard told him.

'How long do we wait for?' the blonde knight asked.

'I'm not sure, but we can't wait forever,' Richard stepped gently onto the ashes.

Bowman nodded. 'No, we can't,' and walked straight past Richard, sending a cloud of thin ash into the air, and slashed his knife down through the ropes in front of them. The first cut set a dozen bells jangling, his second cut sent half of them to the ground, and his third finished the job.

'There,' Bowman said, 'hardly any noise at all.'

Richard didn't have time to worry about it, he dug Sir John's dagger into the tent canvas and sliced it through the fabric with a loud rip. Richard pushed himself through the tear and into the pavilion.

The inside of Saladin's tent was a peculiar shade of yellow, the canvas and its golden decoration tinted the light that passed through it and cast the contents into a golden glow. The chamber contained piles of stores and led into a corridor separated by a decorated carpet hanging from a pole across the doorway. Insects buzzed around in the roof of the canvas and spiders spun webs to catch them.

Richard eased his way through the carpet-door and Bowman followed. 'Where are we going?' the blonde man whispered.

As Richard didn't have an answer, he kept going along the corridor, also bathed in a yellow hue, and came to another room. It had cushions and tables set up with shining drinking vessels and plates full of brightly coloured fruits.

'I think this is an audience chamber,' Richard said, 'so his bedroom might be at the back of it.'

'I think you're right,' Bowman whispered.

'Really? Why?'

'Because there's a guard inside it.'

Richard peered at the curtain which covered the doorway and noticed a pair of feet under it. They walked back and forth.

'If it's only one,' Bowman looked Richard in the eye.

'We don't want to kill anyone,' Richard said, 'it will ruin the effect.'

'Go on then,' Bowman said, 'if you have a better idea.'

'I only need a moment. Can you get the guard to leave that chamber and get out of the audience room for just a little while?'

Bowman cast his eyes around the room and settled on the serving table. 'Aye, young lord, I think I can.'

Richard nodded and pulled back into their corridor where he crouched down out of sight of the audience chamber. Bowmen walked into it and out of Richard's view. A moment later there was a loud crash of crockery and an orange rolled across the floor and came to a rest against the wall of his corridor.

The guard rushed out of Saladin's bedchamber, past Richard's corridor, and out towards the entrance to the pavilion.

Richard jumped up and without another thought he burst through the audience chamber, under the curtain, and into the sultan's private bedchamber.

He'd expected gold, but instead the canvas walls were undecorated and the chamber practically unfurnished. An empty wooden chest lay open, a helmet and a pile of unused mail armour still in it, and a finely decorated sword hung from spokes in the tent's ceiling that ran to a central pole. The bed was low to the ground and covered in white silk sheets. Richard reached into his bag and withdrew Ishmael's cardamom cake. He placed it in the centre of the bed, and next to it he laid down one of Ishmael's knives. That should send a clear message, he thought. Richard ran out of the room and into the audience chamber, the floor of which was covered in fruit, and then back into his corridor. He crouched down for a moment and caught his breath. His feet stung and he prayed he hadn't left a bloody trail behind him.

There were some shouts from towards the entrance to the tent, and he wondered if he should wait for Bowman or not. The blonde man had run towards the pavilion's entrance, and Richard wasn't sure how he would actually be able to escape because there were still guards there. But then, he thought, it would be better to rescue Bowman by killing the guard who chased him. Better to leave a dead guard and rescue Bowman, than leave a captured Bowman. For then Saladin would know it hadn't been the Assassins who'd left the cake. Richard stood up to go and find his friend.

The tip of a blade stabbed through the corridor wall beside him and Richard jumped out of the way. The blade sliced down far enough for a blonde head to push through it and look up. 'Help me through, young lord.'

Richard pulled Bowman through the wall, then the blonde knight reached back through the tear and pulled out a rolled up carpet. 'We can hang this over the rip,' Bowman said, 'then they won't know we cut it.'

'We? You cut it,' Richard grinned and took the carpet. It was made for hanging and he laced it to the pole above the rip.

'They won't know until it's too late,' Bowman grinned, 'and we can do the same thing to hide our entrance.'

'That's a great idea,' Richard went back to the storeroom they'd entered through, and Bowman moved a hanging carpet from another wall and laced it over the tear in the pavilion's outer wall.

Richard squeezed back through it and stepped over the fallen bells and lanterns. He got over the ash and looked back as Bowman joined him. 'Is it even worth smoothing that down?'

Bowman shook his head. 'They can't see it unless they go looking, we should probably just get out of here.'

The blonde man helped Richard back up and over the screen, and then Richard and Sarjeant hauled him over the top of it and back down the other side.

The trumpets sounded again, loudly and urgently.

'That's typical,' Richard said, 'when we don't need them.'

Bowman shrugged. 'We got in, didn't we?'

'Somehow. Now we have to get away,' Richard said.

'Finally,' Sarjeant said.

Brian stood up against the screen, his eyes moving between the smaller tents which surrounded Saladin's. 'This is terrifying, I can't wait to join the army.'

Richard paused.

Bowman chuckled. 'Sorry monk, I think our leader has other ideas.'

'What else do you need to do?' Brian asked.

'We need to raise the cross.'

'That's not a joke, is it?' Bowman asked.

Richard walked towards the nearest line of tethered horses. 'What do you think?'

The stolen Arab horses made good time out of the camp. They happily galloped up the mountain too, although Brian tried to hold his back in fear and succeeded only in annoying it.

Richard reached the clearing where Otto still lay and dismounted. Only then did he see the three horses tied to a branch of a rosewood tree.

Bowman halted his horse and noticed them. 'This is bad,' he said.

Sarjeant arrived as the dust cloud from their ride caught up and blew over them. Brian arrived next, trying to pull his horse back, but the animal had simply lowered its head to evade his bridle and charged on. It charged right past Richard, and into the other three horses, who tried to get out of the way, but their ropes held firm and they could only clatter their hooves on the ground and rear up on the spot.

Brian fell off when his horse decided to stop so suddenly that he slipped over its shoulder.

Richard and Bowman ran towards the treeline without a word, both knowing the commotion would draw out whoever owned the horses.

Richard picked up one of Otto's maces on the way, which Bowman copied. They reached the trees and dove into the bushes to catch their breath.

Sarjeant gathered their horses and started to tie them to a tree of their own.

Brian rolled on the floor, out of the way of the hooves of the agitated horses, and moaned.

Two men burst out from the undergrowth, Saracens with

drawn swords and mail armour with small metal plates sewn onto their chests.

Richard and Bowman, now behind them, attacked together. They ran silently, but the Saracens heard them anyway and turned to face them.

Richard swung his mace but his opponent was quick enough to step aside and out of range.

The blonde knight's enemy wasn't as fast, and Bowman's mace crushed his shoulder. The blow forced the man onto a knee, but that just made his head the perfect target, and Bowman didn't miss.

As the man's head crunched and squelched, Richard attacked again and the Saracen stepped into the blow and grabbed Richard's robes to pull him over.

Richard couldn't swing the mace now, so instead he poked the end of the handle into the Saracen's face and caught him square in the jaw.

Bowman's mace cracked some bones in the back of the man's neck and he fell to the stony ground.

The blonde knight's mace swung down and crushed the back of the Saracen's skull before he could get up. The mace came away bloodied, and Richard winced at the mess it left behind.

'There were three horses,' Bowman looked back into the trees.

Richard looked at Brian instead, the monk had rolled up onto his knees and rubbed his shoulder.

'Come on,' Bowman said, 'we need to find the last man.'

Richard followed him into the rosewood trees. They crouched as they walked, trying to be silent, looking through the foliage for movement and listening for sound.

Bowman stopped and narrowed his eyes. The bush next to him exploded in a flurry of leaves and branches, and the swing of a sword made Bowman fall backwards where he hit his head on the ground.

Richard spun round and came face to face with the kind-looking man.

The Saracen glanced down at Bowman, but the blonde man didn't move, then pointed his curved sword at Richard. 'You. Allah rewards me.'

Richard held his mace out and with his other hand he drew Sir John's dagger.

The now angry-looking man drew a dagger of his own. 'You have only succeeded in living for a little while longer. And I have found your cross. Saladin will reward me when I return it, he will personally speak to me.'

Richard gripped both weapons tightly. 'That isn't going to happen,' he swung with the mace and followed up with his knife but the Saracen side-stepped one and parried the other. His curved sword countered and sliced a hole in the robe on Richard's arm.

'You westerners fight like children once you are off your horses.'

Richard thought of his children, gritted his teeth, and swung the mace again and again. The solid iron head flew through the air and the angry-looking man backed into a bush, his eyes less certain now.

Richard pressed his attack until his arm started to tire and his enemy blocked the mace and stabbed with his dagger. It caught in the folds of Richard's robes, and he struck back with Sir John's dagger but it hit a metal plate on his foe's chest and did nothing but dent it.

The Saracen cut back with his sword and the tip of the blade cut Richard's cheek. He ignored it and jabbed the mace at the surprised-looking man's face. The Saracen stepped back, tripped on Bowman's leg, and fell over.

Richard lunged at him while he was still on the ground and brought the mace down onto the man's foot. Bones broke under the force of the blow and the Saracen screamed. But he didn't give up, he snatched his foot away and tried to get to his feet.

Sarjeant charged through the undergrowth, following the sounds of the fight, and with his knife he grabbed the surprised-looking man from behind and stabbed him in the neck.

Richard relaxed and watched him die. 'I suppose Allah had other ideas,' he said as Sarjeant pushed the dying man into a bush.

Bowman groaned. He opened his eyes and took in the scene. 'I see you still needed help, young lord.'

'I always need help,' Richard replied, 'and I'll need help to drag the cross out of here.'

'Allow me,' Sarjeant showed him where it was, and as Bowman recovered, they dragged it through the trees and back into the clearing. Brian dropped to his knees at the sight of it and prayed.

'Why are you praying?' Richard asked. 'You know it isn't real.'

They raised the cross up against a tree so it looked out over Kerak, and then they all took a breath.

'I cannot believe we managed that,' Bowman rubbed the back of his head.

Brian moved over to Otto, closed the man's eyes, and prayed for him.

'I suppose we can't pray for Ishmael,' Richard said.

Bowman shrugged. 'I have no idea, we can't pray to his God in his language.'

'It's our God, too,' Sarjeant said.

'Fine, I'll ask Brian to pray for him just in case it works,' Richard watched the siege.

He could hear trumpets echo around the cauldron and could see tiny figures fighting around Kerak's gatehouse. There was a breach in the wall next to it, with ramps of rubble on either side of the wall and men fighting on top of it.

'They are right on the wall,' Richard said.

'Aye,' Bowman nodded, 'but there are many more men waiting to join the fight on the enemy's side.'

Richard looked over at the camp of the Christian army. 'We need them to attack now. There isn't much time.'

'It doesn't look much like they're moving,' the blonde man said.

'No it doesn't,' Richard sighed.

'This is the moment the Kingdom of Jerusalem rises or falls,' Sarjeant said, 'that castle cannot be taken.'

'So you keep telling me,' Bowman said, 'but the cross is here now, give the army a moment to see it.'

'Well, get out of the way then,' Richard pushed Bowman aside, who'd been standing right in front of the tall golden cross.

'How long do we wait?' Sarjeant asked.

Richard frowned. 'The sun is behind us again, so no one can see the cross, can they?'

'We're in the shade,' Bowman said, 'so, no.'

Richard wondered if Gerold was one of the men fighting at the breach. It wouldn't surprise him if he was. 'Bowman, set a fire under the cross. Sarjeant, gather as much dry wood as you can. Brian, pray for Ishmael next. I'll get our weapons and armour out from the bushes and we'll re-arm.'

'Then what?' Bowman asked. 'Are we going to charge into Kerak to lift the siege by ourselves?'

'Yes,' Richard said, 'someone has to.'

Richard slipped another of Otto's maces into his belt, then put his torn bedouin robes back on over his two layers of mail and his sword. He felt much better coated in so much metal, and as bright flames rose beneath the cross and Brian finished a reluctant prayer for their guide, they prepared their horses.

'This wood burns fast,' Bowman tightened the girth on his horse.

'It only has to last longer than the siege,' Richard mounted his slight Arab horse.

Bowman snorted. 'We'll be fine then.'

'Very funny,' Richard looked down on Kerak. The battle on the wall still raged, but up on the mountain where the Christian army waited, something stirred. Small groups of riders moved around outside the camp.

'I think they're arguing,' Sarjeant said, 'I think they've seen the cross and they're arguing.'

'This does mean the leper king isn't here,' Bowman said, 'because he is brave and would have already attacked.'

Richard thought his friend was doubtless right. 'I'm convinced it's Guy.'

'Some are riding forwards,' Bowman watched some horsemen ride out towards the nearest Saracen camp, which sat on the next rise in the landscape.

'That's not a full attack,' Richard said, 'I think it's just turcopoles.'

'The Templars and Hospitallers will attack because they do not need Guy's permission,' Sarjeant said, 'but alone they will not prevail.'

'Then we'll have to stop the attack ourselves,' Richard said, 'pile up the last of this wood, we'll have to bury Otto and Ishmael later.'

'So we're going to cut our way through an entire army?' Bowman grinned.

'What choice do we have?' Richard said. 'We need to save my children, and we need to save the Holy Land.'

# CRUSADER

The sun was at its midday peak as they rode around the first Saracen camp and through the town outside Kerak. Richard sweated under his armour and robes, and their horses dripped with sweat from the speed their riders insisted on.

Brian rode a different horse, and this one followed Richard's without overtaking and scaring the monk, who had never gotten to grips with fast riding.

The town was empty of fighting men, for they all swarmed towards the breach eager for plunder, and the only people Richard saw now were camp followers and traders. No one challenged them, especially with their bedouin robes, as catapult stones from the castle crashed into the town around them and sent a shower of rubble across their path.

Richard's horse stumbled on the loose rocks and had to slow down.

'We can't ride in,' Sarjeant said, 'and you can't seriously want to fight your way to the castle?'

Richard held his horse still even as it gibbered on the spot and wanted to run.

Bowman caught up. 'Do you have a better idea?'

'Go on foot,' Sarjeant said, 'sabotage their ladders, kill a catapult crew. Do something small that will have a large effect.'

Bowman halted his foaming horse. 'He's got a point, young lord. We can't do anything about the horde of men charging up the breach, but we can help reduce the pressure on it.'

Richard couldn't argue with that, so they left the horses with

Brian in the shell of a broken building and proceeded towards Kerak's castle on foot. Which hurt Richard at every step. He'd needed Brian to help him into his chausses, slipping on the mail leg armour for him and tying it closely around his legs. The blood didn't show through the metal on his feet, but the wounds were still there and they still hurt.

Bowman picked up a bow and a bag of arrows from a fallen Saracen, the man's head removed by a small catapult stone, and they threaded their way through the husk of the town.

Crossbow bolts whizzed overhead as they reached the back of the pressing enemy army, men who talked and shouted, shot at the defenders, and died when they shot back.

A catapult on the other side of a low wall released its load and its wooden frame shuddered from the force of it. The stone launched high into the air.

'Can you knock the pin out of this one?' Richard whispered to Bowman.

'Not with all those men around it.'

'Fine,' Richard replied, 'then we'll see if we can break some of the ladders.'

Bowman drew his bow as a horseman arrived to shout at the catapult crew.

They edged forwards, pushing through those Saracens who were happy to wait for their turn to fight, until Richard could see the wall in front of him and the breach next to the gatehouse. The pile of rubble leading up to the breach was large, and Saracens clambered up it and fought hand-to-hand with defenders at the top. Richard could see the defender's red shields, but their line was a thin one.

Half a dozen ladders lay up against the walls to one side of the breach, and men streamed up them. Richard knew if men could be freed from defending the walls, the breach would hold a while longer.

He ducked a crossbow bolt he sensed more than saw, and Bowman loosed an arrow high into the air to make it look like he was on the attacker's side.

Saracens swarmed everywhere, men in mail, robes, or just tunics waited to climb ladders or the rubble, while a hundred men with bows peppered the walls with arrows.

A bolt shattered the thigh of the Saracen next to Richard as he neared a ladder, and the man's screams joined the noise of battle that crowded Richard's ears. He'd forgotten how loud it could be. He didn't really want to be fighting again, but he didn't see another way.

Richard elbowed between some actual bedouins and reached the foot of one of the ladders. Bowman held his bow drawn behind him, their beards and tanned faces no different to those surrounding them. Richard wasn't sure where Sarjeant was, and certainly wasn't going to call his name to find out.

Instead he put a foot on the ladder. He tried to kick the rung out with his heel, but it didn't break.

A man fell from the ladder above, took the man below him with him, and they landed either side of Richard in a cloud of dust. One of them moaned loudly as the men on the ladder moved up to take their places. Richard climbed up three rungs and tried to kick a new rung in two. It didn't snap. He drew Sir John's dagger and sawed at the rung. The blade, once razor-sharp, had dulled since it had last been sharpened, but it gradually cut into the wood. Not quite quickly enough, Richard thought, and then the men on the ladder advanced again and he followed. He slammed his heel down on the weakened rung and this time it snapped with a crack. The man below Richard yelled at him angrily, Richard couldn't understand him but could guess what he was complaining about. He saw Richard's dagger, then grabbed his ankle.

Richard clung onto the ladder as the man below tried to pull him from it. Richard went to kick him away with his other foot but couldn't, and out of the corner of his eye he caught the flash of a drawn blade. He braced for it to stab into his leg.

The man screamed out as an arrow pierced his lungs. He let go of Richard and tried to climb down the ladder as his strength waned. Richard quickly sawed with his dagger at the next rung, smashed it in half with the pommel, and then jumped from the ladder in a way that he hoped would look like a fall.

The bedouin landed on his back, with the point of the arrow sticking up into the air. Richard fell onto the arrow, but luckily the shaft snapped and the head tangled in his robes and mail as he crashed to the ground. A fresh wave of dust washed over those nearby and Bowman's arm reached down to pull him to his feet. Richard took it, and Bowman led him away from the ladder where some eyes watched with suspicion and confusion. He hoped the whole thing had looked just like an argument.

They regrouped at the back of the throng as a stone from the defenders decapitated two Saracen archers with a single shot.

'Did he get you?' Bowman whispered in Richard's ear.

Richard shook his head. He looked back to the ladder, and although two men at the top fought with the defenders, no one climbed up behind them.

'I think you somehow did enough to break the ladder,' Bowman grinned.

'Maybe,' Richard coughed, 'but it's just one ladder.'

'But did you see?' the blonde man's grin was full. 'Did you see the arrow?'

'Yes, I practically landed on it.'

'But I shot it,' the blonde man said, 'I shot it, and it hit my target.'

Richard grinned back in realisation. 'It was only two paces away, but well, that's something.'

Sarjeant pushed his way out of the massed ranks of the enemy, blood across his robes. He nodded to tell Richard the blood wasn't his own.

'We won't get away with that again,' Richard said, 'we can't affect matters here.'

'I could have told you that before,' Bowman hissed.

A crossbow bolt caught an archer in the thigh and as he fell, he loosed his arrow which shot straight through the neck of his neighbour.

'We're going,' Richard whispered.

Wounded men were carried away from the battle by their comrades, and nearby a drumbeat started up.

Sarjeant nodded.

Bowman licked his lips. 'Where the hell is Guy?'

'Come on,' Richard said.

'This is worse than Baginbun Head,' the blonde man groaned, 'at least there we fought with real men, not Guy.'

313

Richard's eyes lit up. 'That gives men an idea, follow me.' Richard led the others back to Brian, where the noise of the carnage was less and they could catch their breath.

'I need a drink,' Sarjeant said.

Trumpets blared again, but the drums hadn't stopped.

The monk nervously watched the streets around, but he'd remained undisturbed.

'We're going to the camels and horses,' Richard said, 'come on, we'll cause a stampede.'

'That won't work,' Bowman said, 'they aren't cattle, and they will be running towards danger, which they will just baulk at.'

Richard shrugged. 'It worked in Ireland, it's worth a try here.'

Brian's eyes lit up. 'I've got an idea too,' he made the sign of the cross, mouthed a prayer up to the blue sky, and scuttled off into the town.

'Where's he going?' Bowman asked.

'No idea,' Richard said, 'but we're going to free their animals.'

Bowman followed reluctantly to the extended lines of camels and horses, but there were thousands of them and they could never free them all.

Richard cut the long lines onto which individual animals were tied, which kept them together, and then Sarjeant waved a flaming torch at them he'd made from the nearest campfire. Bowman tried to do it to some camels, but they instead charged at him and he had to throw himself to the floor to avoid them. Covered in dust, he spat out sand and swore.

Sarjeant waved his torch and a hundred horses were pushed into the town. They filtered through the main streets towards the castle, going fast but probably not fast enough, until they were out of view.

'That should at least disrupt the attack a bit,' Richard watched Bowman brush himself down.

'I hate camels.'

'I think someone saw us,' Sarjeant gazed over to the next line of horses, where a pair of boys shouted at the top of their voices.

'To the army now,' Richard said, 'we've done all we can here.'

'What about the monk?' Sarjeant asked.

'He ran off,' Bowman said, 'leave him.'

'For once I agree,' Richard said, 'he knows where we'll have gone. We can't find him before those boys find some adults with weapons.'

They remounted their horses, and the three men galloped around the mountain road and away from the town. They left behind shouts as Saracens mounted horses and gave chase.

Between them and the Christian camp stood one Saracen camp. It straddled the road into Kerak, and its inhabitants had not joined in with the siege, instead they waited to defend against an attack from the army of Jerusalem.

Which at least meant Richard could canter into the back of the camp unopposed, his horse sweating under the sun and his feet burning from their wounds. Bowman and Sarjeant were behind him, their horse's heads low and their hooves thundering over the stony white ground.

The wind rushed through Richard's hair, thin crisp air, but it cooled him even as they flew past campfires and strings of camels.

Ahead, on the border of the camp, Saracens waited, fully armed and nervously watching the road. At least they were looking the wrong way, Richard thought, and urged his horse into a gallop. The animal strained but was happy to run and Richard gave him his head. He steered it straight at the low wooden barricade that had been dragged across the road. The enemy heard them coming, but saw only bedouin and although confused, didn't see a need to get in their way.

Richard jumped the barricade, worried too late if there were caltrops on the other side, and landed safely on the far side.

Bowman's horse followed and Sarjeant's wasn't far behind.

The Saracens cheered them.

'They think we're attacking the Christians,' Richard shouted as their hooves took them swiftly away from the enemy.

'Then the Templars will think the same,' Bowman cried, 'get your robes off.'

Richard eased his horse down into a canter, but it didn't want to obey and fought him until he pulled on the reins and slowed the creature. Sarjeant's horse bumped into his flank as all their mounts struggled to control their enthusiasm.

'I do like these horses,' Richard said, 'but they have their own mind.'

Bowman grunted as he tore his robe down the middle and peeled it away from his body so it hung from his waist.

'We stopped too soon,' Sarjeant glanced back to the Saracen camp as the first arrow flew off to one side. The horsemen who had chased them from the town entered the camp and educated their comrades on who Richard's party were.

Richard was caught with his robe half over his head and couldn't see anything.

'You should have split it apart,' Bowman told him.

Richard heard Bowman's bow twang as he struggled inside the fabric.

'They're through the barricade,' Bowman told him.

A knife tore through the robe and Richard saw Sarjeant's face grinning at him when the big man tore the clothing from him.

'About time,' Bowman loosed another arrow and cantered his horse away from the camp.

Richard flung the robe to the ground and followed after catching a fleeting glimpse of the enemy. A body of horsemen formed inside the barricade as those who had come from the town charged past them.

'They're coming after us,' Sarjeant said as they rode up the hill that led to safety.

'We can see that,' Bowman cried.

'Their horses will be fresh,' Richard cried and pressed his legs onto his horse, who gladly obliged.

They rounded a bend in the mountain, and then another that bent back on itself, and as they did they saw the Saracens charge behind them. A few loosed arrows but the shots were wild and the projectiles flew wide.

They traversed another bend as fast as they could and the road cut through a shallow ravine that sloped upwards. At the top of it, they ran straight into a formation of horsemen who walked forwards towards the ravine. The horsemen were turcopoles, wearing their Templar surcoats and holding long lances. At their front rode two white-clad Templar knights and one who wore a black Templar surcoat.

The face of the black-surcoated knight smiled. 'Richard,' the Marshal said.

Richard pulled his horse to a stop just before it crashed into the Marshal's animal.

'I see you still can't ride,' the English knight grinned.

'I thought you were wounded close to death?' Richard asked.

'I still am,' the Marshal held up his right hand, to which his sword had been lashed tightly into his fist. His left hand hung loosely by his side and his reins were hooked onto his belt. 'But I'm not fleeing from the fighting.'

'I can see that,' Richard replied, 'but there are Saracens after us, will you see them off?'

'See them off?' the Marshal laughed. 'We'll destroy them.'

The Templar knight next to him shouted an order, and the turcopoles moved forwards down the ravine.

'Who leads the army?' Richard shouted after the Marshal.

'Guy,' the knight replied, 'but half the barons refuse to fight under him.'

The turcopoles broke into a canter and flooded down the ravine like an unstoppable torrent of water. The Saracens rode unwittingly around the bend and up the ravine, seeing their assailants far too late to do anything about it.

The turcopole attack smashed into them in silence, apart from the splintering of wood and the screams of the men they killed.

'He's finally done something to help us,' Bowman sniffed.

'That's harsh,' Richard replied, 'but we need to find Guy before he drives all the barons and lords away from him and Kerak.'

The Christian camp was not much further along the road, and Templar sentries allowed them through. The Templars were formed up in order of battle in the open ground before the sea of tents, rows of white-clad knights and brown or black-surcoated sarjeants and squires stood ready. The black surcoats of the Hospitallers were behind them, the white crosses on their chests displayed just as proudly as their Templar cousins.

Behind them though, in the camp, the secular knights and infantry huddled in groups or cooked over their fires. Their horses were saddled but remained tied together in long strings.

Richard headed towards the highest point of the camp, a small hill rising above the rest, where the banner of the kingdom fluttered in the breeze. The white banner with its golden crosses looked glorious, but the scene beneath it felt lacklustre.

Richard heard Guy's laugh before he saw him. A red tent was pitched behind a dais with painted chairs on which Guy sat next to Sibylla. She had both of her hands clasped around one of his, leaning over from her chair and staring up at him.

Guy completely ignored her. Instead he jeered at some of the men who stood around him. Many wore fine cloaks, lined in the furs reserved for high nobility, and some were confident enough in themselves to shout back at the man who was clearly now the regent of the kingdom.

Richard stopped when two guards didn't get out of his way.

'I need to speak to Guy.'

'Only if he has summoned you,' a guard said, 'and he hasn't summoned anyone.'

Richard looked at the men around Guy for someone who would vouch for him, and his eyes rested on Gerard, who was shouting back at Guy. 'The true cross is right there,' the seneschal pointed up to the golden cross with its fire still burning under it, 'what clearer sign could you need? We should attack the infidel at once.'

'God will provide for us,' Guy replied, 'isn't that what you always say? Let the Saracens tire themselves against the walls of Kerak. Once their force is spent, we can clear up the survivors.'

'That is sheer cowardice,' Gerard raised his voice, 'especially when the enemy is distracted and their forces spread out across the hills and mountains. Attack. Attack their closest camp, smash through it and destroy the others one at a time. We can trap Saladin's army between our lances and the walls of Kerak.'

Guy crossed his arms and rolled his eyes.

'Seneschal,' Richard shouted to get the Templar's attention.

Gerard craned his neck towards the guards who kept Richard away from the nobles. The seneschal frowned, then his face broke into a smile. 'You aren't dead?'

'No,' Richard stopped struggling, 'and I can help you win your argument.'

Guy groaned as he saw who it was. 'I suppose the cross was

318

you?'

'Let me through,' Richard said.

'Do not speak to the regent in such a manner,' Sibylla said.

'I am the regent of the kingdom,' Guy said. 'Address me as such.'

'I gathered that,' Richard replied, 'Tell these guards to stand aside.'

The new regent sniffed. 'This council is for the greater men of the kingdom, and you are not one of them.'

Gerard walked towards the guards who wore white surcoats with the five golden crosses of the kingdom emblazoned on them. 'Allow this man to pass.'

The guards looked back to their regent.

Guy shrugged. 'Don't.'

'Why not?' Richard asked. 'Are you afraid of what I might say?'

Sibylla looked at Guy as if to ask what Richard might mean. The regent himself didn't change his expression.

'I'm not interested in the packhorses,' Richard said, 'I don't care if no one else ever hears of it, I only care about relieving Kerak.'

Guy shook his head again.

Gerard stood behind the guards, so closely he could breathe down their mailed necks. One of them flinched. 'This man might not be dressed like it, but he is a Templar knight. Therefore he belongs to me and I decide where he goes, and I have decided he is coming in. Let him through or find yourselves enemies of the Temple.'

The flinching guard pulled his spear aside and his comrade chided him, but didn't dare stand up to Gerard on his own. The seneschal turned and walked back towards Guy and the nobles arrayed around him, Richard followed.

He came to a stop in front of the dais and with the dozen nobles all staring intently at him.

Richard swallowed.

Two men stood with yellow surcoats adorned with red crosses, one looked to be in his fifties and the other maybe Bowman's age. They shared an average height, dark hair, and long faces, and the elder of them watched Richard. 'Who is this man? His face is as scarred as an Ascalonian snake-handler.'

'This is one of my knights,' Gerard said.

'Yours?' the older knight scoffed. 'Are you the Grand Master of the Temple now?'

'Come now, Baldwin,' Gerard replied with a wry grin, 'not yet.'

Richard went to tap his foot but caught himself.

Baldwin's younger relation looked down at Richard's hands. 'He is missing several fingers,' the man said, 'which either means he is a seasoned warrior, or tends to block with his hands.'

Bowman laughed from the other side of the guards.

'His name is Richard,' Gerard said, 'I cannot remember from where, and he came to us with all his scars and the lack of fingers.'

'What happened to your ear?' Baldwin asked.

Richard touched it without thinking. 'A Martel,' he said ruefully.

Both of the men in the yellow surcoats with red crosses snorted and exchanged a glance. 'What happened to the Martel?' the younger one asked.

Richard thought how he should answer. 'That depends on who you are, and how you know the Martels.'

'I am Baldwin of Ibelin,' the older knight said, 'and this is my younger brother, Balian. We came across Geoffrey Martel when he journeyed to the Holy Land.'

'No one calls me young anymore,' Balian nodded with appreciation, 'not since I suffered my fortieth year. Which Martel was it?'

'It doesn't matter,' Guy said, 'and his words are unimportant. We will wait before we attack.'

'I care,' Baldwin of Ibelin said, 'more than I care for your opinions.'

Gerard raised a hand. 'We can argue with each other later.'

'That's all we've been doing until now,' Balian said dryly.

'What do you want to tell us?' Gerard asked Richard.

'Now is the time to attack.'

'Nonsense,' Sibylla smirked.

'Let him speak,' Gerard roared. 'You are here only because of who your father was, not because we want to hear what you have to say.'

'You overstep,' Guy said.

'Stop it,' Richard balled one fist and pointed over the valley towards the castle of Kerak with his other hand. 'Enough of this squabbling. If you continue like this, the kingdom will be ruined and then you'll be arguing over ashes.'

Baldwin leaned over to Gerard. 'Where did you find this one?'

'Saladin will shortly be on the verge of wanting to leave Kerak,' Richard continued, 'all you need to do is push him.'

Guy laughed. 'Why would Saladin want to leave? His men are fighting on the walls.'

'Because he thinks the Assassins are coming for him.'

Gerard's body stiffened.

'Are they?' Baldwin asked. 'And if they are, how would you know?'

'I don't,' Richard carefully kept his gaze on the Ibelin brothers and away from Gerard. 'But I left a cardamom cake on his bed next to an Assassin's dagger.'

Balian laughed and Guy looked confused.

Baldwin raised his eyebrows. 'And how did you come across an Assassin's blade? Or their cake?'

'That doesn't matter,' Richard said, 'it matters that Saladin thinks he is vulnerable.'

Gerard nodded. 'The Assassins have made an attempt on Saladin before, which frightened him.'

'Frightened of a cake?' Guy sneered. 'Perhaps he is not as mighty as I've been led to believe.'

'Says the man cowering away from a battle,' Baldwin said.

Sibylla went to complain, but Guy silenced her with a look. 'I do not need you to fight my battles for me,' he said.

'Then lead the army yourself,' Balian said, 'unless you do need the princess to do the fighting for you?'

'I can deprive you of your lands,' Guy said.

'Do that and every baron will be raised in arms against you,' the younger Ibelin said.

'Let them,' Guy waved his hand as if that would make the matter go away.

'That is not the question at hand,' Gerard said, 'Saladin will find the cake and if our army sweeps down the mountain, he will flee. He is a cautious man.'

'It's only a cake,' Guy cried, 'he won't flee from a cake.'

'He will flee from what he signifies,' Gerard said, 'it will appear to be a clear message from the Assassins. Leave Kerak or die.'

Guy drummed his fingers on his armrest. The drums around the assault could be heard dimly even from where he was, and Richard could hear their trumpets blasting again.

Guy flicked at the armrest. 'You never set foot inside Saladin's tent,' he said coldly. 'At best, this is an elaborate lie to damage me, and worst you are in league with the Saracens. How else would you have managed to raise a cross on that mountain and get here alive?'

'Do not call me a liar,' Richard said, 'you know me well enough to know why I do things. You remember when we stood on the walls of Rocamadour against the world. If you delay here and lose Kerak, then your reputation will be in tatters. Attack now and avoid it. Make a name for yourself as a warrior.'

The Templar seneschal nodded. 'Better to lose in a battle than lose Kerak while you watch. A regent must act to save his kingdom.'

'You try to soothe me with honeyed words,' Guy said, 'but I already made my decision, we wait. We just saw a herd of their own animals stampede through the town, it will take them half a day to restore order. That it even happened is a sign of their imminent collapse.'

Richard groaned to himself. 'We did that to cover our escape.'

'Your stories grow more elaborate with each telling,' Guy said, 'you have learnt to lie.'

Richard pointed over Kerak and to the wooded mountain top where the golden cross reflected burning firelight. 'Look, the true cross is above us all, the Lord wills us on to attack. If nothing else, you must push the Saracens away so that they do not steal the true cross from you. You have a sacred duty to recover it.'

The regent stared at Richard and said nothing.

'It is clearly a golden cross,' Gerard said, 'when I left it, it was mere wood. Christ has turned it to gold to give us a sure sign of his intentions. This is a true miracle, his message is clear.'

'Attack,' Baldwin of Ibelin said, 'it is your duty as a Christian.'

Guy went to make a snide comment, but remembered he was now the regent of the Kingdom of Jerusalem and decided not to.

Richard reached into his bag and withdrew the pouch containing Christ's deciduous teeth. 'These,' he said, 'are the milk teeth of our Lord Christ. Does His will mean nothing to you?' Richard scooped out the small white teeth and hurled them at Guy.

The regent and Sibylla raised their hands to defend themselves from the tiny projectiles.

'You can't throw those,' Brian's voice rang out from where Richard had left Bowman.

'What are you doing here?' Richard asked.

'You'd rather I died in the camp?' the monk asked.

'That's not what I meant,' Richard said, 'I just didn't think you'd make it here so quickly.'

'This horse wouldn't stop either,' Brian said with a shrug, 'and some turcopoles were distracting the Saracen camp.'

'See,' Gerard said, 'the battle has already begun, commit your forces.'

'Don't let that monk in,' Guy turned to the seneschal, 'or are you going to tell me he's a Templar, too?'

'He is,' Gerard replied, 'although I do not think he has anything to add.'

'I do,' Brian said, 'something very important.'

Guy looked up to the heavens and shut his eyes.

'The well in the town,' Brian shouted, 'it's been poisoned. So the Saracens will have to leave.'

'Poisoned?' Gerard asked. 'How do you know?'

Brian scratched the back of his neck.

Richard couldn't help himself forming a small smile. 'The monk did it.'

'What monk knows how to poison a well?' Baldwin asked.

'Trust me, this one does,' Richard said, 'but the point is that the Saracens have no other well. They will now have to leave within a day or two, or die from thirst.'

323

'Those who drink from the well now will soon start to become ill,' Brian lowered his voice, 'were those Christ's teeth that you just threw?'

Richard shrugged. 'They're of no use to me.'

Brian pushed past the guards, who wilted when Gerard looked at them, and collected the teeth one by one.

'Please, Guy,' Richard said, 'what other signs do you need? What other reasons do you need?'

Guy sighed. 'I will consider attacking sooner than planned,' he said, 'perhaps tomorrow, once the sickness from the well has overcome them. Wise generals do not seek battle when waiting will grant them a surer victory.'

'It's not a victory if the castle falls,' Richard said.

Brian finished scrambling around on the floor and returned to Bowman with a handful of teeth. 'Do you still have the golden box?'

Bowman grinned.

Guy ignored them. 'I have no reason to believe anything you said is the truth.'

'I like this man,' Baldwin said, 'his manner is sincere even if his words are hard to believe.'

'Templars do not lie,' Gerard said.

Both the Ibelins and Guy burst into laughter.

Richard pointed again at the golden cross but his hopes were fading. 'The true cross, miraculously turned to gold, shines above us. You don't have to believe my words, it is right there for your own eyes to see.'

'How do we know it's even the true cross?' the new regent asked.

Richard couldn't believe his ears. 'You were there when we recovered it.'

'But it was not gold, so this one cannot be gold. Surely it is some trick of the light,' Guy said, 'or some dark Saracen magic. Are you in league with them?'

Baldwin stepped forwards. 'We do not doubt your passion, Templar, but we do not know you. I am inclined to believe your stories, and agree we should attack now, but Guy clearly requires a sign that cannot be argued against.'

Brian gave Bowman the teeth and stormed back. 'A sign?

After everything we've done for you, for this land, you all still need a sign?'

Guy watched the monk's rage with amusement. 'No regent would go against God's will, but that will must be clear and beyond any doubt. Show me such a sign and I will acquiesce.'

Brian's small eyes shone brightly with anger as he faced up to Guy. 'The Lord will provide, the Lord always provides. Your unarguable sign is already here, the keeper of the cross is here, and he is bound to the suffering of Christ. The last keeper was this knight's father, but since his death the duty has passed to Richard himself. There were rumours the true cross had been stolen from Jerusalem, but it had been hidden under his father's protection all along. This man's father died and now the duty has passed to him. The keeper himself is the sign.'

'Him?' Guy glanced at Richard. 'He doesn't look like much of a sign. You'll have to do better than that.'

The monk wasn't finished. 'I just told you, the keeper of the cross is bound to Christ's suffering. Richard, take off your chausses.'

'What?' Richard stammered. 'I'm not taking anything off in front of other people.'

'I am repaying your faith in me,' Brian told him, 'everything you have done for me when you didn't have to, now I am repaying. Take off your leg armour.'

'Fine, just hold me up while I do,' Richard asked, and the monk put a hand on his shoulder to steady him. Richard untied the leather points which held the mail leggings up to a wide belt around his waist and then bent over to unlace the ties which pulled the mail rings closely around his lower legs. Then he shook off the legs one at a time. Each leg landed in a pile on the ground, and all the nobles watching gasped.

Because on the top of each foot of Richard's woollen leggings, there was a large spot of red blood.

'Behold,' Brian held his arms to the heavens, 'the unarguable sign of the crucifixion.'

The Ibelins were silent and even Gerard was hushed.

Guy peered at the feet. 'I'm not sure about unarguable, monk. You could have just stabbed him in the feet before you got here. This is the sort of elaborate ruse I'd expect from Richard. Also, did the crucifixion not also involve wounds to Christ's hands? Monk, you shall have to do far better than this.'

Brian didn't move. The breeze ruffled his hair slightly and Richard was sure he could see the traces of a smile. 'How many times do I have to tell you?' Brian mustered his grandest voice. 'How little faith in Christ do you have?'

'Not all that much,' Guy muttered, which drew an angry look from Gerard.

'Richard,' Brian said, 'hold out your hands.'

Richard's eyes widened and suddenly the genius of the monk's plan hit him. He held out the palms of his hands, the palms which many years ago had been scarred by a red-hot iron bar.

Baldwin made the sign of the cross and fell to his knees.

Balian came closer and took Richard's hands in his own to inspect them. 'By all that is holy, this is remarkable,' he said.

Baldwin's eyes filled and he placed his hands together in prayer. 'Those scars are old, Guy, there can be no doubt here. This man is the keeper of the true cross. His words are sacred.'

Brian stood triumphant as the onlookers prayed or dropped to the ground in reverence. 'The keeper's hands are his legitimacy, but his feet are the Lord's call to action. As blood flows from the keeper, blood must be spilled from the enemy. This is the surest sign a Christian army has ever received. March forward, forward to victory, and claim the true cross for our faith. Act now to save the kingdom.'

'That is good enough for me,' Gerard wiped a tear from his cheek.

'And me,' Balian returned to his older brother as the secular lords around Guy exchanged quick and excited words.

'We shall attack now,' Gerard said, 'even the Hospitallers will join us. With God's grace in our hearts, we shall sweep the infidel from this place.'

Baldwin got back to his feet. 'Regent, you need only to give the command and all these lords will join together under your leadership and fight. This could be a new dawn for the Kingdom of Jerusalem.'

All eyes turned to Guy and waited for him to signal the attack.

The regent tapped his armrest. He sniffed. 'No.'

A chorus of jeers and complaints filled the air.

'Coward,' Balian cried.

Baldwin put a hand over his face and sighed.

Brian blinked at the regent.

Richard couldn't believe his ears. 'No?'

'No,' Guy repeated. 'This is all a cheap trick.'

'We shall speak after this,' Gerard said to Guy, 'but now, now, the Templars will advance.'

'Order the attack,' Balian pleaded, 'allow us to join the holy orders.'

Guy grimaced. 'You will stay where you are.'

Baldwin and some of the other nobles begged Guy to change his mind. 'There can be no excuse,' the elder Ibelin said, 'to ignore such an obvious message from our Lord.'

Gerard's face had grown red. 'Enough delaying,' he said loudly, 'the holy orders will strike and we shall strike now. To horse, sound the call.'

'Brian,' Richard said, 'help me put my chausses back on.'

'You're in no condition to fight,' the monk said, but helped anyway.

'Who is ever ready to fight?' Richard said as the monk laced on the first leg. 'But sometimes you have to fight when you aren't strong.'

Gerard whirled around with a flourish of his white cloak and pushed the two guards out of his way as he left.

Once armed, Richard left Guy arguing with his barons, and returned to their resting horses who drank from a bucket Sarjeant held for them.

Gerard's Templars already waited for him with his horse to mount. 'Fetch helmets from the baggage,' he shouted over towards Richard, 'and lances. But we will not wait for you.'

Richard went with Bowman and Sarjeant to the Templar baggage and took for themselves three new full faceplate helmets.

'I hate these,' Bowman said as he put it on. 'I can't even see my horse to mount it.'

'You'll get used to it,' Richard said tentatively as Sarjeant found shields and lances for them all and handed them out.

The Templar trumpets sounded the call to march, and outside the camp the massed ranks of white-clad knights began their advance. Once Sarjeant was also armed and mounted, they pushed their horses into a canter to catch up.

The sight of the Templar formation filled Richard's heart with hope. Their serried ranks of uniformly dressed knights looked indestructible, and the piebald banner at their centre flew proudly and surely.

Trumpets sounded again and a company of turcopoles charged off ahead towards the ravine and the first Saracen camp.

Behind the knight brothers rode squires and sarjeant Templars with spare lances and towing spare horses, saddled and ready. Richard had never seen such organisation, even King Henry's campaign in Brittany hadn't looked quite like this.

'Who do we join?' Bowman shouted as they cleared the tents and caught up with the squires and sarjeants.

'The front,' Richard said, 'to the piebald banner.'

They pressed on, but as the Templars squeezed into the narrow ravine, Richard realised he couldn't get near the front. Instead they funnelled down the ravine, pressed in between hundreds of Templars who advanced in silence. All that could be heard was the sound of a thousand hooves on the hard stone, the snorting of horses, and the rattling of armour.

At the bottom of the ravine, Richard's horse stumbled on the fallen bodies of the Saracens the Marshal's turcopoles had killed, but the Templars kept advancing.

Richard could see the piebald banner ahead as they reached the enemy camp and saw the smoke rising from its fires. The sun glinted upon the fresh spear tips of the Templars as the turcopoles in the vanguard charged the camp's defenders. Richard and everyone around him were stuck in a walk as they jostled to get ahead, and he heard the battle begin more than he saw it.

The Saracens showered the turcopoles with arrows, and many horses fell, but the weight of numbers behind them pushed them straight through the barricade and into the camp. The defenders fell as the Templars surged through them, sparing no one, and leaving a trail of bodies, extinguished fires, and collapsed tents in their wake.

As the Templars swept out of the road and into the camp they could spread out, and Richard found the space to canter. His Arab horse took him forwards, around pieces of canvas flapping on the floor, and over the bodies of Saracens who lay still or cried out in agony. An archer crouching behind a pile of sacks took aim at Richard, but his horse was so fast the arrow never had a chance to leave the bow before his lance caught the Saracen in the chest. The lance pushed him over and remained intact so Richard rode on. His only thought was to get through the camp and fall on Kerak, and when he looked over to the castle, he heard horns blow and the drums change their rhythm.

Bowman caught up with him when they reached the boundary of the camp and the Templars bunched up again to file along the mountain road that led to the town. 'I think they've seen us,' he shouted over the sound of horses and hooves.

'Quiet,' a Templar snapped at them.

Richard wasn't keen on the silence rule, so he watched the distant battle around the castle to see if the Saracens would leave that fight in order to counter the Templars.

Some infantry returned to Saladin's pavilion, and horsemen wheeled about on the mountainside from the other camps. 'I think they're mustering at Saladin's tent,' Richard said.

Bowman nodded as their horses pushed together and their legs almost tangled up.

The fighting around Kerak's breach continued, which Richard couldn't decide was for the best or not, because there was now more than one point of organised resistance standing between him and his family.

The Templar trumpet sounded the attack once more, as the white column wound around the mountainside and approached Saladin's camp that merged with the town.

The road headed to the town, with the camp to its left and the castle, accessible only through the town, to its right.

Gerard aimed the Templars at Saladin's great pavilion, and the vanguard of turcopoles and knight brothers crashed into the infantry companies which stood in their way.

'Look,' Bowman shouted above the sound of their horses as they broke back into a fast canter, 'is that Saladin fleeing?'

Richard looked to the pavilion, but he could only see the top of it above the knights in front of him. However, on the hill that rose up behind it, a band of horsemen galloped away along the road that led towards the two Khirbets. Richard's eyes weren't good enough to be sure, but he thought he recognised the back of one rider's helmet as Saladin's.

'He's running,' Richard cried with joy, 'I think he's running.'

'Quiet,' a Templar shouted at him, but Richard was too happy to care.

'His men don't know it,' Bowman said more soberly, 'they are still going to take the castle if we don't stop them.'

Richard calmed himself and gripped his lance more tightly as the Templars around him poured out of the road and moved to attack the Saracens defending their main camp.

Richard found himself curving around the infantry and charging into their flank. The rank of knights in front of him speared some of the enemy, then their horses rode up and over their bodies and trampled down the hapless Saracens beneath their iron-shod hooves. Richard's horse slipped on the spilled entrails of a man, but his lance still found an enemy's side as they turned the flank of the infantry, who quickly started to break and flee.

'Run them down,' Gerard shouted from far away, and as the infantry fled, the engagement became a slaughter.

Richard pulled his horse up and turned it towards the town. 'That's the way we need to go,' he said, 'we don't need to chase defeated infantry.'

'You have to follow your orders,' Sarjeant rode next to him with his lance gone and his sword drawn. 'You cannot disobey the seneschal, and he ordered a pursuit of the fleeing enemy.'

Richard gritted his teeth and tasted blood. He'd bitten the inside of his mouth during the charge. 'We have to stop the siege.'

Knights and squires rushed past as part of Saladin's tent was torn down with a great crack of poles and ripping of canvas.

'We're going to regret that the monk poisoned the well,'

Bowman grinned at Richard, 'he really shouldn't have bothered.'

'I'm not worried about that at the moment,' Richard replied, 'and if it wasn't for him, we'd still be sitting in Guy's camp watching Kerak fall.'

A Templar bumped into Richard's horse and told him to get out of the way.

'Enough of this,' Richard moved his horse into a walk, 'we're going to the town, maybe some of the Templars will follow us.'

'Gerard will remove you from the order for this,' Sarjeant said.

'He is welcome to,' Richard eased his way out of the torrent of Templars and broke clear of them. The town stood ahead, its shattered walls and broken roofs looked menacing enough, but the rubble strewn across the streets would slow them down, and infantry ran between the houses, spears and bows in their hands.

'This isn't going to be easy,' Bowman said, 'and our horses aren't armoured.'

'It won't get any easier if they're given more time to prepare,' Richard spurred his horse, but he wouldn't have needed to because it squealed and launched forwards with all its energy.

The first arrows flew over their heads and Richard hoped some Templars were following him as he raised his shield up to his eyes and couched his lance into his armpit.

His horse made its own way down the street to avoid piles of rubble, which threw Richard left and right in the saddle, but also meant the first volley of arrows aimed at him largely missed. He felt one embed itself in his shield, but he couldn't see much through his new helmet, so he just charged. He needed to break this siege.

Richard thundered past the first four houses before some spearmen appeared in the roadway to confront him. His lance outreached them however, and the point tore through the neck of one of them and Richard's horse knocked another aside with its chest and furious hooves.

An arrow rang his helmet's face-plate, but he could see archers ahead and leaned forward to urge his horse ever on. A spearman lunged out from the doorway of a building and jammed his weapon at Richard, caught his shield and sent his horse staggering sideways. A stone from the castle plummeted down and knocked some archers to the ground as Richard's horse composed itself and Bowman cantered past and lanced the spearman.

Under his helmet, Richard didn't notice the Saracen who grabbed his right leg and pulled it. He fell from the saddle and his tumbling lance cracked his assailant on the head and he let go. But Richard was on the ground, his horse reared away from the noise of it all and ran off.

He got up to his knees, slipped Otto's mace from his belt and swung it at the stunned Saracen, breaking his ribs and winding him. The next blow smashed his jaw away, and Richard looked up through the small eye slits of his helmet. Sarjeant careered after Bowman, and behind him three black-surcoated men followed. Their surcoats sported the white Hospitaller cross. Bowman and Sarjeant crashed into a roadblock of spearmen and a brutal melee broke out.

Richard ran to help them, but his feet slowed him down and each step brought fresh agony. A crossbow bolt from the castle slammed into the wall of a building he strode past and stones fell down and landed on him. His helmet took the worst of it but his ears rang.

Bowman pushed his horse out of the melee and got off it as more Hospitaller knights joined the fray, but their assault had been halted by the wall of spears that was three ranks deep across the road.

Richard caught up and Sarjeant staggered out of the battle on foot, blood streaming from his nose and his helmet knocked off. 'I can't see anything through this thing,' he moaned.

'But it saved your life, didn't it,' Richard said.

Sarjeant nodded, wiped the blood away, and turned to the melee. Archers from deeper in the town shot their arrows up into the air and they rained down here and there along the street, usually hitting nothing but sometimes landing on heads or shoulders.

'We need to break through,' Richard said.

'Evidently,' Sarjeant raised his shield above his head after an arrow snapped in half on the ground next to him.

Richard adjusted his helmet and then looked at a house to one side of the battle. 'Follow me,' he said and ran to the door.

The door opened with a push and Richard entered the house. A boulder from the castle lay in the room, beneath a jagged hole in the roof, and Richard squeezed around it. He climbed up onto the stone and out of the hole it had made on its entry. Richard jumped from the shattered wall of the house and landed in the alleyway beyond it. He looked up the alleyway and saw it came out behind the enemy spearmen who were holding the Hospitallers up.

Those spearmen had to be dislodged, so Richard ran, although it was more of a fast hobble, into the side of them, his mace bludgeoning the first man he reached and then quickly smashing the shoulder of the second.

An alert Saracen brought his spear over towards Richard, but in the close press he struck the wall of the house instead and Richard grabbed the spear with his left hand to control it, and bashed the terrified man's face in with Otto's mace.

Richard hated what the mace did, but he was far better with it than he was with his sword, and he swung it to his right to make the two men who now charged him pause. Both spearmen hesitated when they looked at Richard, covered in dust and more than a little blood, the face-plate helmet covering his face and hiding his eyes in darkness.

A third man turned from fighting the mounted Hospitallers, and suddenly Richard didn't feel as powerful. Time wasn't on his side, so he lunged at the newer man, deflected the spearpoint away from his body, although it cut his hand, and brought Otto's mace down onto the top of his iron helmet. The helmet dented and the man's eyes rolled into the back of his head. Richard spun around as both other spearmen jabbed at him, their pointed weapons cut his arm through his mail and half severed the neck strap of his shield.

Richard advanced on them without thought, between their spears he darted, the fingers on his left hand poked at that spearman's eyes and the mace thrashed out at the other. The Saracen raised his right arm to block the mace, and the iron head crunched into it and forced the arm back into the man's face, stunning him.

Richard went to finish him off, but an arm reached around his neck from behind and jerked him backwards, nearly pulling him off his feet.

The unhurt spearmen shook his eyes clear and then lunged at the defenceless Richard.

Sarjeant, who had found the climb over the house wall far more difficult than Richard, finally appeared and knocked the lunging spear away with his sword.

Richard rammed the handle of the mace into the arm around his throat, but it didn't give. The Saracen who had Richard in his grasp grunted as he tried to strangle him, his left arm helping his right to choke Richard to death.

Richard couldn't hit him with his mace, so he drew Sir John's dagger with his left hand and pushed it into the torso of the man who was pressed against him. The dagger popped open some links of mail and the man gasped as it sliced into flesh, but his grip only increased in force.

It was a race now, Richard pulled the dagger out and jammed it in again, as high as he could, and he felt its path being deflected by a rib.

The Saracen cried out but his arms were making Richard dizzy, and his own limbs were losing their strength as he pulled the dagger out in front of him and tried to aim a stab at the arms strangling him.

The Saracen coughed some blood onto Richard's neck from over his shoulder as Sarjeant dispatched the spearman he'd blocked and the nearby Saracens all noticed their presence.

Sir John's dagger reached up to the Saracen's arms, but Richard didn't have enough strength to push it through the mail rings protecting them. His world started to fade and for a moment he was flushed with a sense of annoyance that now, even as he was about to be choked to death, both of his feet still hurt.

That thought gave him an idea and he lifted a leg and stomped his heel down on the Saracen's toes. The man, already weakened by the holes in his lungs, yelped and released his grip for an instant. Richard gulped down a breath of air and brought his left elbow back into the Saracen's face. The man reeled backwards and Richard took another deep breath.

The Hospitallers were close now, their horses pushing slowly through the enemy even as their horses were brought down beneath them.

A spear caught Richard in his lower back as Bowman howled a war-cry from down the alleyway and charged. Both men used their maces to keep the Saracens at bay, and distracted so many of them that the Hospitallers punched through to reach them.

An arrow clattered into the side of Richard's helmet and he had to wrench the helmet off to breathe. Light flooded into his eyes and he had to close them before trying to see again.

A sword ripped mail links out of Sarjeant's shirt, and Bowman killed the man who wielded it before Richard regained his senses just in time to block a spear thrust aimed at his heart. Sir John's dagger, now with the proper force behind it, thrust up into the man's armpit and Richard pushed him aside.

The Saracens retreated now, but only so they went beyond another side street in which more of their spearmen lurked. They attacked the Hospitallers from the flanks and pulled knights and squires from their horses.

'We need to get past these men,' Richard cried.

Bowman kneed a man in the groin and then pounded his back with his mace. 'We can, but there's only three of us.'

Richard pushed past the blonde man and out behind the Saracen company. Sarjeant was with him, his lungs heaving as he rubbed his chest.

'To the castle,' Richard hobbled along the street.

Bowman and Sarjeant joined him, and Bowman picked up a bow from a fallen archer. Behind them the battle still raged as Hospitaller infantry charged in to relieve their mounted brethren. Bodies lined the street, Saracen's with black and purple faces who had been trampled by the earlier stampede.

'The Hospitallers will prevail,' Bowman said, 'and they'll do it quicker if we help them.'

'There's only three of us,' Richard's neck felt raw, 'and we nearly didn't survive this long.'

His Templar shield had been over his left shoulder and now Richard swung it to his front as they rounded a building which stood at the edge of the short space of open ground between the town and the castle.

Where the assault continued, but the Saracens had given up on their ladders and catapults no longer shot over their heads. No trumpets blared either, and Richard couldn't hear the drums anymore. All he could hear was a company of Saracens on the rubble before him, still fighting on its crest with the wilting red-shielded defenders. Bodies lay piled up on either side of the ramp, and Saracens rolled their fallen comrades out of the way as they advanced up to the line of battle.

'There's no one defending the walls, either,' Bowman said.

'Both sides are exhausted,' Richard said.

Sarjeant leant on the corner of the house. 'So am I.'

The Saracen archers had gone too, but the company on the rubble was fifty men strong and they were pushing Kerak's defenders back into their own castle.

Richard's body was too hot. He couldn't breathe fast enough to cool down and he would have killed for a drink of cold water. Thanks to Brian, however, the only safe water nearby was now inside the castle. His head cooled as the sweat that had formed under his helmet went away with the breeze, but it also meant his head was now undefended except for his mail coif. His two mail shirts were rusted and tattered, and his shield had gouges cut out of it, but his mace was intact and Sir John's dagger seemed to still thirst for blood.

'We can shoot arrows at them,' Bowman said, 'kill a dozen of them before they charge back at us.'

'That sounds sensible,' Sarjeant said, 'we can't charge them, we'd be fighting up that pile of rubble against an entire company.'

'That's exactly what we're going to do,' Richard said, 'we cannot leave it to chance. There are probably more men in that company than are left to fight in the whole of the castle. This company can still take the castle, and look, they're pushing the red shields off the rubble. We don't have a moment to waste.'

Richard pushed himself from the wall of the last house and strode across the ground that was littered with hundreds of bodies, plenty of whom clung temporarily on to life.

Bowman caved in a wounded man's head, who clawed at him forlornly for help.

Sarjeant frowned at the carnage, but the blonde man shrugged. 'It was a reaction, I didn't think about it.'

Richard didn't have time to reply, didn't have the energy to, because he needed to stop this company before they reached the dark and crowded house where his children were cowering up against Alice.

That thought spurred Richard on, angered him, made him forget the pain in his feet and his back and his neck. He put Sir John's dagger away and then slipped Otto's mace back into his belt, and at the foot of the rubble he stopped.

Bowman bumped into him, and as the nearest Saracens were only a few paces up the huge pile of broken stones, he whispered. 'What are you doing?'

'Stand either side of me,' Richard said.

Sarjeant and Bowman exchanged a questioning glance.

Richard drew Roland's old sword with a flourish, held it up, and looked at it for a moment. Yes, he thought, this was the right thing to do. He knelt down, held the sword by the bottom of the blade, with the cross-shaped hilt and pommel high in the sky, and recited the psalm of David as loudly as he could.

'Not to us, Lord, not to us,' he shouted.

Bowman and Sarjeant looked up as the Saracens in the rear half of the company turned around and stared dumbfounded at the three men below them.

All three of their Templar shields faced the enemy, telling them who they were, as Richard sang at the top of his voice.

Sarjeant joined in, but Bowman didn't know the words.

The nearest Saracens looked over Richard's head for signs of more Templars, but could see none, and some of them readied to advance down the rubble.

'Tell them there is a way out,' Richard said to Sarjeant, 'tell them they can still live if they run now. Desperate men fight to the end, and I don't want them to fight.'

'What?' Sarjeant stopped singing.

'Tell them,' Richard hissed, 'before they overwhelm us.'

Sarjeant spoke in their own tongue, and some of the Saracens ceased their advance.

Above them, many of their comrades fought on, oblivious to what was occurring below, but then two Saracens bolted down the rubble in a cloud of yellow dust and sprinted across the open ground and into the town.

'Our father,' Richard shouted up at the rest, 'that art in heaven.'

Three more men ran. Two Saracens shouted at the rest to stand firm and one waved his curved sword at Richard as he bellowed at his company to fight on.

One whole group of Saracens decided they wanted to live and skidded down the ramp of broken masonry, right past the trio beneath them.

Bowman shook his head. 'This can't possibly work.'

The leading Saracen stepped down the slope, raising his round shield before him as if challenging Richard. Some of his men followed, but a few more peeled off and made their escape.

'Or maybe it won't work,' the blonde man sighed and raised his mace.

Richard flipped Durendal around so it was the right way up and shouted the psalm of David back up to the Saracen captain.

Half a dozen men stepped down the broken stones and dust towards them.

'Don't show fear,' Richard said, 'now charge.'

'Now what?' Bowman looked up.

Richard stepped up onto the rubble, which dug into his painful feet. Sarjeant followed and Bowman, shaking his head at it all, bounded onwards with them.

Some of the Saracens paused at the unexpected charge, but the captain and a few of his men shouted war-cries and rushed down the rubble.

Richard raised his shield and used it to push aside the first of them, whose momentum carried him right down the breach.

Richard's sword cut into the next man's thigh as his round shield failed to cover all of him, and Bowman traded blows with two Saracens.

Sarjeant killed one enemy, but then slipped over and raised his shield above him as he scrambled to get back to his feet.

The Saracen captain kicked at Sarjeant's shield and sent him face first into the cracked and shattered stones of the ramp.

Richard slashed Durendal at the back of the captain before he could finish Sarjeant and caught him in the hip. The Saracen spun around but tripped on a larger stone and landed next to Sarjeant. Who brought the rim of his shield down onto the side of his face and sent red teeth flying from his mouth.

A round shield pushed into Richard and a curved sword half-winded him as it dragged across his stomach. His double mail held yet again, even though the outer layer was now nothing but threads of loose metal, and Richard jammed the crossguard of Roland's sword into his assailant's eye.

The next Saracen hurtled into Richard, who again stepped out of his path, but the man's sword cut a line across Richard's forehead just under his coif.

Bowman thumped the man's shield with his mace, then another group of the enemy ran down the slope and away from the fight.

Richard found breathing sent a stabbing pain through his lungs, so he had to make do with shorter breaths. Sarjeant had split the captain's skull in two, and the men who had attacked alongside him were dead or running.

The rest, over a dozen men, still fought with Kerak's defenders, and were on the other side of the crest of the breach.

'They're inside Kerak,' Richard gasped for air as blood from his forehead ran into an eye. It stung.

Sarjeant pushed himself up but couldn't put weight on one leg. 'I caught the foot in the stones,' he said and had to use his shield for support.

'Just us then,' Richard said to Bowman, 'one last time.'

The blonde knight's helmet was still on, but the face plate had half bent outwards. He tore it off. 'I'm not dying with that thing on,' he glanced at Richard's sword, 'although maybe we won't, seeing as you haven't dropped it yet.'

Richard climbed up the rubble, the sharp stones cut into his bleeding feet and he narrowly avoided falling over twice, but then he crested the ramp and stood at the very top of the breach.

Beneath him, the Saracens pushed back a single line of defenders, the bodies of dozens of them piled up all around. Severed limbs lay next to pools of blood and large catapult stones, arrows, and broken bolts littered the ground like flattened grass.

Behind the defenders, and blocking the doorway into the inner bailey, stood but four men, one of whom held aloft the lord of Kerak's banner.

The Saracens killed a defender and pushed through the middle of the line.

'Now,' Richard said. He ignored his feet and clattered into the back of a Saracen halfway down the rubble. The man fell forwards and onto the sword of a defender.

Bowman's mace caved in a helmet and the head inside it, and then the nearby Saracens panicked at the sudden assault into their rear.

Richard thrust his sword at one's face, the man pulled his head back, but fell over and was finished on the ground by an old man with a red shield.

The three Saracens who had broken through ran towards the men defending the final gateway, where they were cut down by the Lord of Kerak and his bodyguards.

Bowman killed a last Saracen as the man's eyes flashed with panic.

The defenders cheered, and with their enemy confused and scattered, they set into them until all of them had either fled or died.

Richard's heart raced, he tried to wipe the blood from his eye but more kept running down into it. He wondered what he must look like, with blood across his neck and chest, his splintered shield and destroyed mail now all but useless. But he'd kept a hold of his sword, for once, although heavily dented, and he thought of the song of Roland and marvelled at whose blade he held. Old things have power, he thought.

Everyone in the castle was looking up at him. Faces peered out from doorways, and the surviving defenders gazed at him with tired eyes and gasping mouths.

The lord of Kerak spat on a Saracen's body and looked across the bailey towards the breach. 'Who is this?' he shouted with a gruff but steady voice. 'Who is this who breaks the siege and saves my castle?'

Richard swallowed. 'I am a knight of the Temple,' he said in a more quiet voice than he'd intended, 'nothing more.'

The lord of Kerak, Reynald of Chatillon, put his sword away.

'That will not do. When they ask who relieved me, I shall not answer that it was some poor Templar. What is your name?'

'Richard.'

Reynald took a step forward. 'Richard of where? Who are you?'

'Of the Temple,' Richard replied, 'nothing more.'

A voice rang out from one of the surviving red shields. Richard recognised the man's face as Gerold's. His left arm hung limply from his side, but his voice was strong. 'This man is Richard, Sir Richard of Keynes. A knight of King Henry of England, who has stormed castles and broken rebellions. He wields the sacred sword of Roland and is a committed crusader.'

'That's more like it,' Reynald grinned. His clean-shaved face was clean of dirt and dust, but wrinkles showed his advancing age. 'Only a great warrior would have broken such a great siege. I will reward you myself for this heroism.'

'I need no rewards,' Richard said, 'if my children are safe.'

Gerold looked upwards at him. 'They are safe, my lord. And your horse lives.'

Richard glanced at the crowded house he'd found them in before, and even though only one eye worked, he saw his son's face peek out from the dark doorway. Alexander's young eyes looked up at his father as Alice held him steady, and for the very first time, Richard thought he saw admiration shine in them.

# LEGEND

Returning to the Holy Sepulchre in Jerusalem after so long in the dust and sand caused a wave of coolness and peace that almost overwhelmed Richard.

Inside the most holy of holy places, King Baldwin and the archbishop said many prayers of thanks for the delivery of Kerak into safety, as a hundred of the most important men of the realm watched on from all around the sunlit chamber.

The tomb of Christ glittered in the warm glow of the light, although the leper king was more frail than he'd been before. Despite his obvious weakness, Baldwin managed to give thanks to the Knights Templar for saving Kerak. Richard stood alongside Bowman and the Marshal to make up Gerard's Templar contingent, the seneschal having swapped their black surcoats to white in order for them to appear more impressive for the occasion.

'The Templars are the cornerstone of this kingdom,' Baldwin said to the hushed chamber, 'and once again, they have shown their dedication to our cause through their actions. These men were the first to reach the castle walls, and the honour and glory of our salvation is theirs.'

Arnold, the Templar Grand Master, had left Jerusalem and sailed west in order to drum up support for another crusade, so Gerard had taken his chance to represent them, and couldn't hide his pride.

'I will send the Temple a hundred iron helmets and a hundred mail shirts,' Baldwin said, 'I would send horses, but everyone knows the Templars have all of mine already.'

A ripple of reverent laughter echoed across the round chamber. The king slowly walked to Gerard, who knelt before him. 'You have shown great courage and have a promising future in the order before you.'

Standing where the king had originally addressed the chamber, Guy snorted. The regent was dressed in almost a regal manner as the king, but he only had sneers for the Templars.

Baldwin moved to Richard, who held his composure to stare back at the leprosy-addled face. 'I hear that you were the very first.'

Richard nodded and bowed his head.

When he looked up, over the king's shoulder he could see both of the Ibelins nodding back at him.

Baldwin faced the Marshal. 'You have fought for your old master's honour and kept your promise to him. The Young King of England shall not be forgotten in my kingdom, and I look forward to his younger brothers picking up his crusading mantle.'

Richard thought he saw the Marshal's bottom lip wobble, but only for a moment.

Baldwin waved for a servant to bring something over, a folded square of white fabric embroidered with golden thread. 'Here, you laid down a cloak for another,' the king said, 'so I would give you a cloak of your own, for when your time comes.'

The Marshal shook his head. 'I cannot take this, both because of my Templar vows, but also because I have already taken a cloak to be buried under.'

Richard frowned when the Marshal looked at him.

'This man's father died wearing a Templar mantle, defending the true cross and teaching me the value of loyalty and duty. I will be buried under that same mantle.'

Richard swallowed and clenched his jaw shut. He had tried not to think too much about his father, but now thoughts of pride overwhelmed the blame he put on himself for the manner of William's death.

King Baldwin nodded. 'You speak well. I implore you to serve your time in the order just as diligently, and when you return to the west, tell them that we need more support here. Saladin will return.'

The Marshal bowed again and promised that he would.

Baldwin ended the ceremony and left, leaning on a staff as he shuffled out of the sepulchre.

Gerard beamed a wide smile around the chamber. 'This has been a beneficial episode for our order,' he said, 'we can use the story to swell our ranks and prepare for the battles which lie ahead.'

Richard had nothing to say to the seneschal, who left them to go and speak to the barons. The Marshal locked eyes with Richard and he smiled back. Then the English knight left Richard and Bowman on their own.

'Can we go now?' the blonde knight almost shivered as his eyes swept around the most holy building in all the world.

'I think so,' Richard replied.

Bowman spun around on his heels and strode out of the church, just as Baldwin of Ibelin reached him. The elder Ibelin caught Richard's arm just as he went to follow his friend. 'You have made quite an introduction to yourself here, Richard the Templar. Or was it Keynes?'

'I think Gerard is receiving all the attention,' Richard replied.

Baldwin's aged face smiled. 'Reynald of Chatillon offered you land once your term of service in the order ends. He does not do that often.'

Richard shrugged. 'I have no wish for land so close to the frontier. My lands in Normandy were ravaged so many times it has taught me to consider all offers carefully.'

Balwin's smile widened. 'As it happens, my family holds lands nearer the coast, west of Jerusalem. We would like to make you a similar offer.'

Richard raised his eyebrows. 'That is very generous. If I am still alive in two years, I will speak to you about it.'

'That sounds sensible,' the Ibelin nodded. 'We need more knights in the kingdom. You may have pushed back the tide for a year, possibly two, but the clouds which darken our horizons shall return. Your men and your family are welcome with mine.'

'Thank you,' Richard said, 'I will not forget your kindness.'

Later, when Richard passed on the news of the offer, Sarjeant laughed. 'I am not a fighting man any longer,' he limped alongside Richard as they walked between trees on the Mount of Olives. 'And nor is Gerold. His left arm will not raise a shield again.'

'He has done enough,' Richard watched his children play with Judas in the distance. 'As have you, my friend.'

'This was not what I had in mind when you rode into my party of pilgrims outside Canterbury all that time ago,' Sarjeant smiled.

'No,' Richard chuckled, 'you were fed up with pilgrims and now you've ended up back in the Holy Land, anyway. I wonder if Archbishop Becket had this in mind for us when he instructed us to go east? Do you want to go back west?'

The large man rested against a gnarled olive tree. 'When we left Normandy, I was starting to feel the cold in my bones. I will feel it less here, that is if I survive two years of Templar service.'

'They'll put you in a garrison in some dusty tower for two years,' Richard grinned, 'I think you shall enjoy a well-earned rest.'

Sarjeant watched the children charge up and down the hill. 'They may not allow me any rest,' he smiled. 'But two pouches of the silver and I will end my days in comfort.'

'You aren't that old,' Richard said. 'And you can have a whole chest of pouches to yourself.'

'I know you are using it to house your family in the city,' Sarjeant replied, 'and in two years there might not be so much of it left.'

'That sounds like a problem to worry about in two years,' Richard grinned. The silver was still safely tucked away in the Templar headquarters, although he worried that Gerard would confiscate it now the Grand Master had sailed west. He decided to head that problem off by offering the seneschal the golden box containing Christ's deciduous teeth.

Bowman cried out in agony. 'Not the box, too,' he complained, 'Gerard doesn't care about the box.'

'You can buy five of those boxes with your share of the silver,' Richard told him, 'don't be greedy.'

'But I found it.'

'You sound like a child,' Richard said, 'and the Templars saved my children by attacking Saladin, so the teeth and the box are a fair gift in exchange for their lives.'

Bowman sniffed. 'Very well, young lord, but the silver better last while you're off playing at being a Templar.'

'It will,' Richard said, 'and if it doesn't, just ask one of the Ibelins for a position and I'm sure they will give you one. Your golden spurs make you valuable out here.'

The blonde knight grinned. 'Maybe the Holy Land will work out for us,' he nodded, 'and finally I will get the appreciation I deserve.'

Richard ignored him, but it gave him an idea. He dug out the battered pair of golden spurs that he had liberated from his uncle, the pair which had belonged to William Keynes. He found his son throwing a stick for Judas and knelt down by him.

'I know what those are,' the child said proudly.

'What are they?'

'They are golden spurs,' Alexander answered, 'they are what knights wear.'

'Very good,' Richard said, 'these spurs once were my father's. I want you to know that one day they will be yours.'

Alexander beamed and reached out a small hand.

'Go on,' Richard held one spur out for the boy.

Alexander grabbed the spur and its dried and dirt-encrusted leather strap. 'I will be a famous knight like you,' he declared.

Richard felt warm, his son's eyes looked up at him with some kind of awe, and Richard wondered if this feeling was the answer to the first question he'd rolled up and tied into Solis's mane when he had been a boy himself. He now thought he knew enough of the answer to let the matter lie. His father had made mistakes but had then tried to do the right thing, and that was all he could have asked of him. He himself had usually tried to do the right thing, and only succeeded in causing himself more problems and loss. But his father had given his life to save Richard in the end, and although that caused him more hurt, it also gave him comfort. His father had cared for him, he had left for the Holy Land despite his family, not because of it. He could forget the two long-lost rolls of parchment now, but he hadn't forgotten his horse.

Solis had been taken into the extensive stables underneath the Temple Mount, where Richard had found that the boast that it contained two thousand horses might actually be true. Certainly, hundreds of horses stood next to each other, tied to the walls of the long stable chambers, and Solis had been tied next to an older palomino horse. The horse was Stultus, the horse of William Keynes, who although greying around his eyes, still kicked at every other horse nearby. Richard had taken Solis to him, and after a sniff and one good bite of each other, both horses had decided they could coexist.

The grooms were amazed, for Stultus had been separated from other male horses for years. Solis caught their attention, and Richard allowed them to use him in their breeding program, for the Templars were experimenting with crossing western stallions with Arabian mares, a task Richard knew his horse was going to enjoy.

He picked out a palomino yearling who had Stultus as a father and a chestnut Arabian for a mother, and dragged the unbroken and ill-mannered horse out of the Templar quarters. He took it back to the two-storey stone house where he paid for Alice and his children to live. The house shared an inner courtyard with two others, as well as a shared stable block. He left the yearling in the stable and then went to find his son.

Alexander grew excited when he realised the horse was to be his, the small size of the horse encouraged him to sit on it, and Richard held him as he placed his weight onto the horse's back for the first time. The yearling jumped a step, but Richard held tight and Alexander was undeterred. Reassured by his father's grasp, Alexander giggled and clapped his hands together.

The yearling didn't jump at the clapping, which Richard knew was an encouraging sign for a prospective warhorse.

Alice stood at the door of the dark stable watching, her hair now brushed and a new silver circlet crowning it.

'For the first time, he looks like your son,' she said.

'It just took him to see me battered and broken on a battlefield,' Richard winced at the soreness in his limbs and stomach which hadn't yet gone away. A fresh scar lay above his eyes, and he wondered if the homeless veterans of Lillebonne would console or jeer at him now, now that he was just as disfigured as they had been.

'He saw what you have been doing when you have been away from him,' Alice said, 'and he is a clever child.'

'He got that from his mother,' Richard said with a smile which then faded awkwardly.

Alice turned her eyes to Alexander as Richard put him back on the ground. 'He will be a fine man.'

'I'll teach you how to brush him later,' Richard told his son, 'now go and find your sister, ask her which colour horse she would like.'

'Two new horses?' Alice asked.

'I can't give him one and not her, can I?' Richard asked. 'Besides, she is as old as him and will ride just as well. She is regaining her strength after the fever, and then she can learn to ride alongside her brother. The Red Child needs to learn properly too, I don't know what to do with him but I expect I never will.'

Alice watched Richard closely as he daydreamed about teaching them. Then he noticed her gaze and coughed. 'What will you do? Your brother is the regent of Jerusalem now, men are still asking him for your hand.'

Alice let out a mocking laugh. 'They can ask him for it,' she said, 'but if they come for it, they'll find that hand clenching a sharp knife.'

She's still a Lusignan, Richard thought to himself.

'I am happy where I am.'

'Are you?' Richard asked. 'You are bringing up my children, that is not your birthright.'

'My birthright was in France, but now thanks to my brother, it is someone else's. I will stay here.'

'Suit yourself,' Richard said.

'My brother has never done anything for me,' Alice said, 'and my family has caused me nothing but hardship. You have protected your family and me.'

Richard felt himself blush.

The yearling swished his tail at a fly and then investigated the bright yellow straw which Gerold had scattered over the floor. The old man still wanted to earn his keep, but now he was one-armed, everything took him longer than before.

'I'm not sure I can protect you from your brother,' Richard said.

'Leave that to me,' Alice smiled sweetly. 'I can handle him.'

Richard was quite sure she could.

Bowman entered the courtyard through the tunnel which led to the outside street, Judas at his heels. Both of them regarded Alice with suspicion, but the blonde man had a bag of something under his arm and looked too pleased with himself to bother with the Lusignan woman.

Brian followed them in, his arms full of bags too, and he dropped one on the way and Alexander laughed at him.

'What have you got there?' Richard asked. 'I expect Bowman to be overly free with the silver, but you are carrying more than he is.'

The monk shifted his load around but couldn't reach the dropped bag. 'Remember when I said someone should write down everything we've done?'

Richard did.

'Well,' Brian said, 'everyone in the city is talking about you. I like writing, so I thought I should be the one to write your story. Writing stories down is fashionable now.'

'You?' Richard laughed. 'Are going to write a chronicle of our doings?'

'I am,' the monk grinned at Richard, 'people should hear about it.'

'Not all of it,' Richard scratched his chin.

'The Lord does not shy away from the truth.'

'I'm not the Lord,' Richard said.

The monk hooked his dropped bag with his foot and managed to grab a hold of it. His load recovered, Brian disappeared into their house.

'I'll ask him to teach the children how to read,' Richard said, 'that should slow down his new project for a while.'

Alice held Alexander back from getting too close to the yearling's back legs.

Richard nodded with approval. 'I want them both to be able to read Eric and Enid for themselves.'

The Lusignan moved Alexander out of the stable. 'They

would like that, they both like the cover of the book and the illustrations inside, although Lora is more interested in learning how to shoot a bow.'

Richard nodded. His sister had enjoyed shooting too, although she had never been very good at it.

Lora recovered from her illness, and when she was a little older, Richard went hunting with her in a wood to the west of Jerusalem. There she stalked a deer with Richard, and when she let her arrow fly, it shot past the deer and into the neck of a mountain lion that crouched in a bush as it hunted the same deer. Richard had not even seen the mountain lion, and as the animal slumped, he found himself pleasantly surprised by his daughter's ability. As Lora grinned up at him with a face that looked exactly like Sophie's, Richard dared to hope that everything might, at long last, be alright.

# HISTORICAL NOTE

After the Young King's death, William Marshal carried his deceased master's cloak to Jerusalem and laid it down at the Holy Sepulchre. But that is all we know about William Marshal's two years in the east. In his biography it is simply said that he did in two years what most men did in seven, but that sounds like the biographer's opinion, seeing as he clearly doesn't know what the Marshal did there. The Marshal must have told no stories of his exploits, as otherwise they would have been recorded, which leaves us with an intriguing black hole in his history. This book is in part an attempt to imagine what he could have done, and seeks to explain why he never felt a need to talk about it once he'd returned to the west. It also provides a story behind the cloak the Marshal took back with him to the west, the cloak which was actually laid over him on his death. He never seems to have told anyone what made the cloak special. The Marshal himself never comes across as particularly pious, but something happened to him in the east which changed him, matured him, and set him up to be the man history remembers him as. One can only wonder what he made of the Holy Land, as he travelled through the green coastal areas which the Franks had heavily farmed and improved the output of. The multitude of exotic items, animals, and people must have been almost overwhelming, as if stepping into an alien world. But it was a mirror of home, too, for the Franks had imported their social structures and systems and laid them over the top of what already was in place. Local Muslim villages were left alone, as long as the headman toed the line and paid taxes, and new villages made up of westerners sprung up away from them. To the locals, the Franks must have seemed like just another bunch of overlords - little different to the Romans or any of the myriad of other occupiers they had suffered for the last few thousand years. A mix of cultures existed side by side and with varying degrees of tolerance, but it was the conflict between the Muslims led by Saladin which cast a shadow over the Christian Kingdom of Jerusalem. The knights of the time surely were hostile to most Muslims, although they tolerated their merchants happily enough, and the term Saracen was widely used as a crude blanket to cover all kinds of peoples.

Another social group in the area were the Assassins. Originally from as far east as Persia, they were a Muslim order founded in the eleventh century and were not just an order of murderers. Their military tactics sprung from their lack of numbers, so instead of fighting pitched battles, they resorted to political assassinations. There are many legends surrounding them, but what is unarguable is that they killed their enemies with knives in public places, and the men who did the deed did not expect to survive. The terror they caused was therefore real, and Saladin did fear them. The idea that an Ismaili cake was placed next to an Assassin's dagger on his bed to compel Saladin to break a siege is a real story, although not one from the siege of Kerak.

The siege as portrayed in this book is an amalgamation of two real sieges in two successive years. Saladin did attack the town just as a royal wedding was taking place, and out of his own courtesy, did announce that he would not attack the tower where it was taking place. The Muslim leader gained a reputation for what would later be called chivalry from this

352

and similar actions, which puts him in stark contrast to the lord of Kerak, one Reynald of Chatillon. This infamous lord was Saladin's nemesis, striking out from Kerak to disrupt his trade and supply lines, and forever causing him problems. Reynald's relentless attacks on Saladin, regardless of what truces might be in effect, have seen him cast as a villain who brought Saladin down onto the Kingdom of Jerusalem. This may well be true, but the lord of Kerak knew that Saladin was coming for the Latin kingdom no matter what, so perhaps his actions could be understood as the last-ditch efforts to keep him at bay.

Gerard of Ridefort, the Templar seneschal, is another interesting historical character. In this book, we see him before he becomes the Grand Master of the order, a position which enabled him to shape the very destiny of the Holy Land. He joined the Templars it seems because Raymond of Tripoli took away a promised wife, but from that moment onwards he seems to have wholly dedicated his life to the order. Gerard would throw the Templars at his enemies again and again, with the same venom as Reynald of Chatillon, but Saladin would prove too much for both of them. The Templars as an organisation are an enigmatic subject. They were early adopters of financial innovations such as letters of credit, maintained a fleet larger than some kings, and could field a formidable army. They followed a very strict monastic life, with some allowances made for their martial lifestyle. The prayers Richard needed to recite several times a day are but one example of this, and the knights were certainly monks first and fighting men second. Their vaunted poverty was a matter of fact, too. In the records of Templars rounded up during their dissolution, the personal effects listed for even the more senior Templars were almost non-existent. The order as an organisation was, however, undoubtedly rich, and this is why the King of France destroyed them in the fourteenth century. He had to invent a lot of juicy stories to justify his robbery though, which is where we get all the Templar's modern conspiracy theories from.


Guy of Lusignan's journey from murdering William Marshal's uncle to becoming the regent of the Holy Land would be too unlikely to write, except for the fact that it is true. Guy went to the Holy Land at an earlier date than in this series of books, and went along with some brothers, but he did inexplicably rise up the ranks to rule the Kingdom of Jerusalem. How he really did this is not entirely certain, for he had no skills in politics or diplomacy, and was generally disliked wherever he went. I therefore went with the idea that he was seen as a 'useful idiot' for others, a puppet who would eventually pull at the strings which held him, and inadvertently plunge the kingdom into turmoil. The seeds of the disasters Guy would ultimately be responsible for are seen in this book, and he is another fascinating character in a rich tapestry of them. His marriage to the sister of King Baldwin, Sibylla, took place earlier than in this book, but it does seem to have been a real love match. When Sibylla later had the chance to reject Guy, she chose to stand by him, to the extent that it eventually killed her. What Guy did to earn her devotion we do not know, which is why I have him rescuing her, but the fact she stuck to him when she could, and probably should, have left him, says something very strongly about their relationship.

Thank you for taking the time to read this series, and if you are interested in the world of the medieval knight, check out the author's non-fiction book "The Rise and Fall of the Mounted Knight" - but although the story of Richard Keynes is over, his son's is only about to begin.

Printed in Great Britain
by Amazon

59911520R00204